Soprano in the Pı

Soprano in the Press Box

Jane Moorman

I dedicate this book to my biggest fans, my parents, Bill and Mildred Moorman, and Dr. Francine Hoffman, my journalism professor, who told me I could reach my dream.

Acknowledgments

I'd like to acknowledge all of the wonderful people I have met during my journalism career. This includes the various group of friends and family members who watch me accomplish my dream of being a sportswriter.

Contents

Introduction

Friday night football in Texas is a community event. The entire town is out to watch their high school team play. As the game began, I found my place in the press box. I was the new sportswriter at the Henderson Daily News. People weren't too sure about having a female covering their sacred sports. They all were in a wait-and-see mode.

As we stood and sang the National Anthem prior to kickoff, I realized I was the only soprano in the press box. In 1981, I was one of a few women sportswriters in the great state of Texas.

During my life, I haven't been aware that I was one of the first women to make a specific career. I was just living my life, doing the things I wanted to do. I think many women have been in the same situation and have helped make headway for women in various careers.

My area seems to have been the sports world, not on the national stage, but at the community level. The first time I contributed to a change for girls' sports was as an eleven-year-old in my hometown of Nickerson, Kansas.

Its little league baseball signup day. I'm excited as I ride my bicycle to go sign up. I've been playing ball with all the boys, now I want to be on a team.

"I'm sorry, but only boys can sign up for the little league," said the man at the registration table. "But if you can get enough girls to sign up, we will form a softball league."

I started riding to all my friend's houses in the mile-long-half-mile-wide town to tell them to go sign up. I pedaled fast because time was running out that day, being the only time to register.

"They didn't know who they were challenging," my mother said that evening. "She got enough girls to sign up to form four teams."

That league has been maintained for more than sixty years.

I lived in this small rural town in Kansas for the first twelve years of my life. From the time I was six years old, watching the big boys play baseball, I have loved sports. I played whatever sport was in season.

When we played our first softball games in school, I was sent to the outfield. I stood out there and thought, *I want to play in the infield where the action is.* I began working on my skills.

I'd play catch with whoever was around, and if there was no one available, I'd throw the ball up on the garage roof and catch it as it rolled back to earth. My brother did not enjoy playing sports, so if I wanted him to play with me, it would cost me—money or candy and him using my better ball glove.

"If you're going to play, I'm going to teach you how to throw the ball like a boy, not like a girl," my dad said. Many summer evenings, when he would get home from his feed and seed store, we would play catch. He'd throw balls high to force me to jump for them or short pop-ups to make me run to catch them.

Soon the coach discovered that being a lefthander, I was an asset as the first baseman. All of the hours playing catch with Dad paid off as I leaped for throws and touched first base for an out just as the runner was reaching the bag.

One time my best friend playing for the other team hit a pop-up on the first base line. I charged forward and made the catch. My opponents soon learned that if they hit a pop-up in my area, they might as well walk back to the dugout because I was going to catch the ball.

My best friend, Tomisha, was a natural athlete. It seemed like whatever we were playing, she did it with ease. Years later, a friend said, "Tomisha was a natural, but you were an athlete. You worked at developing your skills."

The television show *Wide World of Sports* had a big influence on me. I learned about a variety of sports, including the Olympics. It also opened my eyes to the vast world that existed, not just in sports but also geographically. From the first time I watched a televised Olympics in 1960, I dreamed of attending this event, what I considered the pinnacle of amateur sports.

Our family moved to Columbia, Missouri, when I was in seventh grade. This was going to be a big change for all of us as we were leaving my father's hometown. While looking for a house to buy, my parents stressed that we needed a good-sized yard and, if possible, a basketball goal for Jane. The realtor found the perfect place in a neighborhood full of kids, mainly boys, to play with.

One evening, we pulled into our driveway and saw a group of boys playing football in our backyard. Mom went out and said they could play there if they let me join in. That was the first and last time she asked anyone to let me play.

Soon the boys discovered I was able to keep up with them. The neighborhood developer had left two lots vacant where kids could play. The two-acre lot was the gathering place for playing baseball and football.

It was the 1960s, a decade before Title IX. The schools I attended did not have girls' sports teams. At Columbia's Hickman High School, we had Girls Athletic Association, where we participated in various sports activities to earn points toward a "letter." I worked hard to earn the points, but moving the summer before my junior year prevented me from receiving the award.

Junior bowling league was where I focused my love of competing. Our neighbor was the secretary of the league, and she made sure kids from our street got to the bowling lanes every Saturday morning. Bowling costs $3.50. My allowance was $5 each week, so I had money left for a donut and a coke.

Not only did we compete in our league, but we were able to qualify for tournaments with other leagues. I won my first trophy in a singles tournament when I was fourteen.

That trophy was very important to me. A line in the hymn *Old Rugged Cross* states, "At last my trophies I lay down." As a child, I told myself I needed to get a trophy. I knew trophies were given when you won in sports. When I received that first trophy, I thought, *Now I have one to lay down.*

Of course, as an adult, I realized that trophies referred to in the song were not ones for sport victories but symbolic of life's accomplishments.

Besides the singles tournament, my team competed in a state tournament that was held in Columbia. The highlight of that day was seeing professional bowler Dick Weber watching his son Pete compete in the tournament. We all knew that Pete had a future as a pro; as a teenager, his handicap was 1.

Weber is widely regarded as professional bowling's first superstar. Both Dick and Pete are members of the United States Bowling Congress Hall of Fame and the PBA Hall of Fame. When Pete won his first PBA title in 1982, it marked the first time in history that a father and son had both won PBA Tour titles.

A second major influence on my life's path occurred when I was in ninth grade. I was beginning to think about what I wanted to do when I grew up. In the 1960s, the opportunities for a gal included marriage or a job as a secretary, nurse, bank teller or teacher. I couldn't see myself working in an office, bank or hospital, so I chose to teach. It seemed to me the physical education teachers were the adults having fun, plus they got to wear shorts to work.

When I asked a student teacher what I had to do to become a PE teacher, she brought me a brochure from the University of Missouri. That's when I realized I'd have to go to college. This gave me the impetus to become a better student.

When we moved to Dallas in 1968, bowling and softball continued to be my athletic outlets. I participated in a church bowling league and a softball league.

Bowling proved to have a major role in my future. In 1970, as a senior at Richardson High School in the suburb of Dallas, it helped me select the college I would attend.

A friend and I went to a Dallas Library branch one evening. She was researching the costs of colleges she wanted to attend. I wandered to the shelves that contained sports books. I found a rule book on bowling from the Texas Association of Intercollegiate Athletics for Women. There were three colleges listed as a finalist in the state championship—Texas Women's University, North Texas State University and Stephen F. Austin State University.

With those names, I went to the college reference book to see where they were located and how much they cost. TWU was too expensive, and North Texas State was too close to home in Denton.

Stephen F. Austin State University became my choice of college. People said to me, "You are only going to apply for one school. What's going to happen if you are not accepted."

I bravely said, "I'll go to a junior college until I am accepted." I didn't bother to tell anyone how I came up with this choice.

After being academically accepted to SFA, the next major step was qualifying for the bowling team. There were no athletic scholarships for women, so there was no guarantee.

On the day of tryouts, I rode to the bowling alley with the coach. On the way back to the campus, I said, "I didn't know if I bowled well enough to make the team."

Later, she told me, "I can't wait to teach you how to bowl like a pro."

Sandra Cole became my coach, professor, mentor, and friend. There was a clock/bowling trophy on her office desk dated the same year as the book I had read at the library. Her name was one of those listed.

Bowling became a major activity in my life. I practiced seven days a week, rolling 16 games each day. I also helped Sandy teach her bowling class. If a student did not attend, I got to bowl since the class enrollment cost had paid for a lane.

Sandy accomplished her goal of making me a better bowler. When I arrived at SFA, I had a 145 average. At the end of my colligate career, I had a 195 average.

We competed in one tournament each year. They consisted of nine games in one day—team, doubles and singles. One year my partner Ruth Ann and I won the doubles. I came close to winning all events a couple of times.

Being a physical education major, I was a gym rat, always hanging out at the Women's Recreation Center. Spring of my freshman year, I was a high jumper on the women's track team. But I had to drop out because my grades were suffering, and if I didn't make a 2.0-grade point average, I wouldn't be able to bowl the next fall.

The coach recognized my enthusiasm for the sport and asked me to be the track manager. I helped her until her career took her to another college in my junior year.

Being pre-Title IX, the imparity between the women's athletic budget and that for men's teams was apparent in many ways. While the men had a team bus, we created a car caravan with the coach and team members' cars to travel to track meets.

While taking a track coaching class in the men's physical education department, we were given the assignment to create a budget with a specific amount of money. The men students were surprised when I didn't budget for workout clothes and shoes. They didn't know that women had to provide their own clothes.

An opportunity arose during my senior year that set me on the career path that ended in the press box. During my student teaching,

I realized I didn't want to be a physical education teacher. At the same time, I discovered I wanted to be a sports journalist.

Ladyjack basketball coach, and future Women's Basketball Hall of Fame and Naismith Memorial Basketball Hall of Fame recipient, Sue Gunter had a job for me.

She called me into her office with a proposal that changed my life. The university's sports information director was not providing press releases about the women's sports teams. He told Gunter he was too busy, but if she had someone bring him the game results, he would write releases about the games.

That job was my introduction to sports journalism.

I worked in the university information office and gathered the results of the women's games—volleyball, basketball, softball, badminton, and track and field. He wrote the stories.

One day he said, "I'm too busy. You write the story." From then on, I wrote the stories.

After graduating, I asked the director how do we make this a full-time job. He asked, "Do you have a journalism degree?"

"No, just physical education," I replied.

So now what? I had a college degree in something I didn't want to do.

For the next few years, I worked in a flower shop, a self-service gas station and an electrical transformer factory.

Meanwhile, Stephen F. Austin State University created a women's sports information position and hired a gal who had a degree in journalism and physical education. I knew her, we were students together. Our social lives intertwined. I must admit I was not very nice to her because she had "my job."

One day on the way to the factory, me, myself, and I were having a conversation in my head. The question being discussed was why she had "my job." Myself and I ganged up on Me and said, "Well, go get the journalism degree or stop whining."

I worked nights in the factory and attended journalism classes during the day. It was hard for me because my weakest skills were spelling and grammar. I nearly flunked my first class. But in the end, my journalism professors realized my desire to succeed outweighed my skills.

One day I visited with the grand dame of the department, Dr. Francine Hoffman. I told her I was a returning student and that if I couldn't do this writing, to let me know because I didn't have the money or time to waste.

Her response was that I could do it if I applied myself.

The graduate assistant edited my stories and I learned from all the red marks on the paper. Throughout my career, the copy editor was my best teacher. One editor explained that my work was a diamond in the rough and the copy editor polished it to be award-winning.

When I earned twenty-four credits needed for a journalism major, I decided to see what I had to do to receive a degree.

Journalism was in the School of Fine Arts, so I visited the dean to learn what I needed to do. Since I had already received a Bachelors of Science degree in Education, he told me I would have to complete forty-five hours to receive the fine arts degree. This was not the answer I was seeking.

Next, I went to the registrar's office to see what I needed to do to get an additional major recorded on my official university transcript. The answer was more doable. "Have the dean of your college sign off that you have completed a major."

I marched into the Dean of Education's office. To my pleasant surprise, his secretary was a friend of mine. I told her that I had completed the 24 credits necessary to add journalism as a second teaching field. She agreed and rubber-stamped my request with the dean's signature, which I returned to the registrar's office.

It was official I had added journalism to my list of majors—physical education and health education.

My first newspaper job came while I still had two classes remaining for my major. The managing editor of the Nacogdoches Daily Sentinel hired me as the Women's Editor with the understanding I would attend the classes during my lunch hour and work late to make up for any lost time.

While this was not sports writing, it was a newspaper job. In January of 1981, I quit the factory job and became a journalist.

Six months later, I applied for the sports editor job at the Henderson Daily News and became a community newspaper sportswriter.

I would soon be reporting on sports at the seven school districts in the county, plus little summer league, adult golf tournaments and anything else sports-related in the county.

Prior to my arrival, the newspaper had only covered the boy teams. Things would change; stories about each school's girl teams now also appeared in the paper.

Each summer photographs of the boy baseball teams were published in the newspaper. I decided that if we could honor the boys, we should honor the girl softball teams as well. I created a full page of team photos. When the advertising manager saw the page, he said, "Who's paying for this." I didn't realize I needed an advertiser for the page. He went out and sold it to a car dealership and the first-ever girls softball team photo page appeared in the newspaper.

Before my first night in the press box, I had to complete a 52-page football magazine that included stories about the high school teams in Rusk County—Henderson, Tatum, Leverett's Chapel, Overton, West Rusk, Mount Enterprise—as well as college and NFL teams.

The printer's ink began cursing through my veins and I never looked back. I was at the Henderson Daily News for five years before moving to New Mexico in 1986. After taking a break from journalism for two years, I returned to sports journalism in 1988 as the sports editor of the Valencia County News-Bulletin, where I covered all of the sports—boys and girls—at the two high schools and in the community for six years.

In 1994 my career shifted to public relations for a school district. At that time, I realized I had been either watching, playing, umpiring, coaching, or writing about baseball or softball for thirty-two years.

After taking that career break from journalism, I returned to the Valencia County News-Bulletin in 2000 as a general reporter covering education, city, county and state issues, including agriculture.

During my twelve years at the News-Bulletin, I received writing awards from the New Mexico Press Association, including first in sports photo in 1993, sports writing in 1998 and 1999, and columns in 2003; and second place in sports writing in 1992, sports columns in 1993, and general news photography in 2001.

In addition to the press association awards, my general reporting was recognized by the New Mexico Farm and Livestock Bureau as Print Reporter of the Year in 2003, and the U.S. Small Business Administration in 2004 as the New Mexico Small Business Journalist of the Year.

In 2002, I received the Estrella Awards: Celebrating the Shining Stars of New Mexico for excellence in journalism from the New Mexico Commission of the Status of Women.

A call from a former News-Bulletin editor in 2006 gave me a chance to complete my dream of working for a university. New Mexico State University was looking for a writer to produce press releases for the College of Agriculture focusing on the Cooperative Extension Service and research farms in northern New Mexico.

The best part of the opportunity was that I could work out of Albuquerque without having to relocate to Las Cruces, where the university's campus is located in southern New Mexico. My career was capped after fourteen years of working for the university. During that time, I produced more than 1,000 press releases.

Following are examples of my writing during my thirty-one-year career. They are divided into two styles—columns from the Henderson Daily News and Valencia County News-Bulletin, and special articles from the newspapers and the university. Some of the columns are sports-related, but most are just about life as I saw it, including my attending the 1984 Olympics in Los Angeles and bicycling across Missouri in 1985.

Henderson Daily News
Henderson, Texas 1980-1986
Reporter Notebook

These are short columns featured on the editorial page. Each reporter was required to submit a paragraph or two about something or someone on their beats. I usually wrote these on deadlines when the editor told me how much space he needed to fill.

June 6, 1983

First Distance Bike Ride

Setting a goal and obtaining it is one of the biggest thrills of life. Last Sunday, I accomplished a goal that I set over a year ago... I rode my bicycle to Overton and back to Henderson.

All those big hills on Hwy 323 that I have been sizing up when I drive to Overton became mountains on my two-wheeler. But with a tailwind, I sailed into Overton after an hour of pedaling.

I decided to take a bicycle tour of Overton, so I circled the city lake and park and then went to the Texas A&M research farm.

On the return trip, I decided not to face the headwinds on Hwy 323, so I went south on FM 2089 to Wright City.

Let me tell you, those hills on the Overton highway are nothing compared to the steep hills between Overton and Wright City. Halfway up one hill was the Ashbury Cemetery. All I could think about was how convenient it was since I was dying from the uphill climb.

The hills finally leveled out and there was Hwy 64. Finally, the last half of the trip was within sight.

I sailed on to Turnertown and Joinerville. I must admit, I stopped at the roadside park between these two oil boom towns for a little nap before making the final large hills back into the Henderson city limits.

The stretch of road from Turnertown to Henderson High School is an old hat for me because I have ridden from Henderson to Price to Turnertown and back three times this spring.

Four hours after leaving my house, I rolled into the driveway, a little tired but full of pride. All day Monday, I walked around singing the theme song to Rocky, for I had set a goal and accomplished it.

June 6, 1983
Going To the Horse Races By KK

I don't know how many people in this area actually go to the horse races at Louisiana Downs or how many would admit to it.

But if you have ever gone and sat up in the enclosed, air-conditioned grandstand or really gotten lucky and sat in a box, you probably think going down to the $1 outside grandstand seats in the heat and standing against the rail would be taking life into your hands.

That's what I thought. Sports editor Jane Moorman convinced me that the outside area was "where it was at," so we joined the rest of the 'railbirds,' and it wasn't all that bad.

Being down in the heat with the regulars in shorts and anything cool gave me a unique perspective on the track and how you go to the horse races when you don't have very much to spend.

Jane likes the rail because you can feel the horses' power as they run by. She says it's the only way to fly.

Before making our wagers, we walked over to the paddock to check out the horses, then we ran in and placed our $2 bet to show as if it were our last pennies. As the horses warmed up on the track, we found a place along the rail and waited for the announcer to say, "And they're off."

I like the jockeys bantering back and forth as they rode by and the spectators yelling to their favorite rider to "bring 'em in front."

Regardless of the heat, the threatening rain clouds and the crowd, our day at the races showed me that I could have a good time without all the frills—even though I lost $14; Jane won't admit how much she lost.

September 11, 1983
No Feline Olympics for Domino

With all the concern in the athletic world about athletes using steroids to increase their strength, I had sad news for my cat.

I had to break the news to her that she would not be able to participate in the 'Feline Olympics.'

For all of you sports fans, this is the lesser-known sports event where cats participate in such events as tree climbing, mouse catching, the loudest meow, etc.

But Domino will have to watch this great event only because she has feline leukemia, which is treated with steroids, so she will not pass the drug test.

The reports about athletes using steroids say that their voices deepen, and they get more muscles and more facial hair.

Well, it is true. Domino's meow has deepened and she is more muscular than before and yes, she has facial hair.

September 11, 1983

What Boys Do

This summer, when my nephew visited, I was worried about what to do and where to take a nine-year-old boy who had been to the World's Fair and Disney World all in one year.

On our list of things to do was swimming, a trip to the East Texas Oil Museum in Kilgore and a trip to the zoo in Tyler.

Of all the things we ended up doing, the boy's favorite was not something that cost an arm and a leg but a trip to Henderson's Lake Forest Park.

It seems the ducks won the popularity contest. Matt gets a real thrill out of feeding ducks.

Also, he added another first to his list. He learned to play miniature golf on the city's course.

It just shows you that money and things don't impress little boys when there are animals and sports handy.

September 25. 1983
Thank You for the Thanks

There is a simple little word that makes all the difference in the world... THANKS!

As a reporter, it is my job to write about things and people in Henderson and Rusk County. I should not need people to say "thank you" for my doing my job.

But sometimes it is nice to know people appreciate or like what I work hard to do.

This summer, I had to make some decisions about my private life and the nice people of Henderson had a big influence on my decision.

Since I don't have any family here to pat me on the back and keep me going, it was nice to have my readers give me some 'warm fuzzies.'

You can't help but want to work harder and do more when people pay you compliments.

So, to all my friends out there... THANKS!

October 30, 1983

Yule Giving

With ghosts and goblins making their rounds this weekend and Thanksgiving dinner still to come, who would be thinking about Christmas?

I have been. Such questions as what to buy a nine-year-old boy. This year rather than buying my nephew, Matt, a gift that would disappoint him, I decided to go straight to the horse's mouth and ask 'the kid.'

With a quick dial of the phone, I was talking to 'the kid' in Kansas City. Matt is not shy when it comes to Christmas lists. He knows that his grandparents will balk at gifts over $15, his parents will go for the smaller things and clothes, and Aunt Jane is the one to ask for $20 or more gifts.

"I want a Star Wars Fighter, a GI Joe jet and a Star Wars ASTA (whatever that might be)," Matt said upon my asking. Not only did I get the name of the toy, but he also told me what page in the catalog it was on.

In the background, I heard his father say, "Some kids ask Santa Claus, and Matt asks Aunt Jane."

I asked 'the kid' if he really needed all three of these airplanes and he said it would be nice.

Well, Christmas buying is done for the nephew. I went to Sears and ordered all three. I know I spoil 'the kid', but he is the only kid in the clan, and, after all, what is Aunt Janes for anyway?

November 6, 1983

Leveling Dad's Bed

Some people are real sensitive about things being "unlevel." My father is one of those people. When he goes camping, he spends hours leveling his bed, which happens to be the back end of the station wagon.

Whether a bed, chair or mobile home is level or not does not bother me. In fact, I have lived in my mobile home for two years and have not taken the time to fine-tune the levels to even up the floor.

So, there was a little downhill slope to the back of the trailer. Big deal. I found it a challenge to walk uphill in the mornings to get that first cup of coffee.

After my father requested that the trailer be leveled on his first visit in 1981, I said, "Sure, Dad, I'll get right to it."

Then after his second visit last Thanksgiving, he said, "When is right to it?"

This summer, after his surprise visit on July 4, the final ultimatum was given, "Get this thing leveled before I return."

I thought I was going to get an extension on that command when the parents called and said they would have to miss the annual Thanksgiving visit, but a week later, a second call came that the visit was back on.

So finally, after having the mobile home at this location for a little more than two years, I had it leveled.

Now I am taking bets on whether Dad will notice the three-inch difference that the leveling made... because I can.

There is only one little thing wrong since the leveling... all of those pictures I hung are hanging crooked, and that really drives me crazy.

November 13, 1983

9

Got Heat?

Ba... Ba... Baby! It's co... co... cold outsi... si... side!

No, this isn't a song, it's a true weather report. As you all know, the temperature dropped to the mid-30s these past few nights.

Well, this cheap, I mean this conservative person, has been caught with no heat on these cold nights.

To save money, I had my natural gas turned off this summer since the only appliances that use gas are my furnace and my stove, which I don't use since I heat my TV dinners with my microwave oven.

Old man winter caught me sleeping, or at least trying to sleep between shivers. The temperatures dropped at the same time my saving account did from buying my nephew's Christmas gifts, so I didn't have the deposit needed to turn on the heat.

As I shiver in bed, I just keep thinking this is good character building. Since I can't tell my future children that "I walked 10 miles to school in the snow," I can now tell them of life without the utilities everyone takes for granted.

I don't think I will freeze before payday... Tuesday, but if you see me around town with blue lips, you now know the rest of the story.

November 27, 1983
Mother's Free Help Can Be Costly

Mother has been visiting this week, and guess what—she washed the windows. Of all the things I have asked Mom to do when she visits, I think the windows were the most imposing task.

At first, her response was a simple NO. But I guess she either got bored since she was at home without a car or she felt sorry for her daughter's cat since Domino couldn't see out of the dirty windows.

Whatever the reason, I came home from work on Tuesday to clean windows.

People here at The News office have been asking if I rent out my mother to clean their houses. But this free help can be trying at times.

Like the time she put all of the blankets in the suitcases during the summer because that was just wasted space. I, of course, forgot what she had done with the blankets until the cold winter winds hit.

The only time I would think of looking for the blankets was at 1 or 2 a.m. when I was cold. One night I almost called her collect at 3 a.m. to ask her what she had done with them, but being the good daughter that I am, I let her sleep.

It wasn't until Christmas when I was preparing to pack for my trip to the family reunion, that I found the blankets.

Some help's nice. Some, however, are questionable.

November 27, 1983

Shooting Star Wishes

Everyone knows that if you see a shooting star, you are supposed to make a wish.

The other evening as I was driving home, I saw a shooting star, so I quickly made my wish...

Then I began to remember some of my wishes from days gone by. As a kid, I would always wish for a horse. But as that wish was never answered and I outgrew the desire to own a horse. I switched to wishing for a boyfriend and then a husband.

As time has passed, none of these wishes have been answered, but my belief in the falling star magic has not lessened. Now I am practical: if you can't pray for material things, why should a falling star be able to give them to you?

Now my wish is very simple... *Please let me continue to have a good life, with good health and good friends.*

January 22, 1984

Curious Kids...

Oh, the curiosity of youth! Those thousands of questions on how and why things are the way they are!

This week I had the opportunity to share something that I really enjoy with a group of fifth graders from Carlisle Elementary when the class of twenty-eight curious kids toured The Henderson Daily News office

I'm basically a ham, so when Jerry Wylie asked if her class might tour the office, I volunteered my services as a tour guide.

The fact that a person had to be able to spell to make a newspaper did not impress the young students, but watching a photograph turn from a white sheet of paper to a picture really was a hit.

But when it was all said and done, the big, noisy press in the back won all of their attention. When pressman Robert Cyphers cranked up the press to full speed, there were fifty-six wide eyes watching as the newspaper came alive before them—from blank paper to a folded newspaper.

I hope that whenever the students open a newspaper, they will remember a little of what we showed them this week. After all, showing the next generation things that you have discovered is what life is all about.

January 29, 1984
The First Move, the Hardest

After Jimmy Watson, Henderson's head football coach, decided not to pursue the John Tyler coaching job, all I could think of was all of the emotions that his family had gone through in the past few months.

It brings back memories of my family's first move. Not only were we moving children from their birthplace, but also father was leaving his hometown.

When Dad said we were moving to Missouri, all this Kansas diehard could think was, why do we want to leave "God's Country?" Needless to say, tears were flooding the Moorman house.

Once the shock of moving was over, the fear of a new place moved in, but with time and prayers, our family made its first move. Like the Watsons might have been, ours was a career move that turned out to be the correct move.

After the first move, the one to Texas was not as hard, though we had established friends in Missouri. Only one thing was different with that move, my brother had graduated from high school, and he remained in Missouri.

My parents' third move turned out to be the one in which I was left behind. They returned to Missouri while I was attending Stephen F. Austin State University, so I took Texas as my home. And I'm glad I did.

Since the first move, our family has become very mobile, but the memories of that day in January of 1965 when Dad said, "Wagon ho!" remains strong.

February 12, 1984
Old Blue Truck Saved the Day

At long last, I will be driving a nice quiet car rather than "Old Blue"—the noisy pickup truck.

My Honda decided to take an extended vacation at Christmas and remain in Joplin, Mo., in the Honda dealership's intensive care unit, waiting to have its motor rebuilt.

Sunday, Henrietta is coming home. Old Blue will get to go back into retirement in my neighbor's driveway.

One thing about being without wheels: I learned the people of Henderson are nice. When I was unable to locate a vehicle to drive after returning from Missouri, my neighbors Brenda and Curtis Fletcher unselfishly gave me total use of their truck.

When Old Blue was unable to travel to out-of-town basketball games, Henderson Lady Lion coach Dennis River and his wife, Jody, offered me rides on the school bus or with Jody in her car.

When the Friday night Lion basketball games came around, Joe and Jerry Wylie insisted that I ride with them. Now they say I must keep riding with them to bring the team luck. And I must not forget my dear friend Garrison Ausburn who gave me his car keys without blinking an eye or asking where I was going.

I must admit it will be nice to drive a car that you can hear the radio in. And one that you don't have to get out and pull the gear rods when the transmission locks in third—or better yet, one with a heater in it.

Needless to say, I'm one happy girl this weekend. Now I can pull up to the store and everyone in the building will not look out at me and Old Blue.

February 19, 1984
Spring Has Sprung... Maybe

Oh! Is it spring yet?

From all indications, it is spring. The birds are singing, the days are warm, and I have spring fever. The sunny afternoons have been beckoning me outdoors.

More signs of spring include the neighbor children riding their bicycles around the trailer park drive, dogs playing with their favorite bones, and cats napping in the sun. Adults and children were trying to get a kite into the sky.

The whippoorwills are beginning to sing at night under the bright full moon and stars.

The sunrises and sunsets are colorful light shows to begin and end the beautiful day.

Needless to say, I like spring. There is nothing quite like sitting under a budding tree in the sun, watching the puffy clouds go by in the clear blue sky, or walking through the woods and seeing the plants coming back to life with buds.

Maybe the Farmers' Almanac will be wrong and there will not be another cold spell. Hopefully, spring has sprung, but if not, and another Northern does come through, then we will just have to go through these pretty days again.

March 4, 1084
Friday Night Freedom

Did you know there is television at night? And that the normal person spends the evening at home? Or at a movie? Or at least with friends?

This great discovery comes to me about this time of the year. Since September, I have worked every Friday night and now I find myself with the evening off. Now, what do I do?

Not only have I worked every Friday night, but since December and the beginning of basketball, I have had every evening booked except Wednesday. Now, what do I do?

Baseball plays Tuesdays and Thursdays, and most games begin at 4 p.m., which means I will be home before 8 p.m.

Don't get me wrong, I'm not complaining about the crazy hours of a sportswriter. I just find a void when a season ends and the routine of that sport is over.

My life changes into a new routine. This is easy for me to accomplish, but those around me find it hard to adapt.

The main animal to notice the change is my cat. Now that I'm home in the evenings, Domino is not complaining. It just means that she can sleep on my lap and get mad when I get up to change the television channel.

This time of the year kind of reminds me of being a kid during summer vacation. "Mom, I'm bored... there is nothin' to do."

If my memory is right, her response was always, "Go read a book." Well, I guess it's time to read all those books I've been meaning to read since football season began or better yet. Go to a movie or go out to dinner with friends or just enjoy a little time at home.

March 11, 1984
She Stole My Heart

Oh, what have I gotten into this time! A birthday party for a four-year-old at Showbiz Pizzeria.

I'm not complaining. Little Amanda stole my heart the first time I met her. Her big blue eyes and big smile tore down all of my "no thank you, I don't want children" feelings.

From the first meeting, this child decided that she loved me. No questions asked, just child trust and love. She ran to me and hugged my leg, and I fell in love.

On that same visit, she cuddled up beside me while watching television. Before she knew it, she was asleep with a smile of contentment on her face.

But one thing nice about being a friend to someone else's child: When they are bad or "break" (as in crying or being sick), they can be sent home. I can enjoy her knowing that I don't have to survive the trying 3's or terrible 4s – that's for her mother to contend with.

I just get to enjoy the days in the park, trips to the ice cream parlor and all of the other fun things in raising a child.

This child may only be four, but she has already learned how to charm a person into loving her. Watch out, little boys, when this one gets to be a teenager, you won't have a chance.

March 18, 1984
You Can Call Him Billy Jack

You can call him Billie Jack. You can call him William Jacob. Or you can call him Wild Bill.

The above man is the apple of my eye. He's my father. I guess no matter how old I get, my dad will always be a knight in shining armor. He can do no wrong.

His mother named him Billie Jack, but the doctor felt that as a grown man, Dad would want to be called William Jacob. As a skinny boy in Kansas, he worked at his father's feed store that one day he would own.

As times got tough, Dad decided he would have to go on the road as a seed salesman if he was going to be able to feed his family. That road has taken him from Kansas to Missouri to Texas, back to Missouri, and finally to Mississippi.

He is one of those self-made men, that breed that came out of World War II with a dream and a desire, plus the drive to overcome all obstacles.

His travel limited the time we had together when I lived at home, so we learned to make every minute count.

The one thing I have learned from my father is that the best teacher around is yourself and an ability to read. By continuing to read books related to his profession, Father has become a leader in the agricultural advertising profession and is listed in 'Who's Who' in the Southeast.

When he reads a book that he feels would benefit me, he will send me a copy. I can almost hear him saying the words as I read the book, knowing that there are important things he wants me to know.

His travels carry him throughout the Southeastern United States. This week he made a momentary stop in Shreveport. Needless to say, the Bill Moorman Fan Club President held a meeting with her hero. This meeting was an unscheduled one; in a normal year, there are only three such meetings.

You can tell whose daughter I am. I have his nose, his eyes and his drive and love for people.

When I entered the world of business and needed to know a good book about public relations, he said, "I know of only one... the Bible."

Once again, he was right.

March 25, 1984

Who's Your Hero?

An interesting question was put to me this week—Who's your hero?

Right off the top of my head, I was unable to come up with a hero.

Then I began to think about it. As a kid, I was a big New York Yankee fan, so I thought Mickey Mantle was tops. In fact, I promised myself to name my first son Mickey. And then there was miler Jim Ryan from Wichita, Kansas.

But as time has passed and I have entered my 30s, I find it hard to name a hero. There are many people I admire, but each one has their own faults.

There are a few people who stand out, including my first track coach. I admire her way of taking people as they are and not belittling a person. She treated each person as she liked to be treated.

With that in mind, a person should mind their "P's and Q's" at all times because someone is watching and learning. I guess what it makes me realize is that no one is an island and that one's actions affect the entire society in the sense that the next generation will copy your acts.

This little fact is pointed out when a child or wife abuser's background is studied. The majority of the time, they were an abused child, too.

All of this pondering has made me re-establish some goals. Basically—live my life in such a way that I will be proud of someone copying it.

Think about it... Who's your hero?

April 1, 1984

Unforgettable Professor

A most unforgettable person is being honored this weekend at Stephen F. Austin State University. Dr. Francine Hoffman, professor of journalism, is being feted with a retirement tea.

Dr. Hoffman is one of those people who knows what it takes to survive in the real world, and she has worked to prepare her students for the life of a journalist.

With a mean editing pen that makes one's work bleed, she has taught an unbelievable number of students about the proper style of journalism.

I feel very fortunate to have had her as my teacher. She took a person who didn't know a thing about writing news stories and patiently whipped (molded) me into a reporter.

She was the type of person who shot from the hip when she saw you needed to be shocked into being the best you could be, but it was her willingness to be totally honest with me that made me love and respect her.

After one semester in journalism, this college returnee went to the Grand Old Lady of the Department and said, "I don't have the time or money to waste in school if I can't do this writing stuff. I respect your opinion and if you say get out, I will."

To my relief, she said, "You can do it if you are willing to work hard and make up for your weak education in your childhood."

I respect this lady and not a day goes by that I don't say a prayer of thanks to God for allowing my life's path to cross hers.

The field of journalism is losing one of the best teachers. The future journalist who will come out of SFA may not have as strong a background in the do's and don'ts of writing. In recent months, the fact that I am not a graduate of a well-known journalism school has been made apparent by professional people, but if they only knew Dr. Hoffman, they would realize the school's name does not make the writer. Good writers are made by good teachers.

April 22, 1984
A Friend Died This Week

My best friend died this week. Loyal friends are hard to find in this modern world we live in today.

I've thought a lot about friendships in the past few months. Some of the things I have realized that describe a good friend include someone who is there with support during bad and good times, a person that will put up with you when you are in a bad mood, someone who knows when to do those little things to make you feel better; and someone who worries when you come home late.

I was very lucky to have experienced the love, loyalty, and total trust that one has with a true friendship.

My late friend has been my roommate for eight years. Like any roommate, she complained when supper was late, the house a mess, or when dates stayed too late. But she was always there when I got home from work with a loving hello.

On those sleepless nights when one tries to solve all the world's problems at 3 a.m., or when something goes bump in the night, she was there trying to calm my nerves.

This special friend did not just die overnight. She fought leukemia for two years, but even during her own bad times, she was still a strong friend to me.

Oh, the memories are strong these days of all the things we did together—the walks in the woods, the nights of just watching television or reading, the trips to my parents and the general horseplay around the house.

No, you did not see an obituary of my friend because she was of the four-legged version. For you see, my best friend was Domino— my cat.

Now don't laugh. The sorrow is as real as if she had been human. Through the years, as people have passed through my life, she has stayed by my side. And there is a very real emptiness—avoid—in my life, but the future looks bright. In time there will be another kitten to raise, another friendship to develop and, of course, another heartbreaking end, but that's life. Learning to love and learning to let go to help those that you love.

May 5, 1984
Mother's Day Azalea

Well, I've done it again. It's Mother's Day and I have forgotten to send Mom a gift.

This is not the first time, nor will it be the last, believe me. I don't forget Mom; I just don't get into gear and send her a card or gift. But I do watch enough television commercials to remember to call the one I love.

But Mom is of the old school of thought, where a card or gift is nicer than a phone call. During the phone call, all she can hear is the dollar meter clicking away. She prefers to have something she can hold and re-read over and over and over...

I think my greatest attempt to send joy to Mother was the year I sent her an azalea plant. How was I to know that in Mississippi, azaleas grow wild and that her yard was filled with bushes?

When I called her to see if she got the plant, she was pleased with the thoughtful gift but not impressed with the plant. She politely said, "At least my indoor azalea is a different color than my outdoor azaleas."

Oh well, at least I tried.

The years that one forgets to get Mom a gift prove to be the most costly. One year Dad forgot her birthday and, boy, was he doomed. Every time she saw something she wanted, she'd say, "You can get me this for that birthday gift you forgot." She did quite well in the gift department that year, quite a haul.

No, this column is not to be her gift this year, but it will probably not be appreciated. The last time I used her in one of my columns, she was visiting, and I got a spanking when I got home.

Oh well, what can I say? I've done it again. Happy belated Mother's Day, Mom. You are in my thoughts even when I don't get in gear and show it.

May 13, 1984
Russian's Boycott Olympic

Well, they did it. The Russians are boycotting the Los Angeles Olympics. I knew it was coming. It is sad that politicians are playing with the lives and careers of athletes in the continuing battles of the Cold War.

Don't kid yourself, the Cold War is still going just as strong as in the 1950s.

Once again, the athletes are the victims. Just as in 1980, when President Jimmy Carter had the Americans boycott the Moscow Olympics, the hard work and dedication of the athletes went down the drain.

What gives these politicians the right to say that individuals cannot participate in the greatest sporting event in the world?

ABC sports announcer Jim McKay made an interesting point on the ABC show 20-20 when he said that the Olympics was not about what country won the most gold medals but about the individuals who had dedicated their lives to the sport.

He said that as long as there are individuals wanting to do their sporting event to the best of their ability, there will be the Olympics. This year without the presents of the Russians or East Germans, there will be an opportunity for those individuals who have worked just as hard to reach the winner's stand.

Maybe McKay has a point. Maybe we have used the Olympics for national bragging rather than praising the individuals. Take the Winter Olympics, so the United States is not strong in winter sports, but at least some individuals set a goal to train for and compete in the Olympics.

Those individuals are the winners, not their governments, for they have accomplished a life dream. How many of us can say we have done that?

I feel for the athletes in the countries that are boycotting the Olympics. These individuals probably have no idea why their government is doing what it is doing.

It reminds me so much of those friends of mine who were at their peak for the Moscow Olympics and had to see their dream die when President Carter made his decree. Their lives to that point, had become a total waste of time and effort. And what good did that boycott do? Nothing, except stealing a life dream from my friends.

May 20, 1984

Sew And Weep...

A historic occasion occurred in the Jane Moorman residence this past week—I used my sewing machine. Now you say, big deal. But for this non-domestic individual, sewing is a real war between woman and machine.

Several years ago, Mother purchased a new sewing machine, so I inherited her machine. When she gave it to me, the comment was made that this machine would be an excellent antique in years to come since I never sew.

The need to make a tank-top fit properly forced me to pull the machine out of its box, take away the plastic bag and thread the 'monster.'

After making my alterations, I looked around for more mending that had been stacking up for Mother's next visit. Maybe I'll get up the nerve to tackle the pile.

It's not that I don't know how to sew. I worked a year in a fabric store and could field all questions about how to put in a zipper and such., but when I sit down at the machine, a normally calm person becomes a basket-case.

I have and can work with the most sophisticated machinery, but it's a different story with a sewing machine. There's just something about the tension control that makes my patience run out... quickly.

I'm one of those seamstresses that sew an inch and rip out two. By the time I finish a garment, I never want to see it again, let alone wear it.

While growing up, my mother was the family seamstress. She would come in from work a nervous wreck and sit down at the machine to relax.

We are a pretty good team when we mass-produce clothes for me. Mom sits at the machine and sews while I do the ironing and pinning. We have been known to whip out three blouses in one day.

There is one thing for sure: dust won't rest on the machine before I get it back in its box.

June 27, 1984
Mourning Over...

The mourning is over. I have put my 'black dress' away and am ready to face the world of the living.

I wrote of my best friend, my cat, dying about a month ago. Well, her replacement has moved in. A 'fresh' kitty of the black and white variety.

Oh, to name a new child. But this one will step into an old family name, Nacle, the II. Yes, it is a strange name.

It all started as a family joke back in 1970. When two kittens moved into my parent's home, we immediately christened the boys: Nacle and Taber.

"Now, as the boys stand at the door crying to go out," Mom said with a serious expression on her face. "We will have the Moorman's Taber-Nacle choir."

Yes, when your last name is Moorman, jokes are always in the air.

Nacle died last year after thirteen years of joy and love, so I will give the title to the new child in the family.

I can't wait to call my parents and tell them they are the proud grandparents of a black cat that looks like it lay down in white paint as its white marking covers its stomach and paws.

The decision to bring life back into the house has been a long agonizing time as the memory of Domino fads and the void began to go away.

I had convinced myself I did not want another cat, but a few nights ago, as I opened the house's front door, I caught myself wishing there was a little four-legged friend there to greet me.

Welcome home, Nacle!

June 10, 1984
Don't Forget Mom's Birthday... You Will Pay

Birthdays are those days that every adult would like to forget, but if you forget them, some folks get very upset.

Mother's big day was Friday, and it always seemed to slip up on me. Finally, I have come up with a way to remember "her day:" it is two days after D-Day. Easy little fact to remember. Just like my parent's anniversary is the day after Halloween.

As I think of past birthdays of my family, I remember the year my brother had to bake his own birthday cake—it was surprisingly good, even his pineapple frosting.

Mother's birthday gift has always been a stumper for me. As a child, I would go to the five-and-dime store with my brother and spend hours looking over all the things I thought she would like and over all the things I knew I would like to spend my life's savings of $10 on for myself.

The year that stands out in my memory was when we gave her two pheasants figurines. It must have been a good gift because she still has them.

Dad really messed up one year and forgot Mother's birthday and he paid for it all year. Every time she saw something she wanted, she'd say, "You can get me this for that present you forgot." She did really well in the gift department that year.

Now when it comes time to confess age, Mom has a scapegoat—Dad. He claimed thirty-nine for years until his black hair turned entirely gray and he moved it up to forty-nine. She says everyone knows she is two years younger than Dad, so she must be forty-seven (at least) by now.

Happy belated birthday, Mom.

June 17, 1984
No Regrets, Dad!

Several years ago, Father asked me if there was anything that I had not gotten as a child that I wished I had received. He was worrying about his quality of parenting and needed to be reassured.

I answered the serious questions with a smile, saying, "Yes, back in 1965, I really wanted a hat from the state fair."

He was mad at the answer. For once, he was being serious and I answered with a joke, but what I was telling him was, how could I say I missed something? You can't miss something if you have never had it.

He raised two children to the best of his ability. He worked hard to take care of our needs, even when it meant going on the road as a salesman to earn a living. He gave up seeing his children grow up to make sure we had food, clothing, braces on our teeth and bicycles in the garage.

How can you ever find fault in a man who spends five lonely nights a week in motel rooms rather than being at home with the people he loves?

Well, this is our 31st Father's Day together. And I can still answer his question with a smile and a joke. I really did want that hat at the state fair back in 1965.

The unselfish man ends up with a daughter who gets so wrapped up in work that she forgets the simple task of buying a card and mailing it. Sunday morning, he will receive a phone call from her, and she will be joking.

In reality, she is ashamed that she cannot remember one day honoring a man who gave up so much for her.

June 24, 1984
Wake Me Again...

I was awakened the other day by a telephone call from a reader who, after apologizing for waking me, told me how much she appreciated a column I had written about the death of the sports editor in Nacogdoches.

I was unable to express to her the thanks that she deserved for making that phone call. As a reporter, I very seldom hear if the reader enjoys my work. You can wake me early anytime with praise, but not a complaint.

But when I do hear praise or thanks for an article or column, it is the crowning of a person's joy because, in every column, I write, I reveal a little something of myself to about 8,000 subscribers or about 24,000 potential readers. When you are a very private person, this task is hard to do.

A footnote to that column about the late sports editor: I received a thank you note from his parents expressing their appreciation for the column. In part, it said, "We were deeply moved and so appreciative of the wonderful tribute you wrote about our son Mark. He has such wonderful friends—we are so thankful for that. Your writing about him has lightened our hearts."

With tears in my eyes, I cannot say anymore.

Thanks!

July 7, 1984
So Many Fireworks!

Fourth of July is just not the fourth without fireworks.

As a kid in Kansas, this was a long-awaited day of fun, picnics, relaxation and the grand finale—fireworks.

Our family joined a group of ten families for an annual picnic and combined fireworks display. By combining all our Roman Candles and other assorted fireworks, we would have quite a show.

But one year, the fireworks just seemed to go on and on and on.

"My, aren't there a lot this year," Lula said.

"Yes, thanks to John (Lula's husband)," another woman said.

"What do you mean?" Lula asked.

"John provided most of the fireworks this year."

"He did? John, where did you get all of these?" the surprised wife said to her husband.

"I bought them last year from the dime store for half price," John said proudly of his great savings.

"Where have they been for the entire year," Lula continued to inquire.

"In the attic of the garage."

"IN THE ATTCI! DIDN'T YOU THINK ABOUT THE FIRE HAZARD? WHAT IF WE HAD HAD A FIRE?"

The alarmed wife also was thinking about the fact that her husband was the town's insurance agent-adjuster and should have known the hazard of his well-intended efforts.

Hazard or not, that was definitely the best Fourth of July the group of families had ever had and probably ever will have.

August 5, 1984
Friend Quits Smoking

Recently, an old friend came to visit. Prior to her arrival, I dug out the ashtrays since she is one of my few friends who smoke.

As the visit progressed, I realized that the ever-present cigarette was not connected to her hand, so I inquired about her habit.

"You could say I have quit, but I say I am just not smoking," she explained. "There is a difference. Not smoking means I can have one if I want to, but I just don't want one. Quitting means that there will never be another cigarette."

She went on to tell why she had stopped the hazardous habit. "There are so many places that you can't smoke these days, such as the airplane, restaurants, peoples' cars and homes, that I carried a pack of cigarettes around for a month before I could smoke one."

Well, I have heard many reasons for quitting or for smoking, but that was the best for stopping the habit.

I think she has kicked the habit, unlike Mark Twain, who once wrote, "I can quit smoking anytime I want to. I have tried millions of times."

August 5, 1984
Tatting Anyone?

I have a request for all of the Daily News readers. I am looking for people who know how to do tatting.

Tatting is a lost art. This handwork was done by my grandmother's generation to decorate dress collars and pillowcases. You also can make dollies.

I have been tatting for five years and would like to meet others who know this art. It is one of those crafts that has been lost but is beginning to revive.

If you know of anyone who does tatting, please call the Daily News office and tell Olga Dorsey who they are.

September 1, 1984
Hundreds of Vacation Photos

The fun of a vacation is getting the photographs back.

My little two-week trip to Los Angeles yielded 300 pictures. I had to float a $125 loan to get the pictures from the processor, but it was worth it.

Needless to say, there is a lot of self-pride wrapped around those pictures, especially when people say they are 'better than postcards.' And that comment was not even forced from them.

So, if you see me coming in your direction with a white paper sack under my arm, I suggest you run and hide because I'm really worse than a proud grandparent with pictures of their first grandchild.

September 30, 1984

Too Many Cats…

Enough is enough!

I like cats, but when my young cat invites the entire neighborhood into the house to play, it pushes things a little.

Each cat has a different personality. Unlike my old cat, who would not allow another cat on her patio, Nacel invites the neighborhood cats in to play.

Playtime isn't at a decent time of the day, but at 5:30 a.m. on Sunday morning.

Sunday, I was awakened by two cats on top of the bed playing with one on the floor. This is great fun for all involved except the human who is trying to sleep.

Boots and Smokey like playing in my house because there is always a paper sack that needs to be explored or a balled sock that needs to be killed.

Then there is the little white kitty, a stray. She is timid but has learned that there is food in the house, so hunger has overcome her shyness as she enters the house for a free meal. When I talk to her, she tilts her head and listens. One of these days, she will stop running back outside when I move around the house.

The neighborhood party begins at 5:30 a.m. each morning when Boots and Smokey are let outdoors. Nacle gets really excited and licks my face until I get out of bed and let her outside to join in the fun.

It's a good thing I love cats. The additional animals in my family are bringing me much joy. I only hope that Boots and Smokey, who are males, don't realize that Nacle's a female, or I will have more cats than the 'old lady who lived in the shoe' had children.

December 16, 1984

Dislikes Sewing, Too

I have found a friend who dislikes sewing as much as I do. She will call me for moral support when she attempts to mend her children's clothes.

As she struggles with tension control and the needle and clothing, I give her many words of advice.

Since the pile of mending seems to grow faster than she can gather the nerve to attack, I have come up with a solution.

There are clothes of her first child that have been awaiting mending for months. It is almost to the point that the child has outgrown the shirt. So, I simply told her not to worry, child number two would grow into it by the time she mends it.

But there was doubt in her voice when I brought up this point. "Do you really think I will get it mended before he outgrows it also?"

"Well, if that one outgrows it, I guess you will just have to have one more child. That will give you five more years to get the shirt mended."

For some reason, she felt throwing the shirt away would be easier than giving birth to another child.

December 16, 1984
Daddy Tamp—a Good Man

The Henderson Fellowship of Christian Athletics honored Dee Tamplin on Thursday by inducting him into the FCA basketball tournament honor roll.

Dee Tamplin is one man I am glad to say I know.

I call him "Daddy Tamp" since he is the father of Henderson baseball coach Skip Tamplin and Bob Tamplin.

Daddy Tamp is one of those guys who has had a positive effect on many people in his life. I'm probably one of them. He has really made me feel special while I have been getting my feet on the ground here in Henderson.

There is a little pre-game ritual that Daddy Tamp and I perform. It may appear to be a simple handshake, but it is our "lucky handshake." Since we both know that if this handshake does not occur before a Henderson game, the team will probably lose.

Yes, sir, that's one powerful handshake, but Daddy Tamp and I know what's good for our Lions.

Some may still call Tamplin "Coach" since that was his profession for thirty-eight years. And though he has been sidelined by age and a heart attack, Daddy Tamp is still a coach at heart. He watches the Henderson athletes like they were his children and comments on their fundamental skills.

He is truly a good coach who never stops coaching. As long as Daddy Tamp's eyesight is good, he will be picking out those little things that can make the difference between a fair athlete and a great one.

Daddy Tamp, it is an honor to know you.

September 1, 1985
Best Watermelon Ever

Watermelon!

Can you remember the best one you ever ate?

Mine was when I was in junior high. Dad was a traveling seed salesman in Missouri, and he was always bringing home produce from farmers.

The time he brought home, the watermelon proved to be his best 'catch.'

After a long journey home in the back end of the station wagon that turned into two weeks of rolling back and forth on every curve, the melon rested for another two weeks under the hickory tree in the backyard.

Finally, we cut into the prized melon and to our joy, it was the sweetest morsel of food we ever ate.

Now I'm not suggesting that you torture your watermelons as Dad did in the back of the station wagon because you must be careful not to let the melon get over-ripe in the heat of the car.

Dad learned the hard way when a melon he was taking to his boss rolled once too often and broke. The sticky mess broke Dad from bringing home 'goodies' from farmers.

Another watermelon tidbit: to tell if a melon is ripe, take a broom straw and rest it crosswise on the melon. If the melon is ripe, the straw will turn lengthwise. Yes, it really does work.

October 6, 1985

Cat Captured Gifts

For many people, the only thing cats are good for is hunting mice.

At my house, the cats are normal. They sleep all day on my bed and hunt all night. Like any good cat, the female brings her catch to the house for praise. Only she brings it in through her opened window.

This is nice, except when the catch is a gopher and it's alive in my house. Then I tend to lose my cool.

On four different nights, I have been awakened in the early hours by the sound of wild critters loose in the house.

The last one was Tuesday morning at about 6:30 a.m. The cat was playing with the animal as it tried to escape and hide under various boxes and clothes in my bedroom.

After watching this 'fun' and telling the cat she had better not lose that animal in my house, the gopher crawled under the closet door. That was all I could stand. I swooped down with a bath towel and captured the dying critter and threw it out the window.

The fall was too much for the already injured animal, and the gopher died. The look my cat gave me was filled with frustration, for I had killer latest plaything.

After a few minutes of watching the gopher from the window, the cat decided that it was dead. She turned and gave me a meow that said, "Well, if you are going to throw out the breakfast I caught, the least you can do is get up and feed me."

October 20, 1985
Missouri World Series

OCTOBER! WORLD SERIES!

There is only one thing better in the fall than the World Series and that's the trees turning beautiful colors.

Since I was a little one in grade school, the World Series has had a special place in my fall ritual.

The principal at Nickerson Elementary School was a big baseball fan and everything thing stopped during the Series. It was an accepted fact that Mr. Houston (pronounced House-ton, not like the city) would pipe the radio broadcast of the afternoon games through the school's PA system.

We would sit and work on our homework while listening to the Yankees and the Dodgers battle it out in faraway places like New York and Los Angeles.

Meanwhile, in Kansas, we devoted young fans took the names of our favorite stars and played our own World Series during lunch break. My team was the Yankees. We had a girl who always wore white shirts, so needless to say, we called her Whitey after Whitey Ford. Then our catcher was dubbed Yogi. And, of course, we had Roger Maris and Mickey Mantle.

To our surprise, if my memory serves me right, while the Yankees won, so did our "Yankee" squad.

This year is even more exciting for me, with Kansas City and St. Louis in the World Series.

After moving to Missouri from Kansas, I began to follow the Cardinals. Many a night, I would listen to the Cardinals on the radio with Harry Cary calling the exciting play-by-play. Harry Car is now announcing for the Chicago Cubs, but there is still a warm spot in my heart for St. Louis.

The cities of St. Louis and Kansas City are as different as Dallas and Fort Worth. St. Louis is the eastern city-slickers, kind of like

Dallas, while Kansas City is the cattle town grown up, similar to Fort Worth.

When this year's Series begins, I will definitely be in a dilemma over which team I want to win. I will be kept busy changing my baseball cap as the teams come to bat.

After watching the American League and National League championships this last week, I will have to go with the Cardinals. Also, I have to go with my feelings after attending a Cardinal game while on vacation and meeting some of the devoted fans.

There is only one thing greater than a Missouri World Series in my book, and that's the fall trees of the Missouri Ozarks.

November 24, 1985

Where Were You When...

Have you ever thought about milestones in your life? Friday was one in the lives of most Americans marking President John F. Kennedy's assassination.

Friday was the 22nd anniversary of the moment in history in 1963 that will stay with everyone for their entire life.

Just ask someone, "Where were you when Kennedy was assassinated?" They will be able to remember that moment like it was yesterday.

I was in seventh-grade noon recess in Kansas playing softball. For the remainder of the day, the radio broadcast was piped through the school's intercom system.

Richard Slaymaker said he was in ninth-grade physical education class when the principal made the announcement.

Jim Robertson said he was in elementary school.

"They made the announcement over the PA system, then later they dismissed school and we went home," he said.

Our pressman Robert Cyphers said he remembers it because he was waiting to run the day's paper when they said, "Stop the press! The president has been shot."

It is interesting that thousands of days that have passed by the death of a non-family member can leave such a lasting impression on people.

Now here's another one. Where were you when the first man walked on the moon?

December 1, 1985

Cowboys or Turkey

Football on TV...

You just don't realize how nice television coverage of a pro football game is until you sit in the stadium freezing.

My traditional Thanksgiving Day activities were pre-empted this year for a quick trip to Dallas to see the Cowboys play St. Louis.

When someone tells you they have tickets for sale to a game a day away, you can't help by jumping on the opportunity. So, when Williams Ashby walked up to my desk Wednesday with two tickets, I quickly grabbed them up and called a friend to go to the game.

Tatum girls' coach Janet Conway and I headed to Dallas on Thursday morning rather than eat Old Tom Turkey.

They may have said it was 40 degrees in Texas Stadium, but my feet will swear that it was 30 below. We lasted until after the Cowboys' touchdown put them ahead 28-17, then we headed to the car, which was parked in Outer Mongolia.

Janet and I agreed that you have to attend a game to appreciate television

It was fun and though I was cold, I'd do it again. Well, maybe again if the weather is warmer and the tickets are on the lower level.

December 8, 1985
Matt's Gifts

Christmas time is upon us. Boy, how I like to shop for Christmas, especially for my nephew Matt.

He is really going to be surprised this year. I can't tell you what I got him because he received this newspaper, but I can say that he was not expecting this year's gift.

Each year Matt sends me a special gift list that tells me not only what he wants but what page it is on in the Sears catalog.

Each year I get him one or two of his requests then I add a gift that is really special.

Last year, it was a radio with a headset which really lit up the ten-year-old eyes. But I must say this year's gift is really special; he'll be the only boy on this block with one of these. In fact, his father will probably play with it more than any of the kids. I'm even having a hard time wrapping it and sending it off to Colorado; I've played with it so much I have to put new batteries in it before I mail it.

Boy, do I love Christmas?

December 29, 1985

Inherited a Rock Garden

I guess I must have been a bad kid this year. The old tale that bad children will only receive sticks and blocks of coal came true at my house this Christmas. I have inherited my mother's rock garden. Yes, I said rock garden.

Through the years, mother has picked up rocks from all over the country as we have traveled from coast to coast. Many miles have been traveled with rocks underfoot in the car.

My parents are in the process of moving (again) and I have been entrusted with the rocks.

In the selection that Mother dropped on my doorstep are lava from New Mexico and Kansas, limestone from Kansas, quartz and rose stone from Arkansas; rocks from the East and West coasts, chunks of blue and red glass from glass factories' scrap piles, and even a brick that was in the Chicago fire.

These rocks have been moved from Kansas to Missouri, to Texas, back to Missouri, then to Mississippi, and now back to Texas.

While moving to Missouri, Mom and my brother Dave were in one car leading the way. Dad and I were in the other. As we crossed Kansas' back roads, we hit some icy places. Mother sailed right through. Dad and I fish-tailed while trying to keep up with the speedster.

It wasn't until we got to Missouri that Dad discovered Mother had her rock garden in the truck of the car, which had given her more traction on the ice.

One rock that was missing was Jane's Rock. This was a rectangular piece of limestone that I had painted green as a child and sat on while playing in the sandbox. Through the years, this 'big' rock has shrunk and the paint has washed off to the point that none of us can identify it now.

Thanks, Mom, for the nice Christmas present. I'll take good care of all your rocks. I promise.

January 26, 1986
Trees Special...

Arbor Day was Friday. For East Texans, trees are just there, and we don't really think about them much.

But for a gal who grew up in the wheat fields of Kansas, where trees were only located in towns, on homesteads, along creeks or in fence rows, they are really special.

Arbor Day began in 1872 in Nebraska when the citizens began to realize how important this natural resource is to the environment.

The practice of planting trees on Arbor Day began in Texas in 1889 in Temple.

We East Texans are fortunate to live in the Piney Woods, but we must remember to protect this natural, renewable resource.

Trees provide us with shade, fuel, paper and lumber. Also, trees are important in controlling erosion from wind and water.

The lumber industry of East Texas is very much aware of renewing this resource and have an extensive planting operation to keep the lumber coming for future generations.

So next time you look at a tree, stop and think about all that it does for you and don't forget the songbirds that make their homes there.

March 26, 1986
Childhood Keepsakes

Have you ever looked at what parents keep in their attics from their children's childhood?

My parents are in the process of moving for the third time since I left home, but they are still moving my keepsakes around. Maybe they are not my keepsakes, but theirs when you look at the items.

Mother called to see if I would like my three boxes. Yes, she has boiled my things down to three boxes. I commented on what could possibly be worth three boxes, so the next time she called, she said it was down to one big suitcase.

If my memory serves me right, there are several bowling trophies still at Mom's. I know the stuffed animals are still there. Also, a few toys. But otherwise, what could be there?

Mother reports that the hair dryer for one of my dolls is still intact. Why has she kept that for so many years? I asked.

"Because it was a neat toy," she replied. I think she kept it for the child in herself.

I inquired about the whereabouts of my favorite teddy bear. You know, the one I told all my secrets to while cutting his fur one day. "What bear?" Mother asked.

"The big red one. Teddy was his name."

"Oh, I think he is long gone."

Well, I hope Teddy took all my secrets to the grave, but he was my best friend as a child and I know he wouldn't tell my tales, not even if they put needles into his paws.

Mother had revealed that some of the things she found in the attic included cards she received when I was born. From the way she talked, they were placed away and will be there when I have to clean up the estate after her death.

She also had the dress I wore to my brother's wedding. "Why Mom?"

"Because you looked so nice in it. Besides, it will probably be the closest you get to a wedding again."

Well, if I were to get married, I would not be wearing that dress, not just because of the color, but because my body would never be that small again.

Parents! What's a person to do with them?

April 13, 1968
Phone Woes...

I'm sure when Alexander Graham Bell invented the telephone, he did not expect it to become a tool for invasion of privacy.

For years I have felt that the telephone is a luxury item, not a necessity. Several times I have lived for more than a year without one in my home.

There are times when the phone is a necessity, but more times than not, they are an invasion of one's privacy. Sure, they are handy to call for help in times of need, but there are more times that they are a bother.

Three of my biggest pet peeves are friends calling to talk just as a good movie goes into its final fifteen minutes, a salesperson calling at dinner time, and obscene phone calls.

Obscene phone calls are the main cause of my complaints. This week I received one at 6:30 a.m. that totally unnerved me.

For four years, I have had a night caller who calls anywhere from early evening to 3 a.m. This gutless wonder thinks he is making my day. Over the years, I have gotten to where I recognize his voice and I know he is harmless, but this week's caller was on a cruder level and, as far as I'm concerned, below talking to.

The Henderson Police Department tells me that a tap can be put on a phone. When an obscene call comes in, the receiver of the call can leave the line open and contact the police to trace the call.

So, you callers, I'm after you.

May 4, 1986
High School Bands Outstanding

The band students from Carlisle and Overton high schools have been making a lot of 'noise' this spring, but only pleasant sounds as they have won honors with their musical ability.

Both concert bands won sweepstake honors at the District 21 UIL competition in Lindale. The sweepstake award is one of the highest awards a band can earn in the UIL competition.

Carlisle received a first-division rating for concert playing and a first-division rating for sight reading.

This annual competition consists of bands playing music for judges without having heard, read, rehearsed, or performed the selection at any time prior to the contest. Judging criteria for sight reading is the accuracy of reading, flexibility in following the director, adherence to the style, interpretation, and musicianship.

I think this is quite an honor for both bands from our area. Music is an aspect of education that helps a person become better rounded. By learning how to play an instrument, a student is getting a lifetime of enjoyment.

Carlisle's competition also took them to New Orleans to participate in the Creative Arts Workshop Showcase and Mississippi Riverboat Holiday Festival, where they competed with band from Oklahoma, Louisiana, Alabama, Canada, Texas, Arkansas, and Tennessee.

The Indians won a rating of excellence in concert playing and a first-place top jazz award in their class.

Carlisle's band program has been under the direction of T.E. McClain for two and a half years. When he arrived in Carlisle, there were 12 students enrolled in music. Now there are 115 students enrolled in band in grades four through 12.

Two years of hard work by the students at Carlisle have produced a band that received many compliments from the judges at the contests.

"This band gets some really nice sounds. Nice flue section."

"Very good job sight-reading, boys and girls. Thank your director for teaching you good basic music skills."

"Very nice job on the piece 'Song of Winds.'"

"March – good style, nice trumpet solo, played with excellent style throughout. Outstanding jazz group. I like your style, neat trumpets, good balance, nice dynamics."

Congratulations band members, on a job well done.

May 11, 1986

Freedom of the Press Important

Freedom of the press has been on display with the nuclear accident in Russia.

With all the reports of the Russian government not telling their people of the health danger, it makes me thankful to be living in the United States.

Sometimes the free world media overplays a story or situation to the point that a person is tired of hearing about it, but at least we hear all the facts.

I would hate to be living in an area that is radioactive and not have anyone be honest with me about the health hazards. I want to know what's going on upwind from me so I can take the necessary health precautions.

When the Three Mile Island incident occurred, the media kept the power company honest by being there and telling the world what was happening. I really feel sorry for the man on the street in Russia. He is not told what is going on. This is not the first time. When the Russians invaded Afghanistan and the U.S. boycotted the 1980 Olympics, the people of Russia did not even know what their military was up to.

One thing about the U.S., the government is not going to be able to lie to its people. This was proven by Watergate, thanks to the watchful eye of the media.

May 20, 1986

Special Olympics Honors Participation

Special Olympics are just that, special. Not just because of the people involved but because of the rewards to all those people.

The first time I was involved in the Special Olympics was while in college when a professor required our class to help with the track meet.

I learned so much from that experience. The main thing was seeing the self-esteem and self-pride grow with the awarding of ribbons to all participants. It occurs to me that it's a shame that in our society of winner-loser, we can't award honors for just participating.

The Special Olympics creed to "To do my best." What more can anyone ask for a person to do than their best at whatever the task maybe?

May 5, 1986

Summer Ball Teaches Valuable Lessons

It's summer baseball time again. Life for many families revolves around taking the children to baseball or softball games.

While we are all out at the ballpark, let's try to remember what the summer program is trying to contribute to this community.

Both the Henderson Baseball Association and the Henderson Girls Softball Association are giving young people a constructive place to burn off energy and learn some important values for their adult life.

Learning the valuable lesson of being a good winner and loser is vital to all involved in the program, from child to parent and coach. Also, learning self-discipline, following directions, and learning how to work together is a by-product of gaining the skills to play the game.

Selfishness has no place on a ballfield or in the stands. Working together to accomplish the set goal is what these young people are learning. Go out and support the children. Remember, children are mirrors of the adults around them, so set good examples for our future adults.

June 1, 1986

Summer Vacation

"School's out! School's out! Teacher let the mules out!"

As a child, this ditty was sung as we skipped away from school after the last bell of the year. Then from the front porch of the house, I would give out a war hoop.

For nine months, we had dreamed of summer and what we would do when we didn't have to be in school all day. I had dreamed of playing all day long, swimming, picnics, going to camp, going to grandma's and much, much more.

The first day of summer was always packed full of activities. I'd start the day with a bike ride around town to talk to all the little old ladies who were gardening in their yards. Then I would talk mother into a first day of summer picnic as I ate my lunch on the back steps.

As the afternoon wore on, I would convince Mom to take us swimming. Then as the evening cooled, the kids from the neighborhood would get up a game of baseball that was called because of darkness, and our parents called us to come home.

These busy days usually lasted about a week then that dreaded day would come when we would ease up to Mom and say, "I'm bored. What can I do?"

Ah! The joys of summer!

July 29, 1986
Unplanned Vacation

Vacation time is just around the corner. I must admit I'm looking forward to it this year. It's been a long year full of long hours.

Usually, I plan a vacation down to the hour: where I will be, what I will do, every little detail. But this year, it will be different.

I have two destinations in mind and nothing planned in between. I'm headed to northern Colorado. I'm not too sure which roads I will take to get there, where I will sleep or what I will see and do.

So, on July 18, I will board the cats, throw my sleeping bag and tent in the car and head out. Who knows what adventure I will experience? But knowing me, it will be something exciting.

August 3, 1986
Rough Road

I have preached to my softball team that it only makes it worse to say it's hot when it's 80 degrees or hotter. But let me tell you that it's hot.

The heat hit me smack in the face in Weatherford on my way back from vacationing in the mountains of New Mexico, Arizona, Utah, and Colorado.

I enjoyed the nice cool mornings, the brisk noon breeze, and the need for a sleeping bag at times.

In two weeks, the car plowed its way over hill and dale for 4,120 miles. I had promised no dirt trails, but I could not resist a road that led through the Valley of Gods in southern Utah.

So off we went over a road that had bottomless potholes, rocky gullies and rocks the size of a basketball to knock the oil pan off the car.

At the point of no return, I hoped two things: that the view up ahead was worth the drive and that the road would reach pavement before forcing me to make a return trip.

We reached the pavement and headed on down the road knowing that we had just seen the highlight of the trip.

August 24, 1986
How Old Are You?

There is something about getting older than forty that causes people to stop counting the years. But to 'stay' 39 until your second child is almost the same age is ridiculous.

Dad has claimed age thirty-nine for many, many years now. Let me get my pencil out here and do some figuring. I guess he's been thirty-nine for twenty-five years.

Mom knows for a fact that she is two years younger than Dad, so if he claims thirty-nine, she must be thirty-seven.

Their first-born child was born in 1950, which makes him thirty-eight this year. Now their second child just had a birthday and is within five years of the magic number.

Isn't it interesting how people can be in their twenties when they give birth to a child, but then the child ages while the parents stay the same age?

Dad said it is one of the miracles of life. The phenomenon occurs at a point in everyone's life when the calendars just stop peeling off. A person just automatically stops aging at thirty-nine.

Now I just wonder what happens next year when my brother reaches thirty-nine. If the numbers tell the story (and Dad keeps claiming thirty-nine), that would mean that Dad was fifteen days from birth when Dave was born. Also, Mother, who is two years younger than Dad, was not even born.

Now that's a miracle.

Henderson Daily News
Henderson, Texas
General Columns

May 9, 1982

Thanks, Mom, For Being There

Through my years of associating with sports, there has been an ever-present individual who seldom gets any recognition.

She is affectionately called "Baseball Momma."

Her physical descriptions are not important because she comes in all sizes and shapes.

There are a few common factors that can identify this woman in the stands.

She can tell you the rules of the game in her sleep. Any coach can ask her for a scouting report on her child's opponents and she will give you a review of the player's career against her child. But her main duty is to support her child's efforts on the field. When 'little Johnny' makes an outstanding play, Momma's voice is the loudest. You can hear her say, "That's okay, Johnny," when her child makes a mistake.

Words of encouragement are what she is there for.

This lady, who will sit through a Blue Norther,' a spring rainstorm or 100-degree temperatures, has many years of experience. She was there the first day her child began participating in baseball in the summer Little League program.

Her duties in the early years were a combination of chauffeur, laundry maid and cheerleader. As the years have gone by, she has had to replace her original lawn chair at least once, and her chauffeur duties have been eliminated as 'little Johnny' now has a car, but her cheering is still echoing across the baseball field.

'Little Johnny' probably has not said "Thanks for being there" recently. It will only occur to him that she was there when she is not around anymore.

There is something about looking up in the stands and seeing 'Old Mom' sitting there. Sometimes it is not necessary for her to say a thing—her presence is enough.

After a bad day on the field, 'little Johnny' probably does not want to talk about it, but just knowing that Mom cares is enough to help heal the wounds of defeat.

'Baseball Mommas' are also good at letting this young reporter and once-young umpire know that they appreciate her efforts. This is how I have been most affected by these women of spring.

On this day of honoring Mothers, it is time for 'little Johnny' and this reporter today to say, "Thanks, Mom, for being there."

June 20, 1982
It's All With Being a Father

Last summer, when my nephew Matt was visiting, he told me that he was playing soccer.

"Your brother! Your brother is our coach," he exclaimed excitedly about his father—and my brother—coaching his team.

Why, you might ask, is this such a big thing? Well, my brother was not the athletic one in our family while we were growing up—I was. In fact, I had to pay him a dollar an hour to play catch with me when I couldn't find anyone else to play.

Surprised by Matt's comment. I turned to my father and said, "What has happed to my brother? He's coaching? I can't believe it."

Dad's reply was very simple, "It's all with being a father."

It's all with being a father. What a statement.

I began to think back on my father's determination to help me not 'throw the ball like a girl.' He would come home from work tired and hungry and play catch with me while we waited for supper.

And then there were the hours in the swimming pool when he taught me not to be afraid of the water. How about the hours of huffing and puffing behind my bicycle until I learned to hold my balance?

It's all with being a father.

Or how about the day he shot a whole role of a home movie film—the whole 50 feet—on my first bowling trophy?

As I grew up and found personal pleasure in athletics, it was Dad who understood the feeling of working hard to be good enough for the team.

He told me of his childhood—as all fathers do—when he was in high school and wanted to play basketball. His father said he could, but only after his farm chores were done. So, every afternoon he ran a mile home, milked the cows, and fed the chickens before going to basketball practice.

On the day of the big district game, he had to go home to do his chores before leaving for the out-of-town game. All of his dedication went up in smoke when he saw the school bus pull out from the school when he was two blocks away. The coach could not wait any longer for him.

Dad knew what it felt like to catch that last out to win the game—and what it felt like to make the last out to lose the game. He was there afterward with a smile and a hug to remind me it was only a game.

His job as a traveling salesman did not allow him much time with his family when I was in junior high and high school, but he still kept up with my athletic accomplishments and encouraged me to purse a college career in physical education.

Today, Dad is still my biggest fan. I get memos from him hurriedly written on an office notepad, bringing words of praise and encouragement.

After all, no matter how old his child gets—it's all with being a father.

June 27, 1982

I Want To Play Ball

A little girl approached the baseball registration table with a form she had clipped from the newspaper.

"I want to play ball," she said to the man behind the table.

"Well, honey, this is a boys' league. Girls don't play in this league," he said.

That's not fair, thought the girl. *I play with them at school and in the evenings. Why can't I play on a team?*

Seeing that the child was disappointed, the man gave her a challenge that he thought would keep her busy and take her mind off baseball.

"I'll tell you what. If you can get enough girls to sign up, we will have a softball league."

The only thing he did not realize was that he was talking to little Janie Moorman, who was strong-headed and determined enough to rally her friends together to form a league.

Off she went on her bicycle. Before the sunset, she had talked to every girl who lived in the small Kansas-farming community of Nickerson, which is one mile long and half-a-mile wide.

"Come on," she would yell to her buddies. "Let's go sign up to play softball."

Out of the 1,100 population, a girls' softball program was started back in 1961. The program was meager in size, with only four teams, but it served its purpose—to give the girls a league of their own.

It Takes Planning To Get There

Anyone who tries to get more than two people somewhere on time knows it is next to impossible.

My mother has a trick—set the departure time an hour ahead of the desired departure and hope you leave no more than a half-hour after the necessary time.

When I traveled with college track teams, we told all the team members to plan on leaving a half-hour before what we knew was the necessary time. We still left late—and that was with only fifteen members.

On one of those trips, from Nacogdoches to Denton, we were somewhere between Kilgore and Henderson when we realized we were missing our star miler.

As the three-car caravan was stopped at the side of the road trying to decide who would go back to get her, here came a friend of the teams, honking her car horn, with the track star in tow.

Can you imagine what it is like to get 380 high school students to a football game on time and then home before the sun rises?

Well, this is the job of Bill Sitton, director of transportation for Henderson Independent School District, who supervises thirty-three bus drivers.

The seven-bus caravan pulled away from the high school at 6:15 p.m. Friday night to get the band, drill team and pep squad to the Hallsville game forty-five minutes before game time. Two buses had already left with the football team.

With luck and preparation, the caravan will make five road trips this year with the precision of a finely tuned Swiss watch.

At the lead of the caravan is the band van, followed by the seven buses and the maintenance truck in the caboose position. Citizen-band radios keep all the drivers in touch in case of an emergency.

70

Sitton does not expect any emergencies this year with the fleet of buses he is using. They are all new and in tip-top shape, plus he is proud of his new diesel buses that will be put into use.

The first time I came upon this caravan last year, I got goose bumps all over. To see seven buses in a row, stretched over a half mile, is quite a sight.

As you pass each bus, the passengers are already warming up their vocal cords with cheers and the excited conversation that echo into the passing cars. All you can think is, "Boy, I'm glad I'm not driving that bus."

The driving duties are rotated among the school system's thirty-three drivers. This year's crew includes Fred Albricht, Marie Autry, Scott Bauer, Denny Baylor, Carolyn Blanton, Sedric Choice, Sylvester Conyer, Lobis Clay, and Henry Coleman.

Also, Ray Durham, Mike Ferguson, Annie Fletcher, Lynn Fountain, Al Gilson, Johnnie Harris, Lyndell Henson, Mack Hollis, Arlander Johnson, Steve McMullen, Susan McMullen, Melvina Parker, and Tom Phillips.

Others are L.E. Powdrill, Annie Price, Williams Renfro, Dan Satterwhite, Lees Terry and Wylie Naomi.

Sideline Coverage: You Really Get Involved in the Game

In a book that I just read, one of the main characters, an ex-football player, said the game was only real if you were on the field. That the spectator only saw an illusion of what was going on.

He was referring to hearing the pads hit and the noise of combat, sounds that round out the game experience.

Well, I agree with him 100 percent. During the last few weeks, I have covered the Henderson Lions from the sidelines. And let me tell you, you really get involved in the game.

Involvement comes when a player is tackled out of bounds and you are in the line of fire. Or when an excited cheerleader hugs you during a big play and you miss taking a photograph because your arms are pinned to your side.

Or better yet—as happened to one of our reporters Friday night—a cheerleader jumps with excitement beside you and lands on top of you.

I think the real involvement comes when you know the players by name and your heart bleeds for them when the big pass of the game is intercepted from them, as happened in the Lions' Dallas Jesuit game.

Sometimes I have found the spectator in me gets in the way of the photographer. Friday night, I watched Vernon Whetstone enter the end zone and in the excitement of the play, I forgot to take a picture.

This missed photo has happened more than once as my enthusiasm turned me into a cheerleader rather than an unbiased, emotionless observer as I had been trained to be as a journalist.

During the game, excitement is contagious. Before you know it, you are standing there throwing your arms in the air and yelling, "ALL RIGHT!"

Once you've been on the field, it's hard to stay an unbiased reporter.

During the Jacksonville game, I sat in the press box for a change, but I didn't leave my enthusiasm on the field. While Clifton Thurmond was scrabbling to avoid a tackle, I was yelling, "THROW THE BALL! THROW THE BALL!" as though he could hear.

Call me a big sister to these players if you want. But after a year of associating with them, I feel like they are family. So, mothers and fathers take pity on your "child" when she misses taking a picture of your star in his glory because I was probably right there cheering him on with my camera hanging on my shoulder.

The athletes know I'm there pulling for them—if not physically, at least mentally.

Some have been kind enough to let me know they know I care, and that makes dodging tackles, missing photos, and losing my unbiased journalist position not seem so bad because, after all, the game is real, not an illusion.

A Week to Honor High School Athletes

Beginning Monday, there is one more 'national week' to celebrate. It seems like if you have a cause, you have a week. But this week is worth pausing and thinking about.

The week in question is National High School Activities Week.

There are more than one-and-a-half million Texas public school students participating in some form of University Interscholastic League activities and competitions.

The first thing that comes to mind when you say UIL is sports, mainly because this governing body rules not only the districting but eligibility and competition rules.

But you must not forget that students other than athletes participate in UIL competitions in music—instrumental and vocal—drama, speech and journalism.

It is estimated that one out of every two graduating seniors voluntarily participates in a UIL-sponsored contest during his (their) high school career.

There are many benefits to this extracurricular program. In the September issue of *'The Leaguer,'* the official publication of the UIL, the state champion in the different sports, was shown in team photos.

There were also some quotes that sum up the UIL benefits as expressed by different administrators from around Texas.

Earl Richardson, superintendent of Palmer Independent School District, said of his school district's athletes, "Values for personal improvement, both in athletic competition and in any contest, instill traits that will be vital in facing the world of work and life."

It has been proven from studies that students who participate in UIL activities score higher in achievement and college entrance examinations, have a much lower dropout rate, and achieve higher college grades than those who do not participate in these contests.

The students learn more than the skill it takes to participate in the competition: they learn how to deal with victory and defeat. The sportsmanship and fair play learned in the competitive arena carry over values to their everyday lives and in the years to come.

It's the old saying, "It's not whether you win or lose. It is how you play the game."

Ed Campbell, baseball coach at El Campo High School, said of his team after winning the state Class 4A title, "As we stood on the turf at Disch-Falk after the championship game, you could look into the kids' faces and see the gleam in their eyes with the satisfaction of accomplishing a goal."

That may be the bottom line of UIL competition—setting a goal and shooting for it. The goal—do the best I can every time I compete.

William R. Jackson, principal of Sharpstown High School in Houston, said of his state baseball championship for Class 5A, "Their success in Austin is an example of the hard work and determination that they have displayed through the years. This has certainly been one of the most positive experiences this school has had."

Learning that it takes hard work in a total team effort helps the youth of today learn good habits that will carry over to their careers of tomorrow.

It is when we, the supportive fans, lose sight of why there is a UIL that we have done a grave injustice to the UIL program and the youth.

Over-stressing winning can cause an average person to give up on themselves, causing them to quit.

These young people can develop self-confidence, self-esteem and self-value by participating in a healthy atmosphere of competition. So let us pause a moment and join Gov. Bill Clements and former President Gerald Ford, chairman of this year's National Activities Week, in saluting these leaders of tomorrow.

This week's goal is to encourage student participation in and community support of extracurricular activities in all schools.

After all, as President Ford stated, "These activities offer experience in human relations as well as physical and emotional development. They are paramount to youths' total dedication."

Best Christmas Ever

Christmas is the time of year when the child in all of us is rewarded. Adults and children alike will be opening presents in less than twenty-four hours in hopes that their "I wants" are answered.

There was always an air of anticipation hovering over the Moorman house on Christmas Eve when I was a child.

Looking back, the best Christmas I remember was the year of the homemade gifts when I was four years old.

Father owned a seed business in Kansas and like all businesses in the small farming community, it depended on the wheat harvest to pay the farmers' bills.

This one year, there had been a drought and the harvest had been so poor that there was very little money for Christmas gifts. But my dad did not let the financial state of our household affect the presents under the tree.

Dad built a play stove from a wooden orange crate. He put a front door on it and used thread spools for the burner knobs. With a little white paint and black painted burners, I had a one-of-a-kind stove that was the envy of all my girlfriends.

That same year he answered my brother's request for a movie camera with a homemade wooden movie projector with a real lens and wooden reel that moved with spring-action pullies.

As all the years and toys passed through our home, these two stayed at the top of our "best toys ever" list and remained in the toy room until we were in high school.

My most surprising Christmases were the two years when I received a bicycle. The first was a small bike with training wheels, the second was a 22-inch Huffy Flyer.

The surprise was in the way my parents gave the bikes to me. The first one was hidden in the laundry room. On Christmas morning, I was told to feed the dog.

Well, like any good child, I complained about feeding old Dixie—I had better things to do, like opening presents. But I took the can to the laundry room and as I spied the bicycle, I quickly closed the door when I thought I was not supposed to see the bike.

"What's the matter with you?" my parents asked. "What did you see?"

I did not know what I was supposed to see, so I acted cool.

Then everyone said, "Merry Christmas?"

The parents had to outdo themselves for the second bike. It was bigger and I had wised up to their tricks.

They made some excuse for the entire family to go to the seed store and we all headed downtown. When we went into the warehouse, there it was, a bright red bicycle. I did not know what to think as they said, "Smile, you're on Candid Camera."

When you look at Christmas past, it is the ones that are a little different that stand out. Through thick and thin, good and bad times, there was always something under the tree to brighten our days.

The economy for some families today is like that of my homemade Christmas. I hope that the parents of those households will be creative and make their children's Christmas one to remember.

I hope that your Christmas is one that you will remember with a laugh or a smile. And as the old overweight, white-bearded man said, so well, "Merry Christmas to all and to all a good night."

May 8, 1983

Mother is Really My Best Friend

My mother is my best friend and I'm proud of it.

Not many people can say that about their mother, but I can.

Our friendship has grown stronger now that Mom lives in Mississippi and I'm here in Texas. Maybe the heart does grow fonder with distance or maybe we just have to work harder at being friends rather than mother-daughter.

I guess the friendship started when we moved to Dallas in 1968. It was the first time neither of us had a lot of friends our age, so we explored 'Big D' together.

The summer of 1969 marked the beginning of a Moorman tradition that has continued through the years. Mom and I decided to return to Missouri to visit our friends.

We asked Dad and he gave his okay, but he really didn't think we would go through with it. Mom didn't like to drive for long periods of time, and I had just gotten my driver's license and had not driven on a long trip.

The look on Dad's face when we pulled out of the driveway, was a total shock, as though saying, "I didn't think you would do it."

That was a great trip. We stopped at every antique shop and tourist trap between Dallas and Columbia, Mo., all those places Dad would not stop. We also did a lot of singing and just general get-to-know-you talking on the twelve-hour trip.

Those summer trips continued through my college days and even included a two-week trip that circled the Rocky Mountains by going to Las Vegas, Salt Lake City and Denver.

One year we even let Dad go to Canada with us, and we let him and his billfold go to the World's Fair last summer.

Mother's annual weekly visit is also another tradition. Now you must understand I'm not complaining. Two good things come from these visits.

First, I clean my house and second, Mom usually does a project for me.

One year she called me on a Tuesday and said, "I've got a ride to Texas and I'll be there tomorrow."

Needless to say, I cleaned the house furiously, trying to 'motherize' my apartment. Her little visit lasted three weeks and terminated with the entire family of brother, sister-in-law, and nephew coming in from Kansas City and Dad from Mississippi to see us all.

That was a total of six bodies in a one-bedroom apartment. Maybe it's the closeness that makes the heart grow fonder.

Our projects usually consist of all those projects I've been too lazy to do on my own. Like cleaning out the closets and building shelves—Mom's a great shelf builder or cleaning out the spare room that had been referred to as my giant closet.

Best of all, Mom is an expert at getting rid of cockroaches. After her visit, those little friends in the kitchen don't have the nerve to show their face back in the house for at least six months.

She mounts an attack that begins with a trip to the store to buy every pest control item in stock. Then she attacks! She was so successful at ridding my apartment of roaches that the apartment manager wanted to put her on full-time staff.

I'm not sure if the annual visit will be made this summer. When she left at Thanksgiving, I told her that the project would be to wash the windows of my mobile home that had never been washed. All she said was, "I don't wash windows."

Mom's also our family plumber. Her biggest mess—I mean project—was the time she tried to fix the toilet.

There was a little trickle coming from a little screw. Mom felt like if she could take the screw out and put in a new one, the trickle would stop.

It was going to be easy, just pull out that screw and put in the new one. No need to turn the water off.

The second she pulled that screw, she had a fountain shooting into the bathroom.

There was only one small problem with trying to put the screw back in: the water force coming from that small hole was the entire water pressure since no other water was on in the house.

She ran to the water main and tried to shut it off, but the knob would not turn. She ran back to the bathroom and tried to put the screw back in the hole.

Water had now gotten to a six-inch depth on the floor and in the bathtub. The walls were soaked, and the water was beginning to seep through to the basement.

She quickly went outdoors to see if there were any men working in their yards. No one was around. It was up to her to muscle the main water valve and stop the fountain in the bathroom.

Dad came home from work to the tales of the plumbers and said quietly, "Please, no more plumbing. That's why you hired plumbers."

All kidding aside, Mom is my best friend. I look forward to those trips and visits because it is hard to stay close when you live eight hours apart or your lives are full of work.

But on this Mother's Day, Mother will get her annual phone call. Once again, I forgot the card and forgot to get a gift.

One year, I called my father's secretary to remind him to save my skin and get her a gift for me. That tactic won't work this year since Dad's office is at home, and Mom is his secretary. But I know she understands that her forgetful daughter loves her and cherishes her friendship very much.

Mom will read this column sometime next week when the mail finally gets the newspaper to her. So, Mom, and every mother who reads this, your children do think about you and do love you.

What a Summer!

Back in May, when I was asked to help coach a girls' softball team, I was not too sure about the new experience that awaited me.

But with the prodding of Gwen Churchill, I agreed to help her and Roger Morris with the Vaugh Kee Gulf softball team and I'm glad I did.

Of all my years of playing and working around summer softball, this was my first coaching experience. It proved to have made this summer one of my best.

At the onset of the season, I wondered what chances this group of 15 girls would have in the league.

We had the usual number of girls who could not get the ball more than a few feet from them when they threw and about the same number of those who couldn't hit the ball.

As the season comes to an end, these same girls are now making those throws for outs and hitting the ball for singles.

Our coaches decided early in the season that we wanted our kids to have fun, so we stressed to ourselves and our players that we were out to have fun and if we win, that's even better. And fun we have had.

I set some personal goals as far as communicating with the ten to twelve-year-olds of today, and I think I even accomplished those goals.

There is just nothing like the smile of a girl who normally has difficulty reaching first base when she makes it all the way to third.

Or the smile that spreads from ear to ear when a gal plays third base for the first time and catches a line drive.

Or better yet, the excitement of two double plays in one game.

Yes, I get excited. Yes, I jump up and down, clapping and yelling because I have seen these girls develop into respectable ballplayers.

As the season wound down this week, they found themselves in a three-way tie for first and had to play Big Oak and Robertson's Jewelers for the right to go to regional in Marshall.

Going to the regional tournament Friday night, Gwen and I were talking about how we were the Bad News Bears in that we had only expected to have a .500 season, but here we were going to regionals.

We expected to get to regionals and be dominated by our opponents, but a funny thing happened on the way to the forum. We discovered that the team from Kilgore that we were to play was beatable.

Our kids gave them a run for their money by taking 5-3 lead in the first and then fighting back to tie the score at 10 and 14 before having Kilgore edge them 15-14.

As this paper goes to press, the girls are back in Marshall, trying to stay alive in the loser bracket. I know they are playing like winners and representing Henderson with good sportsmanship.

This group of kids last year was among the "and others" at the end of the season.

This year not only have they won, but they have developed team loyalty, self-pride and confidence that will stay with them after the taste of victory and the agony of defeat have long gone.

From the first time I participated in an organized softball game as a skinny little kid, I have known many benefits. I never thought that those same benefits applied to the coaches.

I would just like to take this opportunity to thank Kim Hall, Tonya Hall, Amy Sawyer, Lisa Woodard, Chris Churchill, Susan Cadenhead, Amy Kee, Kristi Walker, Rebecca Whitaker, DeeDee Howeth, Lisa Morris, Deshani Jones and Tracy Walker for making this a summer to remember.

Sidebar

The team reached the quarter-finals in the regional tournament... battling their way back through the losers' bracket.

I had no voice after cheering them on from the first base coach's box.

The next year I coached many of the same girls in the 13-15 age group. This year the biggest thing the team learned was the 70-degree rule. I told them—when you read a book in the summer that is set in the winter do you get cold and want a blanket. I said we were not going to complain about the temperature, instead, we were going to say, "70 degrees, 70 degrees." To help our bodies adjust to the temperature.

One day was in the high 90s with 95 percent humidity and hardly any breeze—I was just about to tell the girls, who were sitting in the dugout, how hot it was when I heard them chanting 70 degrees, 70 degrees, 70 degrees. I kept my mouth shut and thought—lesson learned.

Can Our All-Stars Win District?

It's not whether you win or lose, it's how you play the game.

That's what they say.

But gee, it's a lot more fun when you win. I always felt as an athlete, that good old saying was just what parents said to make you feel better when you lost.

It was hard watching the Henderson Little League All-Stars take such tough losses at the Dixie League district tournament in Nacogdoches this week. What do you say to a kid who has just been beaten 16-0, 19-4 or 13-3?

After the losses, I began to think how Henderson could be a contender against the teams from Nacogdoches and Lufkin.

Nacogdoches and Lufkin have a much bigger field of boys to select their All-Stars from, so the players' skill level is higher.

When you watch your best athletes playing their best and having difficulty, you begin to wonder about the selection of the teams.

First, you have to think about the two sides of the All-Start argument.

One side is that All-Stars and tournament play are to give as many kids as possible the opportunity to play at a higher level, plus give as many kids as possible the honor of being an All-Star.

This is a wonderful idea if you are willing to go to the district and take defeats against the tough Nacogdoches and Lufkin teams.

If you want to win the tournament and advance to the state, the other side of the argument goes into effect.

Rather than selecting two teams, select one team of the best fifteen boys in the summer program. This is what Panola County's baseball association does, and they are competitive with Nacogdoches and Lufkin or even keep two teams, and have an A squad that is the fifteen best and a B team composed of the rest of the players.

This would put Henderson's best 15 on one squad rather than spread them over two teams with the remaining slots filled by average players. As you can easily see to win will hurt a lot of feelings of kids and parents. I do not propose to have the answer—only the question.

I personally think All-Start tournament play is a good experience for the youth. It gives them an opportunity to play some different teams plus get more playing experience.

I worry about the effect of the loss on the boys' self-images, but if the coaches, parents and fans can prepare the kids for the loss mentally, then the present system is fine.

But if winning is all that there is—which I personally don't believe—then maybe changes need to be made.

As the years have clicked by in my life, I have become that adult standing on the sideline saying, "It's not whether you win or lose. It's how you play the game."

If our selected All-Stars go to tournaments and play their best—as the Henderson boys did. What more can you ask of them?

September 2, 1983

Friday Night 3-Ring Circus

My first encounter with high school football as a child was an experience I would never forget. Each fall on the eve of the schoolboy season, these memories come alive.

Football in my hometown was better than a three-ring circus. There was never a slow moment on or off the field.

The evening began as the cars arrived at the field. There was no parking lot. It was first-come, first-serve for the best seat in the house as the drivers parked their cars around the field.

This gave the riders a portable bleacher. They could sit in the car or on the hood. I always thought that this parking arrangement would come in handy if the stadium lights went out. They could just turn on all the headlights to light the field.

The more passive spectators could sit in the cars while the students went roaming around the few bleachers that were provided, but the true fans were the 'sideline coaches.' These men would station themselves behind the retaining wire that circled the field. As the ball moved up and down the field, this huddle would move with the down maker.

If that was not enough of a show, there were always three or four kids, myself included, in the end zone playing football. When the game's action neared, we would put our game on hold and watch the 'big boys.'

Halftime was also a once-in-a-lifetime experience as the band marched in not-so-straight lines and played slightly out of tune. This proud group was led by the band director's grade-school-aged daughter with her drum major boots and baton.

Through the years, as I have attended football games on all levels—Super Bowls, Dallas Cowboys, University of Missouri, and Stephen F. Austin, not to mention my own high school in Dallas—these memories have prevailed.

I can't promise you a three-ring circus at Henderson Lion games, but I can promise you an exciting evening as the Lions open their season against Hallsville tonight at 7:30.

You won't be able to park your cars around the field, huddle along the sideline, or watch the kids play in the end zone, but you will be given some exciting moments as you watch those long passes fly down the field.

Also, you will be entertained at halftime by the Roaring Lion band—they are definitely better than my childhood memories.

November 4, 1983
Sing Out With Country Pride

Cold chills go up my back when a marching band strikes up the first measure of note of the national anthem, but then a disappointment set in... very few people are singing the words.

This could very easily be one of my pet complaints. The average sports fan either doesn't know the words or is afraid to sing or (heaven forbid) doesn't care to sing the national anthem.

Oh! Say, can you see, by the dawn's early light,
What so proudly we hail at the twilight's last gleaming?
Whose broad stripes and bright stars, thro' the perilous fight,
O'er the ramparts we watched were so gallantly streaming.
And the rockets' red glare, the bombs bursting in air,
Gave proof thro' the night that our flag was still there.
Oh! Say, does that star-spangled banner yet wave
O'ver the land of the free and the home of the brave?

My respect for the song and pride in my country causes me to sing the verse as loud as possible, as though singing these few words will tell the world that the United States is still strong as ever.

I think the time that I saw real country pride shown through the singing of these words that were scribbled down by Francis Scott Key on September 14, 1814, on the deck of a British battleship in the Chesapeake Bay, was in 1980 following the Winter Olympics.

The sporting event was in Nacogdoches when the Russian women's basketball team played Stephen F. Austin State University. The fans seemed to know that the Ladyjacks were not going to defeat the Russians because of their 7-footer but that we fans would show them that Americans are proud of their country.

At the top of our lungs, the standing-room-only crowd sang the verse with such vigor that the coliseum vibrated with spirit and love of country. For a moment, it seemed that the people who could sing the loudest would erase all the world's problems, for in the back of our minds was the fact that these Russians were from a country that had invaded Afghanistan.

The spirit that caused Key to write the words in 1814, as he wondered if the troops at Fort McHenry had held strong as they defended Baltimore from the British attack in the later years of the War of 1812, was still alive briefly that winter night 168 years later in Nacogdoches.

I know that just singing the words is not going to save the world for justice, but, at times, I think if we Americans can't at least sing a song that congress made our national anthem in March of 1931, how can we have enough pride in our country to fight for what it stands for?

People have told me that they didn't sing because of no musical ability. So what? I have a tin ear and a voice that will never earn me supper, but I let it rip when it comes time for the "Stars and Stripes."

Old Glory has been drug through the mud in the past as the Americans question their government, but for a brief moment before every sporting event, our countrymen have an opportunity to show their pride—so please show it.

Racers, Start Your Elephants! What?

Mother never told me I would have a day like last Thursday. She also never told me I would be taking up a new sport.

Jim Wallace of KGRI and I participated in a new sport at the Ford Brothers Circus held at the Rusk County Rodeo grounds on Thursday.

Well, actually, the sport is not new. It's just new to Henderson. Yes, folks, we did it. We had an elephant race and we have photographs to prove it!

Why is it that some days you wonder why you say yes to the wildest offers? When the circus representative called to see if there were any takers at The News for an elephant race, I jumped at the opportunity.

Yes, there is a fool born every minute. And, there is nothing quite like an old fool. I said sure, "I've never ridden an elephant. But only if Jim Wallace also rides."

So, Thursday evening, we mounted our mode of transportation and under the watchful eyes of the elephant trainer, we rode off into the darkness.

The first step to being an elephant jockey is getting on the animal. I sized up the situation and decided the smaller mammal was for me. As I stepped up to Mabel, I put my foot on her leg and did my imitation of Roy Rogers mounting Trigger.

Jim was not as quick to straddle his elephant. After two tries, he finally did the 'ally oop' and pulled himself up.

I had no idea what was going to happen next, so I said a little prayer to the heavens, "Please get me through this one. And don't let me fall." This wish came from a person sitting on an eight-foot elephant who doesn't like to climb ladders and who could never get down from trees as a kid.

The proper place to sit on this mountain of dry skin and bristling hair is up on its neck. So, I wiggled over its shoulders and wrapped my legs around its neck.

You have heard of white-knuckled flyers. Well, for a brief moment, I was a white-knuckled elephant jockey as I wrapped my fingers around the chain on Mabel's head.

On command by the trainers, the elephants hit it in high gear. I figured an elephant at high speed could not be half as terrifying as riding a horse at full speed without a saddle. But let me tell you, as we charged from the lighted circus area into the dark parking lot, all I could tell was we (Mabel and I) were headed for a parked car. *Oh no, we're going to cream a Chevy,* I thought as I heard the trainer say Mabel stop.

Thank goodness for human beings who keep both feet on the ground. Mabel veered left, came to a stop, and lowered to the ground. And I asked is that it? Yes, the trainer said, and I crawled off Mabel and patted her on the head, "good girl."

As for the race, well, after all of my mouthing to Jim about my winning, I made a strategy error. You see, I took the follower of the herd, not the leader. Jim was the winner of the elephant race as "good old Mabel" stepped in behind his elephant and latched on the leader's tail. (The elephant's, not Jim's)

Mabel was no fool; she wasn't going to be the leader into the darkness that was for us foolish humans to do.

Well, chalk up another experience to the records. I must admit I prefer elephants to horses. The last horse I mounted ended up walking on my ribs, then racing to the bard a mile away.

December 25, 1983

All I Want For Christmas...

All I want for Christmas... is a dream trip that I have wanted since 1968.

In 1968 while watching the Mexico City Olympics, I made a promise to myself that someday I would go to the Olympics. This promise didn't state that I had to be a contestant. I just said go.

Well, on the eve of 1984, and the Los Angeles Olympics' just nine months away, all systems are go to reaching that dream and promise.

I have my ticket confirmation papers in hand and a house rented in Long Beach, so now it is just a matter of staying alive and well for nine more months.

The Olympics... the sporting event of sporting events. It will be like a dream come true to just be there in the stands watching the greatest athletes in the world going for the gold.

In 1968 I watched on television as my ideal miler Jim Ryan had to settle for a silver medal after having been proclaimed the fastest miler and being the first man to break a four-minute mile.

Time went on and four years later, I sat in total shock along with the entire world as terrorists took captive and killed members of the Israeli team at the 1972 Munich Olympics.

Those great Games had been tarnished in my eyes. How could they kill those athletes at their finest hour for a political cause?

When the Montreal Olympics rolled around in 1976, I was a foot-loose college graduate who was starving. My family wondered why I didn't head north to the game, but I had just started a job that appeared to be a good deal, plus it paid well. But I was there glued to the tube every evening watching the games. That year the Olympics were of special interest to me—I knew one of the coaches.

Stephen F. Austin State University women's basketball coach Sue Gunter was the assistant coach for the U.S.A. women as they settled for a silver medal when the Russians defeated them in the finals. Just knowing someone that was there calmed my desire to be there.

As far as I'm concerned, the 1980 Moscow Olympics didn't even exist. An Olympics went by, and I did not get to see the thrill of victory or the agony of defeat.

To this day, I feel President Jimmy Carter did a grave injustice to those American athletes who had dedicated themselves and orchestrated their lives to peak physically for that year's games.

Again 1980 would have been a special year for this Olympic fan since Gunter was to be the women's basketball coach and two SFA Ladyjacks, Rosie Walker and Barbara Brown, were on the team.

Now four years later, the dream is beginning to form into reality. When asked what I wanted for Christmas, my family quickly answered their own question with money.

I said, "That would be nice, but I would just like to wait to collect in July when I see how many bucks I will need."

The agenda for the first week of August calls for a four-day car drive to Los Angeles via the southern route through El Paso and Phoenix. I hold tickets for the women's volleyball semi-finals, women's fencing finals and a day at the track.

Since there will be time on my hands, and I will be staying within walking distance of the ocean, I will view the yachting. And like any good tourist, I will tour Hollywood, Disneyland and all of the other Los Angeles attractions. There will also be a day trip to San Diego to the zoo before making the four-day trip home stops at Las Vegas and the Grand Canyon.

This definitely will be the Christmas present of all Christmas presents. The year of all years, one to remember until the day I die and to tell my grandkids in years to come.

I hope you all receive your Christmas wishes... as I know (at last) I will.

Another Record Falls

World-class athletes are something to watch. This weekend I went to the Dallas Times Herald International Track Meet held at Reunion Arena to watch some of the best in America and the world compete.

Carol Lewis set two American records in six leaps at the long jump pit. On her third run, she broke her own American record of 21-61/2 with a 21-11 leap. But the University of Houston coed was not through for the evening. On her last jump of the night, she flew to 22 feet-2 inches.

Meanwhile, on the track, the second athlete of the Lewis family, Carl, was edged in the 60-yeard dash by Ron Brown. Brown ran a personal best of 6.06. Lewis was hoping to better his world indoor record of 6.02 that he had set at this meet last year.

Track fans will have something to watch this year as these two speedsters go against each other during the indoor and outdoor seasons as they prepare for the Los Angeles Olympics.

Elsewhere in the arena, the 15,520 spectators watched Billy Olson win the pole vault with an 18-foot 8-inch jump. Olson had hoped to set a new record of 19-1, but it just was not in the cards.

Watching the best pole vaulter in the world charge down the runway with a fiberglass pole and catapult himself into the air to clear a pole that is 19 feet in the air is quite a sight. For a brief moment, man defies the laws of gravity as he soars over the pole.

World-class high jumper Dwight Stone was also present. The athlete was something to watch as he prepared for his jump. The total concentration on his face is something. He talked to himself and traced the steps of his approach over and over again until he felt like he was ready to jump, then he charged toward the pit.

Of all the athletes, I must say I was most impressed with Carl and Carol Lewis. There was no trace of stardom on these two athletes. When not competing, they were visiting with reporters and fellow athletes, never acting like it was an imposition.

I was proud to think that these two, along with the other athletes present Saturday night, represent the United States. They are truly great people.

Yes, We All Still Miss Larry

Class reunions.

Those events are where you see how much weight your slim classmates have gained. Or if the most likely to succeed did. Or did the football captain and the head cheerleader get married and are they still married?

My first class reunion will be in a week. When the list of more than 750 names came this winter, I realized I only knew four of those names, counting my own. There midway down the list was my high school sweetheart's name, his best friend and a gal whose father works for the same company mine does.

As you can see, I really have close ties to old Richardson (Texas) High.

Reunion time reminds me of my brother and his high school buddies. Their friendship began as freshmen and has continued through the twenty years since. They were a real slice of the '60s and '70s generation.

Dave, my brother, and his buddies, Larry, Doug and Frank, were in one of those gangs of highly intelligent fellows that were weird and walked to their own drum. Their common bond was their band that practiced all the time but never performed a note for money.

My connection with the group was through the band, plus all my girlfriends were dating Dave's friends.

As their high school days came to a close, the Vietnam War and college loomed on the horizon. While Dave, Larry and Doug headed to college, Frank went to Vietnam.

Each faced the perils of war in a different way. Frank faced it, while Doug stole a motor worth $50 to get a criminal record which prevented him from being drafted. Larry got married and Dave suffered a should dislocation that kept him out of military service.

Through the '70s, each went through their lives with ties to their buddies, remaining strong. Dave got married and had a child. Larry also fathered a son. Doug went through several relationships and marriages while getting heavily involved in drugs.

Larry's walk in the fast lane of life caught up with him when he was twenty-three and had to declare bankruptcy. Once Larry's life began to straighten out, a tragedy occurred that affected each member of the gang in a very strong way.

In the spring of 1980, Larry was diagnosed as having rare heart cancer and died within three months. Each member of the gang reacted differently, yet similarly, to their thirty-year-old buddy's death.

Doug, the lost sheep of the gang who the group had been unable to locate until after Larry's death, blamed his drug addiction on his missing to get to say goodbye to his best friend. In turn, he cleaned up his life and got off drugs.

Frank, who has been a policeman since his return from Vietnam, and his family of four face his own cancerous illness caused by Agent Orange with renewed faith and understanding. And my brother, the wandering sheep of the family, has settled into a new conviction and is preparing for the Methodist ministry.

He reports that the time span from the discovery of Larry's illness to mid-June is blank. He knows he worked and supported his family, but he remembers nothing else. Their friendship with his minister helped him through the time and also guided him into the ministry.

Since 1980, life has had to go on, but when the buddies get together, they may be the only three in the physical sense, but they still stand four-strong emotionally.

As my nephew, age six at the time of Larry's death, said to Larry's widow the night of the funeral, "I miss Larry."

We all do, kid. We all do.

A day doesn't go by that I don't think about Larry and the guys of the Class of 1968.

Athletes' Dedication and Sacrifice Are Inspiring

"I wish you were here."

How many vacation postcards have you received that say that? As you read this column, I will be on my way to Los Angeles for the Olympics.

If I could send a postcard to Russia, that is the message I would send the athletes of the Soviet Bloc. Their absence will be missed in every event as the 1984 Games have become the "Free World Games."

As a spectator, I will miss seeing the challenge that the Russians, East Germans, and Cubans give our athletes in basketball, track, boxing, gymnastics, swimming, shooting, and many more.

The prediction for gold medals for the United States is high, with the men's and women's basketball and volleyball teams at the top of the team lists. In the individual events, there will be many "sure" golds. But the thing one must remember is that there is nothing sure about winning a gold medal. There have been many unknown athletes that have stolen the show from the "sure-fire winner" in the past.

Two that come to mind are Olga Korbut and Nadia Comaneci, the gymnastic darlings from 1972 and 1976, respectively.

As I sit in the stands at the volleyball, fencing and track events, I will not just cheer for my countrymen but any athlete who gives an outstanding performance. Once you remove the team colors from an athlete's back, they are just another human being trying to give their best.

Not every individual at the Games will be a contender for the gold, but they are still there. There will be 142 nations represented by 7,800 athletes. Needless to say, not everyone can take home a gold, silver or bronze medal.

Some athletes have worked for years for a chance to reach the victory stand, but some will not make it to that celebration. Some will not make it to the Games, but as they worked to exhaustion, each of these top athletes from around the world had a chance for a medal and the dedication to sacrifice for a dream.

Once every four years, a weary world looks away from familiar scenes of crisis and conflicts. For a few short weeks, our attention shifts to a single arena, where young athletes strive to find the best within themselves. And in so doing, encourage us to look for the best within ourselves.

Since the first footrace was run in the Elean Plain 2,700 years ago, the example of Olympic competition has inspired mankind to do better, to reach farther, and to excel.

I wish it would also inspire politicians to strive for understanding and peace.

Forget the political boycott, forget the nationalism, just try to remember, while watching the Games on television, that these people have dedicated their lives to hard work for this one moment.

Don't just watch the leader of the pack, watch the "and others," for they too are champions.

While watching the games, also remember what the Olympics stand for, peaceful competition among the athletes of the world. This gathering is not an easy task, as the boycotts of the past three Olympics have proven.

In a letter to the spectators and athletes in the Official Olympic Program, President Ronald Reagan stated, "All of us recognize the worthy aspirations of the Olympic movement in seeking to bring together the nations of the world in fulfillment of the historic ideals of peaceful athletic competition, dedicated to excellence and the commitment to good sportsmanship. For people around the globe, these games serve as an inspiring display of international cooperation and a celebration of the finest in the human spirit."

In a letter from International Olympic Committee President Juan Antonio Samarach, it is stated, "The Olympic Games offer an opportunity for the youth of the world to gather in a spirit of friendship, enjoying each other's company as they learn the importance of values that transcend difference in nationality, culture and geography."

And from the Los Angeles Olympic Organizing Committee, "The Olympic Games have a rich tradition of excellence in human athletic performance. Equally important, however, is the spirit of international youth that pervades the Games. The fact that people from all over the world gather to celebrate the Olympic festivities is indeed a tribute to mankind."

Please do not think about which country has won the most medals, for that is not what the games are about, they are about the individuals and the personal efforts they are making to give their best performance.

As they say in the opening ceremony, "Let the games begin."

And yes, I wish you were here.

The Olympic Spirit Lives on in Hearts

Editor's Note: Jane Moorman has just returned from a week in Los Angeles, where she attended the Olympic Games. This is the first of a series of articles about her experience.

The Olympic torch that burned over the Los Angeles Coliseum was extinguished Sunday night, but the "Spirit of the Games" lives on.

For the past two weeks, the world has watched as peace, friendship and goodwill dominated the athletes, fans, and volunteers of the 1984 Los Angeles Games.

I was fortunate to be among the masses that had the opportunity to experience the 'Spirit.' I only hope that the effect the experience had on me will last my lifetime.

From the moment that I stood with 80,000 proud spectators and sang the National Anthem during the medal presentation for Carl Lewis' 100-meter-dash victory to the comradery along the route of the women's marathon, the spirit engulfed me and all who were present.

One would think that with 80,000 people trying to get into and out of the coliseum, there would be short tempers and problems, but instead, there was a tranquil, easygoing, peaceful atmosphere.

People were concerned for their fellow man. As one spectator, who was confined to a wheelchair, tried to move into place to look at the souvenirs, I paused from my "got to get some more t-shirts" panic to allow her in line first.

Sharing was the first and foremost rule.

While sitting on a street curb waiting for the women's marathon, cups of coffee and breakfast rolls were shared among our newfound friends.

The ever-present portable television was also a common point of comradery as people would gather around to watch what was happening at other event sites.

Along with peace and goodwill, national pride became the vogue. To chant U.S.A.! The U.S.A.! was the norm. To wave one's national flag was the order of the day.

For two weeks, we Americans have had something to be proud of. Our athletes collected 174 of the 684 medals. The national anthem was played 83 times as fans sang while watching Old Glory fluttering in the breeze.

As the "spirit" engulfed me, I only wish that the spirit would settle over the leaders of our world's governments. Why is it that people from all nations can exist for two weeks in a potentially explosive environment, but our leaders cannot participate in a peace conference?

There were more nations participating in the Olympics than are involved in the United Nations.

The Olympic Spirit is so strong that talks of the end of the Olympic movement are a thing of the past. The athletes of the world will gather in Seoul, South Korea, in four years. Already talks are beginning about a return to Athens for the 100th anniversary in 1992 and then possibly to China for the first time.

Yes, sir, I really think the Olympic flame is no longer burning over Los Angeles: it is burning in the hearts and souls of the people of the world who attended the Games or watched them on television.

More to Olympics than Gold Medals

Editor's Note: This is the second of a series of columns about Jane Moorman's experiences at the Los Angeles Olympics. Sometimes there is more going on at the Games than what is being reported by the media.

While the world was watching the first three finishers of each event, other Los Angeles Olympians had stories to tell.

Arsene Randriamahazoman was one of 7,800 athletes who came to the Game not expecting to win a medal but came just to compete.

The 400-meter runner came from Madagascar, an island off the southeast coast of Africa in the Indian Ocean. His personal best time for his event was not a world-shattering record, but 48 seconds compared to the Olympic and world record 43.86. But Arsene was the epitome of the Olympic Creed that states, "The most important thing is not to win but to take part."

I met Arsene through his coach Alfred Rabenja. Alfred was sitting beside me when his athlete ran in the preliminaries. That race was his one and only. He traveled halfway around the world to run 400 meters.

As the runner took his mark, Alfred sat nervously watching, "I know he will not win because he is so slow," the coach and president of the nation's athletic organization said. "I just don't want him to be so far behind that it is embarrassing."

As the runners rounded the track, Arsene held his own but was left in the dust by Erwin Skamrahl of West Germany, who finished first at 45.94. Arsene was clocked at 48.86.

What was important was not the time on the clock but that the man had set a goal of running in the Olympics and had met that goal.

Many times, we are so busy celebrating the glory of the medal winners that we forget the true reason for the Olympic movement.

The movement is for the world athletes to come together to compete and to do their personal best.

Arsene was not the slowest 400-meter runner that day. Only the top three in each of the ten heats could advance to the semi-finals, so fifty of eighty competitors ran only one race. Issaka Hassane of China, Messaqu Rizvi of Pakistan and Alberto Lopez-Davila of Guam were slower than Arsene.

Alfred and I talked about the Games and his athlete in a broken conversation since his main language was French (which I do not speak), and my main language was East Texan (which he did not speak). In broken English, we talked about the meaning of the Games.

"I am disappointed that he (Arsene) did not do better," Alfred said.

"But at least he had the determination to come and compete," I said.

"Yes, many men would not put themselves into a situation where they knew they would not win," the Madagascar coach said.

"Tell Arsene," I added as Alfred left to go console his runner. "That I admire him for coming to the Games and that it is not winning that is important but competing."

"Thank you, I will," he replied.

A footnote to the brief meeting: Alfred asked me to take a picture of his runner. When the picture comes in, I will send it to Alfred in Antananarivo, Madagascar.

August 15, 1984

Friendship Main Language of Games

Editor's Note—This is the final part of a series of columns about Jane Moorman's experiences at the Los Angeles Olympics. There are many brief moments and encounters that will be remembered forever by this reporter.

The realization that the long-awaited 1984 Los Angeles Olympics is over has not really sunk in yet. It may be a year before all concerned realize the greatness of the event they participated in.

A dream came true not just for the athletes in Los Angeles but also for the spectators. People came from all over the world to experience the historic event.

At one point, while dining, I realized that the people at the table to the left were speaking Japanese. To my right, Spanish was being spoken, behind me, I heard French and in front was German. When the waitress asked me for my order, I was almost unable to understand her because she was speaking English, which had almost become a foreign language to my ears.

There was a common language being spoken at the Olympics, competitive spirit and country pride. A person did not have to understand what the Brazilian or Korean women's volleyball teams were saying as they set up their attacks from opposite sides of the net; the final result was exciting, excellent competition.

One did not have to understand the words of the proud Peruvians, who chanted cheers from the balcony while their women's volleyball team battled Japan for the bronze medal. Before you knew it, you were clapping with the countrymen and chanting Peru! Peru!

Or the lone Brazilian woman who waved her country's flag and made signs of despair as her women's volleyball team faltered to Korea. Her pride was as strong as the thousands of Americans that were getting the limelight with their display of patriotism.

People came from across the United States. One couple had taken a month's leave of absence from their jobs to drive from Pennsylvania to California, not only seeing the Olympics but their country as well.

Those in the stand were an interesting group. Many did not even know the rules of what they were watching; their attendance was just to take part in the historic event. Many times, I heard a patient husband or friend explain the game's rules to the newly-born sports fan.

I found myself sitting beside some very interesting people.

One proud but disappointed Mother from Canada told me that her son was Canada's leading fencer, but he was not participating because the Canadian team had been selected a year prior and he had just begun to dominate his sport this year.

At the women's marathon, I sat on the street curb for two hours with a misplaced Texan now living in Santa Monica. She lived in India for two months last winter.

There was also the man at the coliseum who shared his television set with me while waiting to enter the stadium. He was a frustrated public accountant that felt the ideal job would be a sports reporter. "I love sports and I would love to spend my entire time watching athletics."

There was also the Los Angeles policeman, whose duty on the marathon route was to control the crowds. But when the runners came by, he was one of the masses, taking pictures and cheering. For an hour, those of us behind the barrier rope had given the officer a hard time, but all was in fun.

My path will never cross those of these people again, but the memories of our sharing a historical moment will live forever.

As we left an event to race to another game or another sightseeing tour, quick goodbyes were exchanged along with business cards.

"If you are ever in the area and need help, give me a call," was the usual parting comment.

Friendship was the common language of the Games.

August 19, 1984

Lost, But Not Exactly Lost

A trip with Jane Moorman is a real experience. There is never a dull moment, especially when she is lost.

Now wait a minute, it is not fair to say I was lost on my vacation to California. I wasn't lost; I just didn't know where I was.

When it comes to traveling, I am a real adventurer. I will head into new country with just a map in hand.

The fear of being lost never occurred to me. This adventurous trait is in my blood. It has been said that our family has been lost in every major city in the United States.

Father is one of those drivers who looks at a map once and then throws it on the back seat. Our family has been lost in Boston, New York City, San Francisco, and Chicago.

But let me correct that phrase 'lost.' We were never lost; we just didn't know where we were at the moment.

My little vacation to Los Angeles was uneventful in the navigation area until I entered the Navajo Indian reservation on my return trip.

The desire to see Rainbow Natural Bridge forced me off the main highway and onto a dirt road that headed toward Navajo Mountain in northern Arizona.

After driving an hour through beautiful country on a sand and rock road that challenged my driving skills, I came upon the Navajo Mountain Trading Post.

Since the road was not on my map, at this point, I was wondering where the Rainbow Lodge was located compared to the trading post. The lodge was the trailhead for an 18-mile hike to the natural bridge.

Well, wouldn't you know it, when I reached the trading post, it was close. I did faintly remember seeing a government agent pass me on the road. Fortunately, there was a Navajo man at the trading post to ask for directions.

"Rainbow Lodge," he said. "Oh, you mean the old lodge. You passed the road four miles back."

That must have been some road because I was looking for a major road all along the way. After visiting a little longer about the pack trail—which turned out to be 18 miles over rough country and the possibility of camping since the sun was getting low in the west—I headed back to the paved highway.

Since the trail turned out to be more than I could handle, I decided that the world's most beautiful natural bridge was going to have to be missed.

The adventurer in me just knew that there had to be a 'shortcut' out of the reservation. This line of thought was foolish since I didn't even know where I was on the reservation.

As I sat at a four-way stop, I decided to explore another way out. On the first road I chose, I thought I was headed toward the lodge until the road began climbing the mountain and became a four-wheel-drive-vehicle road.

The second road appeared to be the right one until the well-graveled road became a truck path and took a turn into a beautiful valley of buttes.

The scenery was wonderful, but the sun was getting closer to the horizon, so I knew I had to find the pavement soon.

The third road went south, and as I rolled along, I just knew it was the one to civilization, that is, until it popped over a ridge, wrapped along the wall of a canyon and into a valley of dunes that were prettier than the Painted Desert.

Oh, how I wanted to sit there and just look at that beautiful scene. But the orange glow of the sunset was beginning to color the view and I knew I had a wild road to drive back to the highway.

My adventure was not over when I found the highway; it had really only begun. Now I had to find a place to sleep. Twenty miles down the road, I came across civilization in the form of a Holiday Inn. But my blissful feeling ended when the No Vacancy sign came into view.

There were only four motels in the next 100-mile stretch, and all were full. Finally, at 11 p.m., I pulled into a roadside park and prepared to sleep in my small car.

I knew I had driven past some of the most magnificent scenery in the country as I passed through Monument Valley, Arizona. But it was not until the next morning, when the sun rose, that I saw the beautiful red sandstone buttes and pillars.

What a way to end one's vacation—with a little adventure and a beautiful sunrise on some of Mother Nature's greatest work. That just shows you: If you are afraid to get off the highway and into areas not on your map, you will never see this great country of ours.

August 26, 1984

Sweet Mary Lou

Every time I see Mary Lou Retton on the television, I have to tell someone, "I've met her."

But I'm not the only person in Henderson that can say that. Mary Lou was in Henderson last summer with Bela Karolyi at a clinic given by the Henderson School of Gymnastics.

On that day, I met two very special people as I spent time with Bela and Mary Lou. They were two people who have not let their national notoriety change them from being very nice.

Also, on that day, over a year ago, I had a feeling that I was watching the next Olympic gymnastic darling. As Mary Lou signed autographs, her bubbly personality just flowed over the young Henderson and East Texas gymnasts.

Somewhere in all of those young East Texas gymnasts' belongings is a crumpled piece of paper with Mary Lou's autograph... oh, what a prize that autograph has become!

Seems I come by 'Pack Rattiness' naturally

Now where did I put that map?

That question came up at 10 p.m. one night this week and the search began. One would think that one person in a two-bedroom mobile home could find anything on a second's notice, but this is not so in Pack Rat Moorman's house.

My grandmother has an attic full of the family's 'keepsakes.' Mother made the sacrifice of throwing away her college class notes twenty years after she was out of school. And then there is Dad, who had every professional magazine and book ever printed.

My pack-rattiness is a little different from my family's, however. Unlike the well-organized attic with boxes labeled Christmas, Easter, or Halloween, my front bedroom is a jungle of boxes of every size and shape.

The room, better known as the 'giant closet,' is a treasure hunt every time I go looking for something.

Take the search for the map. It began as a quest to locate a United States map on which I have marked every road I have traveled during vacations. But soon, I was sidelined as the elusive map was replaced with looking at a yearbook from high school.

"Oh, look, here's that book I was looking for last month," I said to my cat, who was busy in her own exploration.

After looking at all those silly people in mini-skirts, I decided to dig to the bottom of another batch of books because I remembered seeing that map about a year ago.

Now my boxes are not orderly or packed in any reasonable way. In fact, the boxes are the final product of my 'quick' house cleaning. When I am cleaning the house for visitors, I will end up with a pile of stuff that has no home, so I put it in a box.

I have the box from Thanksgiving of 1981, 1982, and 1983, and boxes for July 1981, 1982, 1983 and 1984, these being the major house cleaning times, or better known as parent visits.

Well, the map was in none of those boxes, but I did find the magazine I was reading back in '82 about the divisions of the brain. Needless to say, I had to stop my search to finish the article.

There are also boxes from times I have cleaned out my car. The car stuff has a different route to the 'giant closet.' Stuffs first moved from the inside of the car to the trunk, where it rides for months (and even years) before being taken into the house when I had to clear the trunk to carry suitcases.

"Look, I just found that pair of shoes I was looking for," I said with excitement to my cat, who had now located an empty box and was trying to go to sleep.

After turning the 'giant closet' upside down, I rest on the rowing machine that is also located in the room and try to remember where I last saw that map.

"Maybe it's in the big box in the bedroom closet," I said to myself since the cat was asleep. "Come on, Kitty, let's look one more place."

Fortunately, the bedroom closet is small, so only one box is located there. This box is known for its ability to eat books that I have borrowed from friends.

Once I began digging in 'The Box,' the cat's interest was renewed. This was a new box and room for the kitty, who is not allowed in the closet. But the search was hopeless.

After coming up empty-handed and realizing it was now midnight, I went to bed.

"Now, where could that map be?" I thought as I fell asleep.

November 4, 1984

Thousand Questions About Olympic Trip

I found a quick way to go insane this week. I spoke to the Carlisle fourth grade about my trip to the Olympics.

A million questions were fired at me before I could even get my little speech started.

"Did you see Carl Lewis? Did you see Mary Decker? Did you see Mary Lou Retton?"

"Yes, no, no," I responded as fast as possible as three more hands went into the air with very important questions.

Jerry Wylie had asked me to be a resource person for her classes and had warmed me about her lively fourth graders.

They were 'lively,' just oozing with the curiosity of youth. Remember when everything was a great discovery, and you couldn't learn enough about things? That's your typical fourth grader.

But I think the sixth graders were my favorite group. They had questions more about my feeling and thoughts. One girl summed up my entire experience in Los Angeles when she said, "I bet you still can't believe you were there."

She hit the nail on the head. After three months and 300 photos to look at, I still can't believe I was there. But visits with interested people help the memory stay alive.

Thanks, Jerry and your students, for making me feel special. The day at Carlisle was the icing on the cake for a very special year for me.

Bathroom Scale One of the Most Intimidating Thing on Earth

There is nothing more intimidating than a bathroom scale.

I don't care if you are fighting a weight problem or not; the little white box can send the skinniest person into a diet.

This week Circulation Manager Olga Dorsey brought a bathroom scale to work. Her alibi was to prove one of our reporters wrong on a discussion of weight. But I really think it was to intimidate us "fatties" back on our diets.

The scale has a permanent resting place beside my desk. I asked Olga if that was a subtle hint. Yes, I have fallen off of my two-year-old diet. But a simple comment about getting chubby would have done the trick.

Not only are the scales there every morning to let the world know if I added a pound overnight, but they are in front of a window that works as a mirror while you check your weight.

If you think the scales are lying, all you have to do is look in the window and see the reflection of a once-skinny, soon-to-be-fat person.

Each morning, the entire office holds their breath as I step up on that itty-bitty box. Will this be the day of milk and honey or bread and water?

As the scales tip toward the larger numbers, all will hear me scream, "It's definitely diet time."

Why does the desire to lose weight always come at the heart of the eating season?

As everyone is getting keyed up to devour all sorts of holiday goodies, all I have to do is look at a family portrait and see the "great fat one" in the back row.

Pictures do not lie. That triple-chinned person was me. But I have decided that the two-year-old photo will be the last of the "Jane, The Great Whale" photos.

There is more to losing weight than dieting. You have to add some form of physical exercise.

Until recently, I could claim that it was too hot to "sweat." But since the cool, sunny days of fall are upon us, it is time to get back on track with the grueling fitness program.

My battle cry this time is "140 or die." That is 20 pounds of blood, sweat and no food, plus a few tears.

So, if you see me watching you eat a yummy holiday treat, please forgive my drooling and longing eyes. All I want for Christmas is to get those bathroom scales away from my desk.

December 23, 1984

Christmas 1981 Best Yet

Each year about this time—two days before Christmas Day—I try to decide which past Christmas was my favorite.

I think Christmas of 1981 surpassed all others.

The meeting place for the family reunion was set for the family farm in Kansas and cousins from across the country came for the weekend of togetherness.

Each year the fear that this will be the last time all will gather makes the event memorable. But it has turned out that 1981 was the last time our entire clan was together.

The relatives from Seattle, WA; Portland, OR; Santa Barbara, CA; Fresno, CA, Kansas City, MO; Columbus, MS; and Henderson, TX, gathered at the homestead.

I was designated as a "driver," so I had to travel to the reunion by car since I was assigned to go to the airport and pick up everyone else.

By the time everyone arrived, I had made the 40-mile round trip three times. The headcount was at 13 by the time we all arrived.

Since there are only four bedrooms in the farmhouse, the rooms are reserved for married couples. The parents get the first pick and the first two married couples of my generation get the other two rooms.

The rest of us bed down on the floor in the living room downstairs.

I dread the day I tell my prospective husband that once we are married, we will not get a bed at the family reunion because we are married too late. And that we will have to join the "singles" on the floor.

Christmas morning is a continuous chorus of "Oh look what I got from..."

"Thank you, it's just what I needed," or "It's so unusual," as gifts were opened as thirteen sets of eyes watched with anticipation.

The only representative of the family's third generation is my nephew. The kid gets the honor of passing out the gifts between opening his own. This is a lot to ask a little one who can't wait to see what is in "that big one."

After all, gifts are opened, a moment is set aside for a "thank you" exchange. The entire room roars as each person gives thanks to the other by calling out their name with a thank you.

"Thanks Jane. Thanks Karen and Marlin. Thanks Janet. Thanks Roger. Thanks Mom. Thanks Dad. Thanks Aunt Margaret. Thanks Uncle John. Thanks Aunt Mildred. Thanks Uncle Bill. Thanks Dave and Sheri. Thanks Matt. Thanks Tom. Thanks Grandmother."

Christmas of 1981 reached its high point when the water pump broke Christmas night.

The first attempt to repair the pump called for a bucket—or, actually, a pan—brigade to be formed from the hand pump outside, up the porch steps, and down the basement stairs to the broken pump that the "repairmen" felt just needed to be primed.

While I was pumping the hand pump and my brother Dave held the pans of various sizes and shapes under the spout, he announced to me that he was going into the ministry. The shock of the news stopped the flow of water momentarily as I congratulated him.

The repairmen were unsuccessful, and the family had to send someone to town three miles away to get water from the city relatives to use until the pump was repaired the next day.

It is real togetherness when thirteen people are using a 10-gallon jug of water for everything from brushing their teeth to cooking. But our family loves adversity and it made Christmas one of the best.

December 30, 1984

Time to Look Back At 1984

Where did this year go? It was just yesterday that I was writing down my annual "want to do's." Now it is time to see if I did them.

Each January, I write down the things I want to do during the next year in the areas of career, travel, home improvements and finances. Then the following January, I took the piece of paper out of my billfold to see how many I had accomplished.

On the top of my 1984 list was "Go to Olympics." I guess that accomplishment will overshadow all others this year and the years to come. It is not every year that you get to see the world's best athletes compete.

It's not every day that you see Carl Lewis, Evelyn Ashford, Sabastian Coe,, Rod Brown, Edwin Moses, Al Joiner and Jackie Joiner, to name a few.

Next on my list was "Go to World's Fair in New Orleans."

Thanks to parents that enjoy traveling and sharing trips with their children, I got to add a weekend in New Orleans to my year's travels.

The fair was so underrated by the media that it suffered financially, but personally, the fair was enjoyable. It is fun to see things and movies from and about other countries.

Using the theme "Water" gave each country a common bond that proved that all countries and people are the same. We all do eat, sleep and work in environments that are similar because nature is the same all over the world.

Mother Nature does not have favorite countries because of their political doctrine.

The major thing I enjoyed from both the Olympics and World's Fair was rediscovering that people are people. We are all the same, no matter what our government leaders disagree about.

Another "want to do" on my travel list was the Texas State Fair. My timing was just not right for that one, so it will have to be put on next year's list.

On my home improvement list, I find "build a front porch."

Well, this little project is in the works. As I looked through the Sears catalog for mobile home accessories, a "friend" said he could make one cheaper. I'm still waiting for the cheaper version.

The lesson to the cheaper porch is that "if you want it right now, pay big bucks. If you want it cheap, you have to wait, and wait, and wait..."

Financially I set a budget for the first time this year, and I kept on target in all areas. I was only over by less than $50 in the utility department and $100 in the telephone department. Gasoline... well, that's another story.

I even put some money in savings. Almost as much as I had on my list.

All and all, this has been a great year. As my mother said on my birthday card, "I hope next year is as great as this one has been, but it's going to be hard to top."

To my readers and friends, I hope you have accomplished some of the things on your "list" and have had a year to remember. Good luck next year.

By Golly, It Snowed Last Night

SNOW! IT SNOWED LAST NIGHT!

What a way to wake up having your brother yelling that the 'white stuff' had at last fallen.

Our family's first winter in Missouri was a learning experience for all of us.

We kids, having only experienced snow on the flat Kansas plains, soon learned that sledding is a lot more fun going down a hill than it is being pulled by another kid or a car.

Dad learned the hard way to park his car at the top of the hill the night it begins to snow. His first snowstorm had the traveling salesman snow-bound in his home office for a week.

Mother found out what friendly neighbors really are as other women, who were headed to the grocery store, would call to see if there "is anything you need."

The first snow of the season was my and my brother's biggest learning experience. The snow had not even covered the grass well and we were out sledding down the hill. But we noticed that no other kids were out and those that ventured out only stared at us.

It was not until the second snow of the year, when there were three inches of ice and five inches of snow, that we learned that Missouri kids don't waste their time if the grass is showing.

Our neighborhood was the "world's best" at building a sled run. The run began in the driveway across the street, the highest point on the hill. The route ran down that driveway, across the street, down our driveway and took a gentle curve to transverse three neighbors' yards before taking a sharp cut to run parallel with the creek at the bottom of the hill.

To pack the snow down and make the 'run' faster, we would have a little kid sit on a snow shovel as we pulled it down the path. By the time the run was finished, it had crossed four acres of land, weaved through bushes and trees, around telephone poles and under swing sets.

Once the construction was completed, all would man their sleds and head to the 'top.'

There were two things that determined a good ride. Completing the run in the fastest time of the day and not rolling into the creek at the end of the run when you cut your sled in a 90-degree turn at the bottom.

We thought of playing in the snow as 'for children only' until one night, I heard voices laughing in the backyard. As I looked out of my bedroom window, I saw the neighborhood parents 'playing' on our sled run.

When I asked Mother what they were doing, she said, "It looked like fun, so we decided to try it."

AT MIDNIGHT!

March 6, 1985

Recreation Complex is a Worthy Dream

The facts are vague, but the dream is solid.

It is very seldom that I use my column as a campaigning arena, but Proposition 2 of the Henderson bond election Saturday is a worthy cause to back.

Proposition 2 is to sell $750,000 worth of bonds for the construction of a recreation complex in or near Henderson.

At this time, the fact of what this complex will include is vague, but the attempt to improve the city's facilities is a solid dream.

Henderson has needed better facilities for recreation for years. After many hours of discussion, the Henderson City Council is putting the issue to the voters on Saturday to see how many taxpayers are behind the dream.

The dream is to have a final complex that would include baseball and softball fields, tennis courts and other recreation facilities, including a jogging route that will give the people of Henderson a wide variety of things to do in one location.

Presently, overcrowding at the city's five fields (three at Lake Forest and one at Fair Park and Yates Park) has been a hardship for many different people. These fields are in constant use during the spring, summer and fall with youth baseball and YMCA softball leagues.

City manager Jack Dickerson, Mayor Lester Brown and all the city council members believe the answer to the over-crowded situation is "build now. The people have waited long enough."

Mayor Brown said in a February 21 article in The Daily News on the proposition, "It has been discussed for years. Now is the time for the voters to spend the money necessary to begin building a baseball and softball complex. We have 700 to 800 people involved in using the present facilities. We are just out of places for their use."

Presently, the city council wants to get the money in hand before going shopping for land. Once the tract is located and purchased, a recreation committee of representatives from the community's different sports leagues will determine what facilities are to be built first.

The final "dream complex" is, in reality, a multi-phase project. What the city officials have in mind is a $3 to $4 million facility. This complex will benefit all citizens with recreational facilities that will reach everyone.

It will also give the people of Henderson something to be proud of when other city teams come to compete.

Phase One is what the $750,000 bond will purchase. After the land is purchased, the city will build as many fields as they can with the remaining money. Early estimates by city manager Jack Dickerson were quoted as four fields with an estimated cost of $100,000 per field with lights.

But further studies of the proposed building have found that more than four fields should be obtained, but until the plans are drawn and contractor estimates are taken, the total number of fields is unknown.

Councilman Lee Allen says of the proposition, "We are shooting for a full-recreational complex developed over the years." He also added that the sale of $750,000 worth of bonds would be "money enough to get started."

"We are high center right now," Allen added. "We have discussed this issue for years. We have a problem of over-crowding with the existing facilities. It is time to take the bull by the horns and tries to get this project started."

"We have contemplated this type of facility before," Dickerson was quoted in the February 21 article. "But with the market, as it is now, with lower rates, this is the time to do it."

Should all four propositions be approved by the voter on Saturday, Dickerson said there would need to be, at most, an 18.5 cents per $100 of evaluation. The present tax rate in Henderson is 41 cents per $100 of evaluation.

Proposition 2 alone is only a 4.56 cents tax increase in the 18.5 figure that has been quoted. That will be an increase of $18 tax increase for a $40,000 home for just Proposition 2.

"These quoted tax increases are on the high side," Dickerson said. "We really don't know how much it will be. It will depend on the cost of the bond, say 9.5 compared to 10 percent interest, which will make big savings for the taxpayers. Many citizens in Henderson have asked for and debated the building of a complex. Now is their opportunity to express their opinion where it counts, at the polls. At first, I feared that we were going into a project backward with no set plan as to how the money would be spent, but after visiting with Allen, Dickerson and others, I feel that the intentions are good and worthy. It is time to get this dream into the working stage. Please go out and vote Saturday so the dream can begin becoming a reality."

May 5, 1985

Pitching in is Great Fun

It is surprising what tidbits of knowledge linger ten years after graduating from college.

For me, there are two phases that a professor at Stephen F. Austin repeatedly used that come to mind almost daily.

Dr. Alvera Griffin, a retired health education professor, had a lot of knowledge to share with her teachers-to-be, but only two seem to still be with me.

The first is her famous question, "Are you having fun? This was asked of me when one career was going sour and the new one was still a dream."

After answering, "I don't think fun is in this career's vocabulary." I re-evaluated my career and changed to journalism. Now I can say yes to that question.

The other point Dr. Griffin made continuously was to "Be a contributing member of the community."

This phase was among other phases in a definition we had to learn. Ten years later, I cannot remember the definition or the work it was defining. All I recall is the contributing member part.

After roaming around Texas and other unknown parts, I have finally settled in Henderson and am, to my surprise, becoming a contributing member of the community.

For the third year, I am working with the Henderson Girls Softball Association as a coach and am serving on the board of directors.

At times, I wonder what I am doing coaching when my schedule seems to be so demanding and I have no children, but then the old phase pops into my mind.

I stop and smile, thinking, *Gee, this is fun. It's really fun to be involved with your neighbors.*

Dr. Griffin was right: it is important to contribute to the community you live in.

What would happen if all of us did not help with community projects? Who would collect for the different fund drives? What would happen if no one cared what happened in their community and helped to make things happen?

The first thing that comes to my mind is that democracy would come to a screeching halt. Then a dictatorship or governed by a select few would take over.

What I wish is that those who sit at home and complain would realize that being a contributing member and getting involved in their community is healthier for both them and the community.

I know that coaching a softball team is not like being active in the chamber of commerce or city government, but it is a start.

There's a little niche for all of us. It takes a lot of threads to make a piece of cloth: likewise, it takes everyone's contribution to make a community. Look around you and see if there is a place for you to get involved.

There is always a set percentage of the community that is involved. If the community is small, then it is just a handful of people. And bless their hearts, it is always the same one who we expect to carry the load.

Between church involvement, community service club activity, charity fundraising, and government, there is something for everyone's liking. Consider, for example, youth work with the YMCA, Henderson Baseball Association and Henderson Girls Softball Association.

One thing I know for sure is that it is fun! Once again, there's Dr. Griffin's requirement—to have fun.

May19, 1985

What About The Adopted Texans Out Here?

NATIVE TEXAN!

We all have seen the bumper sticker that proclaims a person's birthright in Texas. Well, how about us ADOPTED TEXANS?

What makes you a Texan? The fact that you were lucky enough to be born south of the Red River, west of the Sabine River, or north of the Rio Grande?

Or is it a personality that fits the image of the tall Texan?

Whichever it is, I want to declare that I have adopted Texas. I couldn't help it if the stork dropped me a few miles north of the Red River in the flat land of Kansas. He got confused thought that the Arkansas River was the Red River. He wasn't a good navigator; it's not my fault.

When my family moved to Dallas in 1968, I did not realize that it was destiny in the works.

Earlier in my life, I had become a trivia nut about Texas. It was really only an economic move on my part that made me such an authority on little-known facts about the Great State.

I ordered a map and facts book of Texas from the back of a candy bar wrapper. My reasoning for selecting Texas was that I knew about Kansas and that Texas was the biggest state in the union. (Yes, I know about Alaska...) I would be getting my money's worth.

Little did I know that, eventually, I would experience this great state firsthand.

When the call came to move to Dallas, our family held one of its famous meetings. At the time, we were in the process of moving back to Kansas from Missouri. The votes went in: my brother abstained since he would be attending college in Missouri. Mother voted yes because she had fond memories of visiting her aunt in Dallas.

And I reasoned that if you are going to move, you might as well go somewhere you have never been, so I said yes.

For years I planned my escape from Texas, or rather Dallas. You see, I'm a country girl at heart and the cement and closeness of Dallas caused me to hate this fine state.

Even after I came east to the Piney Woods of beautiful East Texas, I still dreamed of returning to Missouri.

Then one day in college, I realized why should I return to the snow country when I had all the good things in life right here in East Texas.

Who do you know who can have the pretty countryside to look at while driving to work? Or national forests within driving distance for camping?

But once again, economics became a factor. NO STATE INCOME TAX were the words that stole my heart.

Thirteen years after moving to Dallas, my friends gave me a Texan Party with gifts of all the symbols of being a native, including a cowboy hat and boots.

You see, thirteen years makes the longest I have lived in any one state. The longest prior to 1981 has been my native Kansas for the first 12 years of my life.

What makes a person a Texan? The drawl. Or using the phrase "fixin' to." Or how about looking at cars with out-of-state license plates and saying, "Go Home, Yankees?" I do all these now.

Every year I look for greener grass. It happens in the spring and summer, about the time the wheat in Kansas is in its most beautiful stage. I think, *I'm not tied to Texas. I can live anywhere I want in the United States.* So, I start looking. But nothing has stolen my heart as East Texas has, not Dallas, the coast, or the Hill Country, let alone another state.

I think that seventeen years of living in a state should count for something. So how about it, can I place an ADOPTED TEXAN bumper sticker on my car?

Don't Lose Sight of Program's Goals

The summer ball is in full swing. Maybe it is time we stopped and thought about what we, the coaches and parents, are trying to teach the boys and girls in the program.

I've thought a lot about this question since I am coaching. Do I want to stress winning or having a good time?

What I came up with is the goal of teaching the kids that if they do their best, that is all anyone can ask. I want the girls to develop good self-image.

It just so happened that while I have been doing this soul-searching, the magazine Sports Fitness came out with a special section on coaching kids in its June issue.

One interesting article titled "A Question of Balance" made some interesting points I would like to share with you.

One of the main points was that we, the adults in the situation, lose sight of the main goal of youth programs.

According to Steve Keener, director of publicity for Little League Baseball, Inc., "Little League was envisioned to be a leadership program for youth using baseball as the vehicle. The attempt has been to develop positive qualities like working together, leadership and striving to win in a friendly, enjoyable, competitive atmosphere."

Keener went on to say, "We do recognize a problem of over-emphasis on winning among some coaches and managers."

A coach can lose sight of what the program is supposed to provide for the child.

Dr. Tom Tutko, professor of psychology at San Jose State University, specializing in sports psychology and the author of "Winning is Everything and Other American Myths," said, "I firmly believe all children should take part in a variety of sports, but I think the present organizations are far from ideal."

Tutko went on to say that organized sports are based on a professional model and not on the needs of kids. "You force the youngster to be preoccupied with winning and fail to take into account the physiological and psychological differences of youngsters at different ages."

"At four to five, kids are learning mastery of their motor activities and want to romp, tussle and play freely. We come along and apply the pro model based on winning and excellence. This is unnatural. It tends to inhibit them. We should be emphasizing fun instead."

He continued by saying, "From six to eleven, kids need a positive environment in which to grow gradually and receive feedback on progress. We destroy this with all the winning hype. I say minimize the need to win and maximize skills improvement, developing rapport with adults and getting along with teammates."

Turko pointed out that from twelve to fourteen, "kids are still getting a sense of their identities. Winning becomes a more important issue, but it is still not critical."

Coaches of youth need to take these points into consideration when working with kids. Can you help a player improve their skills with positive words rather than negative ones?

Bill Bruns, author and former sports editor of Life, Little League coach and father of two children playing in organized sports, said, "I try to teach kids a few simple basics of baseball during the season, and yet there are coaches out there trying to teach a sophisticated double play."

"That's a joke to me. I just want my kids to make an out. I think there are coaches asking far too much at too young an age. I feel that such intensity undermines self-confidence and takes away the fun."

Don West, national president of American Youth Soccer Organization, says, "We believe in keeping competition in perspective, that is, winning kids come first, winning games is second."

Dr. Rainer Martens, professor of physical education at the University of Illinois and author of 'Joy and Sadness in Children's

Sport,' points out that "under the right leadership, organized sports are wonderful for kids. Under poor leadership, they can be devastating. Sports for kids are as good as we, the adults, make them. With good leadership, you enable youngsters to acquire an appreciation for their bodies, to develop confidence by learning physical skills, and learn cooperation in a competitive context, which is so important in this society. You also have the opportunity to teach psychological skills like managing stress, concentrating intensely, setting goals and achieving them, and responsibility toward others. And perhaps most importantly, you provide the chance to have fun."

The best teacher is an example. When a child sees his coach ranting and raving, yelling insults to the umpires and just generally being a bad sport, of course, he will act the same way.

These points have been made not to criticize the people working with the Henderson Baseball Association or the Henderson Girls Softball Association but to remind them of the great responsibility an adult has when working with youth.

After all, that is what the article did for me.

July 28, 1985

Vacation Is More Than 'R And R'

Vacation—Freedom from any activity; rest; respite; or intermission. A period of rest and freedom from work, study, etc.; time of recreation, usually a specific interval in a year.

Rest and relaxation: that's what most people dream of for a vacation. But a few adventurous souls use that brief break in their daily routine to live a dream.

I decided that this year I wanted to take a "physical" vacation. Something that would make me use my idle muscles. Such as hiking, camping, canoeing or the like.

After contemplating the possibilities, I came up with taking a bicycle tour, a vacation I have fantasized about for years.

Since spring, I have been pedaling my little heart out to get in shape for this vacation. After conquering the "mountains" of Rusk, Smith, Nacogdoches, Panola and Gregg counties, I am ready to take on the world.

Now, where to go on this dream vacation?

Another dream, floating down the Missouri River, has been modified and added to the bicycle tour idea to form this year's vacation.

Bicycle across Missouri from Kansas City to St. Louis following "Old Muddy."

As you read this column, I will be on the first leg of the trip. Traveling to St. Louis, then west to Kansas City. Going by train is another dream trip and now is the time to take this venture since President Reagan wants to stop the rail system's passenger service.

The bike route will take nine day—three days of 60 miles, three of 40 and three of 30. While huffing and puffing over hill and dale, I will be seeing land that played a big role in American history.

Reading about the Lewis and Clark expedition as a schoolgirl, I wondered what the land looked like and what sort of human effort it would take to traverse that terrain.

133

My trip will go through Independence, Lexington, Sedalia, Boonville, Jefferson City, Hermann and Washington. I know that these towns mean nothing to many of my readers, so here are some tidbits of history.

Independence is the home of President Harry S. Truman and the Reorganized Church of Latter-Day Saints. The Truman House is a mandatory stop on tour.

Lexington, which is located on the south banks of the Missouri River, is the site of an important Civil War engagement that became known as the Battle of the Hemp Bales. The Union soldiers were undone by the pro-Confederacy troops of the Missouri State Guard, who used huge bales of hemp as mobile breastworks in their assault on the Union fortification.

A highlight of Lexington is the courthouse, which is the oldest one in Missouri. It was built in 1849, and a cannonball from the Battle of Lexington remains embedded in one of its columns to this day.

Lexington was also the home office for the operators of the Pony Express.

The second day of bicycling will take me by silos housing intercontinental ballistic missiles. I must remember not to take pictures of this for fear that the government might think I'm a low-budget spy on a bike.

Sedalia's claim to fame is that it's the home of the Missouri State Fair. The town should be sprucing itself up the day I'm in town since the fair is the last two weeks of August.

The little town of Arrow Rock is the high point of the next day's ride. Eighty-one people call Arrow Rock home, but in pioneer days, the city's streets were abuzz with activity. Wagon trains formed here to head out on the Santa Fe Trail.

American artist George Caleb Bingham, whose paintings depict life on the river, was a native son of Arrow Rock.

In recent years Arrow Rock was the location of the filming of a musical version of Tom Sawyer, starting Celest Holmes and others.

The trail will continue on to Boonville along the original route of the Santa Fe Trail. Boonville was named for Daniel Boone, who traveled this area, and it is said he gathered his salt supply at the "Boone's lick," a salt deposit north of the river.

Jefferson City is the capital of Missouri. Sightseeing will include the capital building.

Hermann is the German community of Missouri. The area is called Missouri's Rhineland, so named for its vineyards. The wine was produced here prior to Prohibition when the wine cellars were converted to growing mushrooms. Today many vineyards are back to producing grapes and wine is again being fermented in the cellars.

Washington is a sleepy little town that American history toyed with. When the United States had expanded from sea to sea, Washington was considered as a central location for the federal government. It was referred to as Washington on Missouri.

Along the way, I will peel myself off the bicycle and hike in the Meramec Caverns. The caverns were used a century ago by the James Gang as a hideout.

See you when I get home. I'll be the person with the weird sunburn (thighs, calves, forearms and lower face) who is 10 to 20 pounds lighter than the last time you saw me.

August 18, 1985

Vacation Soul Searching Experience

Have you ever set a goal, worked toward it and accomplished it?

I know most of you have. The goal could be very small or seem unimportant to anyone else, but to you, it was a mountain. The accomplishment of the goal was the high point of your life or you, at least, deserved a pat on the back.

Dr. Robert H. Schuller calls the accomplishment of the goals of life a peak experience. He also states that once you accomplish a peak experience, you get to peek at your next goal.

In his book "The Peak to Peek Principle," he states, "A peak experience is a positive experience that affirms who you are and leaves you with an awareness that you are more than you ever thought you were."

He added, "You succeed at something that may seem small to others but is a mountain scaled in your mind. It becomes a self-congratulatory experience that reveals present worth and, in the process, releases an early glimpse of your undeveloped potential. You begin to believe in great possibilities for yourself."

As I told my readers prior to my vacation, I took an unusual trip—a bicycle trip across Missouri.

Now, to many cyclists, this was nothing. I have met people who have ridden across the United States, through the Rocky Mountains, and from Louisiana to California, so an eight-day trip that averaged 40 miles a day is not all that great.

However, to me, it was a peak experience. I learned a lot about myself while peddling up hills of which I could not see over the crest.

After 320 miles in eight days, I feel like I have just seen the tip of the iceberg named Jane Moorman.

I learned that I could face unexpected challenges and work through trying times with a positive attitude. Three days of rain did not dampen my spirit. I saw them as cool days without the blistering sun.

Once I realized that while pushing my bike up a steep hill, if I took time to look at the woods and wildflowers on both sides of the road and the beautiful view over my shoulder into the valley, it made the physical strain of pushing the 70 pounds of bicycle easier, plus I got to see the country up close and personal.

Many of my friends were concerned that the trip was a solo. They worried about the 'crazies' I might have to face. But when you walk in faith that nothing will happen to you... nothing does.

I met only people interested in what I was going through, no crazies. One thing about being by yourself all day long, when you come in contact with people, you talk their ears off.

After this trip, I can see what Will Rogers meant when he said, "I've never met a person I didn't like." If you approach people with a friendly smile and treat them like a friend, they will be warm and considerate of you.

The country store manager in Arrow Rock told me about moving from Los Angeles to a small town of sixty-five people and loving it.

The restaurant owner in Hermann sat down and ate lunch with me while sharing her story about telling the world about her little German community.

Another solo bicyclist, who was going south into the Ozark Mountains, told me of her trip across the southwest United States in search of a place to live and go to college. After talking to her, I felt rejuvenated and ready to finish the last half of my trip—after all, it was only four more days, not four more months.

I think one of the things that I will remember the most is passing a church where a friend of my brother preaches and reading his message to his congregation. "God challenges but never overwhelms." Thanks, I needed that at that moment.

Prior to that moment, I was willing to consider quitting and sending the bicycle home when the going got tough. But once I began to take each challenge head on and make the best of each situation, the trip became a downhill glide to the end.

I also got a peek at the future and what I need to do to be ready for it. Next year a six-day ride across Iowa with 5,000 other bikers.

Between now and then, more riding and more serious weight training to get in better condition. I bet you if I had been stronger, I would not have been pushing the bike up some of those hills.

Next time you have a dream idea, go for it. Set a goal, no matter how small, and complete it. Then pat yourself on the back. I have and it's quite a growing experience.

October 6, 1985
At Least Mom Has Sense Of Humor

Every day I visit the mailbox in anticipation of a letter from home. But they seem to come few and far between these days.

Mother went on strike from letter writing after her children forgot the art of correspondence and discovered the 'reach out and touch' way of life with the telephone.

After her children stopped writing, Mother's first move was to buy stock in the phone companies. Now when her kids call, she at least feels like she is making a profit.

Out of the blue the other day, a letter was waiting in my mailbox, along with the junk mail and bills, with Mother's handwriting on the envelope.

In anticipation of all the latest news from the family, I read the following letter:

Dear Jane

I write to let you know we are still alive. I am writing slowly so you will have a longer letter to read.

You won't know the house when you come home – we moved. We had trouble moving especially the bed – the man wouldn't let us take it in the taxi and we were afraid we might wake your father.

Your father has a nice new job, and very responsible. He has about 500 people under him. He cuts the grass at the cemetery.

Our neighbors started keeping pigs. We got wind of it yesterday.

I got my appendix out and a dishwasher put in.

There is a washing machine in the new house here, but it doesn't work too good. Last week I put 14 shirts in the washer and pulled the chain. They whirled around really good, but then they disappeared. I think something is wrong with the machine.

Your uncle drowned last week while working at the distillery. He fell in a vat of whiskey. Four men tried to save him, but he fought

139

*them off. We cremated his body the next day and just got the fire out
this morning.*

*It rained only twice last week, once for three days and once for
four days. Things are a little soggy here.*

Your loving Mother

Write us soon

P.S. – I do need a vacation!

Needless to say, Mother has a sense of humor. The letter
brightened my day much better than the latest family gossip.

I would write her back—but since they moved, I don't know the
address. But I expect if I sent it in care of the funny farm, it would
reach her.

Discovery: My Brother and I Find Each Other Again

This summer, I met a long-lost friend: my brother Dave.

Dave has not been gone physically. I have spent Christmas with him and his family every year. What was mission was just the personality of the guy I grew up with and loved no matter how much we fought as kids.

He was the big brother who came to my calls to get me out of trees when I was afraid to drop to the ground. He was the guy that knew how to doctor me when I fell and bit my tongue.

He was the fellow who played catch with me even when he hated baseball and sports. And the guy who let his little sister tag along with his buddies.

The hours of adventure we had together bring back fond memories of fun times in the little town in Kansas, on our grandparents' farm and along the creek in Missouri.

Then something happened in our relationship. He went to college in Missouri and I experienced city life in North Dallas. We both changed and our souls lost contact with each other.

A sarcastic college kid would come home during the early '70s and lock horns with an independent-minded sister.

No more experiencing things together. No more sharing the ideas that keep people growing in the same direction.

Dave was the artist child of our family—the musician, artist and actor. I was the outdoors type who found my joy in physical activity.

He was the philosopher; I, the practitioner. While I charged a path through life with a goal in mind, Dave struggled to find himself.

Then he found the answer to his quest for a meaning in life—the ministry.

As his little sister I was shocked, for he was the first minister in our family. But with time, I have grown to admire my big brother again. Listening to his sermon last Christmas brought back that pride.

For years I have only remembered the fights, the hate. Now I can say what I hated was that my big brother was not living up to my expectation. Since I am a person who charts out life, I get frustrated when others have floated through existence.

While I will still try to understand why Dave went into the ministry, he said, "Where else can I use all of my talents."

I thought, *You could be making money in advertising or the film industry.*

He is truly using all his talents now, not just the gifts.

I think what caused me to rediscover my brother was meeting one of his college friends while on vacation. There was the sarcastic, cynical person that I hated. It was not Dave that I disliked, just the personality he had become but now has outgrown.

Once I realized this, my memories of him began to flower with fondness, not hate.

Recently, Dave honored me more than he will ever know. He used one of my columns in his sermon.

Our souls have reunited though we are not experiencing life in the same environment. He is in Colorado; I'm here, but our souls are once again growing in the same direction. And I must tell you, it's nice to be back together.

December 24, 1985

Your Love is the Best Gift of All

"I'll be home for Christmas."

This is one of my favorite Christmas songs. It conjures up memories of Christmases past and the family reunions that coincide.

This year's Christmas will be a little different for the Moorman clan. My brother and his family will not be with us

I guess I am fortunate that this is the first Christmas in my life that Dave has not been with us.

As our family moved around the country, with each branch in a different state, my father has only made one request, "Let's make a special effort to have Christmas together."

This special effort has found us traveling to Utah, Mississippi, Kansas, Missouri, and Florida for a holiday.

Each year something special happens to bring our family closer. Fifteen years ago, my grandparents celebrated their golden wedding anniversary, so the entire family went to Florida.

Eleven years ago, we awaited the arrival of the newest member of the family. My nephew Matt was a few days late for Christmas that year, but he got in on the fun by being born on December 31.

Four years ago, Dave announced to the family his decision to go into the ministry.

Each year the family wonders what funny or trying thing will happen, which in turn, I will use in a column,

Last year the late arrival of my Christmas box on the next airplane seemed to be the column and all would go smoothly, however, more was to come.

Our family's love for my grandmother was tested when we were called at 10:30 p.m. Sunday and informed that she had a mild heart attack.

143

Our family's Christmas goodies were spread out in Missouri, but we packed up two cars and drove to Kansas in an all-night affair to be with the matron of the family.

When we arrived at the hospital, she was quietly resting. The scare was over. Fortunately, she is still with us this year, as healthy as can be expected for a 91-year-old woman.

Good comes from sad times. The five-hour car ride with my parents was a very heart-warming experience. To keep Dad awake at the wheel, we talked about life, death and religion. Why is it that people tell their deepest feeling in the wee hours?

I think last year's 'midnight ride' will remain with me my entire life because of the sharing we experienced in our car.

One thing about our family is that we adapt quickly to change. Last year's moving of Christmas gifts did not tarnish the love and giving.

If anything, it showed me that it is not what's under the tree that counts but the love of the ones there sharing the day. Gifts seem to mean nothing when you realize that one you dearly love was almost taken from you forever.

This year I have had a hard time finding gifts for the family because you just can't buy something to show love. You have to share a part of yourself emotionally and verbally to really give a Christmas gift.

Maybe that is why we honor Christmas. God shared with us the ultimate gift, his son.

I wonder sometimes if maybe we forget this fact when we are running around like madmen buying gifts and worrying about matching the dollar values of gifts received.

So tomorrow as you are ripping the wrapping paper off the gifts, stop and look around. What would you do if one of the people with you last year were not there this year?

Take time to give those people the best gift possible—a loving hug and a quiet personal 'I love you.'

Life's Not Same Without Red Dye

Life just isn't the same since "red dye number" whatever was removed from food use.

Gone are the red M&Ms. Gone are red hot dogs.

What do the kids today have to look forward to or fight over without red M&Ms? Who wants to eat brown, tan, orange, green or yellow M&Ms anyway? It was always the red ones that had the best flavor.

A hot dog is just not a hot dog when it's brown. A red one always tasted better. The contrast of colors between the white bun, red dog and yellow mustard always caused the taste buds to come alive.

But the government told us red dye number, whatever was bad for our health, along with all of the other goodies in life that it is trying to protect us from.

It reminds me of the year they decided cranberries caused cancer. Mom wasn't fooled. She said, "I'd rather die than not have cranberries with my Thanksgiving dinner."

"After all, what is Thanksgiving without cranberry sauce or that other tasty dish with cranberries and oranges all mashed up."

We ate the cranberries and I'm here to tell you that no one in our family died.

All of the worries over food that's bad for you makes me recall a book that was on my dad's bookshelf while I was growing up. It was titled "Got a Match?"

In this fiction, a tobacco industry president was tired of the government studies that proved cigarettes are bad for people's health. So, he hired a scientist to run tests on food and find something that was hazardous to health.

Now I know in real life that cigarettes are bad for the health, and I don't smoke. I know that doctors are proving too much red meat is bad for the heart. But a little thing like red dye, how much worse can that be than artificial sweetener?

As I said, life just isn't the same without red M&Ms. The next thing you know, they'll be saying that red Life Savers are bad. Then what will there be to live for?

Dozier Family Showed What Faith in God Can Do

Brooks Dozier's death, like his life, was a God-sent message.

While Brooks lay fighting for his life in the intensive care unit in Henderson Memorial Hospital after suffering a ruptured aneurysm, the people of Henderson and his friends from around Texas learned an important lesson from the Dozier family about the Christian faith.

There are four ways to cope with the sudden change that the death of a loved one brings. A person can decide to cope with the sorrow with the hope gained through faith in God and Jesus Christ. Or a person can turn to the other three methods of groping in the pain of sorrow, moping during the loneliness, or covering the pain with doping.

For the Dozier family, faith and trust in God carried them through the week of waiting at the hospital. They knew Brooks was in the hands of God, and their sorrow was lessened with that knowledge.

"Brooks was runner-up and district champion many different times as a basketball coach," his wife, Faye Dozier, said. "Brooks has had a victory of life and now sits at the victory table with God."

As friends came to console the Dozier family, they turned their pain into an opportunity to demonstrate what living Christian faith is all about. They showed that with their faith, they knew that death is not the end of the road but a bend in the road.

With that knowledge, they were able to cope with the hours of prayers that they spent in the hope that Brooks would be given a miracle and return to consciousness, but with time they knew that his and their ministry in life would continue through his death.

In their sorrow, they could have just groped around and asked the big "Why" question. "Why did he die?" But instead, the family realized that it is not a matter of duration of life but donation that counts.

Brooks donated more than can ever be counted to the young people whom his life touched. His advice was heard by all. Some chose to accept the advice and live their lives as they saw he lived his.

For the Dozier family, it was not "Why" that they asked, but "Now what?" Life is made up of facts and mysteries. Faith is the only possible way to face the mysteries of "What next?"

To continue Brooks' dedication to young people's future, the family has set up the Brooks Dozier Jr Scholarship Fund for black athletes that are unable to gain a college scholarship through athletics.

Brooks was always there encouraging the young black people that came through his life. He would tell them the best way to change their environment and make something of their lives was by starting with a college education.

He told many an athlete who had received a scholarship that they were not going to college to play a game but to get an education; that they had an opportunity to make something of themselves off the court or field as much as on.

In dealing with their loss of Brooks, the Dozier family would never run from the sorrow by doping with artificial substances.

They know that doping is just a distraction from reality. If dope nips the tears, it also dulls the joy. The family members have lived their lives with smiles on their faces during all of the trials that were put before them. And even in the final minutes of the funeral on Wednesday, they were facing their piles of trials with smiles.

While it is easy to mope over loneliness caused by the death of a loved one, this is also an unhealthy thing to do. The Dozier family knows that one of the most dangerous things a person has to watch out for is self-pity.

They are not allowing self-pity to take over their lives. They know there will be long hours of loneliness, but they also know that there are many more hours of happiness from having Brooks in their lives.

"Brooks was such a loving person. We feel so fortunate to have loved and to have been loved by him," Faye said. "We're so grateful that Brooks got to spend his life doing the thing he loved most. We feel so fortunate that he got to coach Tres (his only son) through high school."

"This year has been so wonderful and so special," she added. "Brooks and Tres had a good coach-player relationship, but they also had the most wonderful father-son relationship. After the Palestine game, Brooks said, 'Well, it's not coach-player anymore. Now we can go back to just being father and son.'"

The family recalls many fun times with the humorous man that was Brooks. I, as a member of the working press, also have many fond memories of this gray-haired coach that always had a smile. He made interviews easy for one who hates to interview.

The Dozier family has opened my eyes to something I believe I had tried to cover up. It's OK to be Christian and to talk about your faith to others.

I am of the generation that was forming philosophies of life during the 1970s and the "God is Dead" era. Though I was raised in a Christian home, over the years, I had developed the attitude that it was not 'cool' to demonstrate and flaunt religious beliefs.

But during the past four years of my association with the Dozier family, I have found myself more and more declaring my faith in Jesus and God. In fact, I had told Brooks this the last time we visited.

I believe that we meet different people to learn things that God wants us to learn.

The life paths of the Dozier family and myself had crossed before we both arrived in Henderson, but it took the second crossing for me to learn the message.

We both lived in Nacogdoches at the same apartment complex. Brooks never knew this, but his dedication to his morning jogging and a dip in the swimming pool inspired me to get my lazy body back into shape.

I would sit and drink my morning coffee and watch this already graying man swim a lap or two in the pool. I finally told myself, "If he can do it, so can you."

But I don't think that was the only thing I was to learn from Brooks. I feel that God made our paths cross again so I could realize that public display of faith is OK.

During our last interview, Brooks and I got off the subject, which happened every time. I was talking about wondering why I had been sent to Henderson. Brooks and I were not sure, but we both knew there was a reason. I had said, "I just wish He would tell me so I could be sure to do it."

Brooks told me a few jokes about the purpose of life, and we went our separate ways. As we walked out the door, I mentioned that I was working out seriously for bicycling, and Brooks' last words to me were, "You need to run for endurance."

I now smile when I think of that last comment of Brooks because he never knew of the Nacogdoches crossing and influence.

So, I have learned a lesson from the member of the Dozier family, who are able to face life's trials with smiles because of their solid faith in God.

May 4, 1986

An Honor to Be a Lady Jack

I took a ride down memory lane Thursday night as I attended the induction of charter members to the Stephen F. Austin State University Ladyjack Hall of Fame and Hall of Honor. Nineteen of my friends from college days were honored.

As I watched the past Ladyjacks being honored, I recalled many things about each person. I reflected on how the college athletic world had changed in many ways but is still the same.

As one of the Ladyjacks received her plaque, I recalled that her first airplane ride and first trip out of Texas was to New York City to participate in the national basketball tournament. Before her college career was over, she tried out for the 1974 Olympic basketball team.

Another recipient was a gal I had watched from her high school days in Nacogdoches. As she developed into a Ladyjack, she exhibited the qualities of a Ladyjack as major surgery kept her from competing at the national track meet.

Before her college career was over, she participated in four national meets and went on to be one of the top six shot putters in the country and attended the National Sports Festival in 1980.

I am proud to proclaim that I was a Ladyjack. Though I participated in one of the lesser-known sports—bowling—I did represent my school at the state and regional competitions in the tradition that had been established by those Ladyjacks that had gone before me. These same traditions are being followed today by the present Ladyjacks.

Our class was the last to be non-scholarship athletes. We came to college for an education and discovered that we could develop our competitive spirit through the intercollegiate program.

When scholarships were awarded, I noticed a change in the attitude of people. Before scholarships, if we played our best and lost, we were congratulated for a good effort. After scholarships, I overheard a faculty member say, "We've got to win now that we're paying."

Playing for the sake of playing was over. It was big business time, with education being the payment.

I grew with the Ladyjack program from the time of basketball games with a handful of faithful friends watching to the international competition with the Russians in 1980 before a capacity crowd at the Coliseum. The night of the Russian game could easily been the high point of Ladyjack history.

I have had the honor of calling All-Americans friends. These friends were ranked nationally in basketball, badminton, volleyball, and softball. I have been traveling roommate with the first Ladyjack to attend a national track meet.

As you can see, during the early 1970s, we women were doing a lot of first at SFA.

Dr. June Irwin, head of the women's physical education department at the time, led us with high standards. Dr. Irwin is a Rusk County native from Laneville and the sister of Henderson's Louise Jacks.

Dr. Irwin was also inducted into the Hall of Honor at the Thursday program. She taught us that you set your goals and strive for them with class and dignity. You are a champion if you perform to the best of your ability.

Also honored was Dr. Lucille Norton, the founder of intercollegiate athletics for women at SFA. Dr. Norton, though retired from teaching since 1977, is still a big Ladyjack backer and travels to many of the away sporting events to back her girls.

Two other inductees were vital for the growth of Ladyjack Land—Sue Gunter, the coach of the 1980 women's U.S. Olympic basketball team and now coach at Louisiana State University, and Mrs. Sadie Allison, present director of women's athletics at SFA.

Both put SFA on the map by coaching teams to national tournaments.

All of these ladies had a dream in the early 1970s and found SFA to be a diamond in the rough for that dream. With their dedication as coaches and administrators, they have guided the program to national rankings in four sports: basketball, softball, track, and badminton.

The thing I realized coming back from Nacogdoches in the rain was that we Ladyjacks are a proud bunch. To this day, we are loyal to the Ladyjack program and if any of us were cut, we would bleed Ladyjack red, white and blue.

I take my hat off to the charter members of the Ladyjack Hall of Fame: Rosie Walker Montgomery, Doris Felderhoff Dennard, Ella Faye Abercrombie, Alnet "Scotty" Bailess, Mary Harvey Beaty, Kay Moody Butler, Janice Lynn Cobble, Jimmie Ann Morrow, Robin Ann Ramsey and Paula Del Schuyler.

Also, charter members of the Hall of Honor are Sue Gunter, Dr. June Irwin, Dr. Lucille Norton, Sadie Williford Allision, Carolyn Ruth Barnett, Dr. Robert Carroll, Lynda K. Lewis, Sharon Arnold Montes and Cindy Kittrell Pierson.

Thanks for the memories.

It Takes a Big Man to Admit to a Mistake

It takes a lot for a person to say, "I make a mistake."

These four words are the hardest to say to one or two people in a group, but to the children and their parents involved in the Henderson Girls Softball Association, it is even harder.

Last week HGSA Commissioner Jim Wallace found himself standing in front of the parents of about 200 girls and explaining how he had goofed.

It seemed he had failed to register the girl's minor and major league teams for regionals before the deadline. And at the time of his announcement Tuesday night, there was a slim chance the league's first-place team would get to participate in the tournament.

"I have learned that the only thing to do in this situation is stand in front of the people and say I made a mistake," Jim said prior to his announcement. "There is no one to blame but myself."

Jim was not saying this off-handedly. He had lost a lot of sleep over this mistake and felt truly bad about the situation. You could tell from the man's face that he was terribly upset about his announcement.

My respect for Jim Wallace grew double fold while watching this chain of events. It takes a big person to admit to a mistake and not try to find a scapegoat, make an excuse, or blame someone else.

Jim could have told the people that the regional director had not sent him the entry forms and had denied ever hearing from one of the HGSA board members with the association's address.

The kids were strong about the announcement. They were disappointed, but they realized that their disappointment was shared by Jim.

Last Tuesday night, there was an outside chance that the regional tournament directors would allow the Henderson teams to participate.

The next day I saw Jim Wallace, he looked like a death-row inmate who had been given an extension on his execution.

The minor league girls, ages 10-12, had received word from regionals that the first-place Bout-Nu Motors team could participate in the tournament held in Tyler on Saturday,

Now he just had to sweat it out over the major league girls.

Thursday night, the word was out that the 13–15-year-old girls' first place them will get to go to the regional tournament in Marshall on July 13-14. Jim was a free man.

All is well at Hall Park. The girls will get to experience playing at regionals.

I hope that the girls also will learn a lesson from Jim. Only good can come from being upfront and honest to the people around you. It may hurt at the time to admit to a mistake, but the reward for doing the right thing soothes the wounds.

My hat's off to you, Jim Wallace. You're quite a guy.

August 3, 1986

Cyclist Pedals Way Through 'Soul Journey'

My vacation is over and it's time to recall the interesting people I met on the trip through New Mexico, Arizona, Utah and Colorado.

One of the highlights of the trip was visiting with a cyclist and his two-woman support crew that was traveling across the country.

Rich Murphy has been a drug user whose body had been convulsed three times too many times. After the final warning, Rich cleaned up his act and life.

While striving to get his life back on track, Rich set the goal of riding across the country and talking to youth about a drug-free society.

The first night on the road, as his crew marked the half-inch of distance covered on a map of the United States, he said, "That's a big country."

His support crew was made up of Cheryl Henderson and Jean Rossa. None of these individuals knew each other before the trip, but now they are lifelong friends.

Each had personal problems to solve and were finding that a challenge was the best way to get things into perspective. Cheryl and Jean had left their jobs that were causing them to compromise their personal beliefs.

All team members had a very positive outlook on life. The trip's adventure taught them that they could do anything they set their minds to.

Rich said the first day he rode 100 miles, he was surprised. He never thought he would be able to ride that distance.

Jean found herself camping and enjoying the experience. She was not misled but had not been told that camping would be the normal mode of accommodations.

Jean told the story of the first night in camp and the raccoon eating the campers' food right by her head after Cheryl had promised there was no way an animal could get in the van. Jean told the story with excited body language but now knows that her little fears are just that—little.

Cheryl is trying to see the world and experience life. After the sudden death of her father two years ago, she has set a goal to live life to its fullest. She said for years, her father had put off living his dreams so that they remained unaccomplished.

The crew members are keeping journals through the thick and thin of the day-to-day transcontinental trip. Each said that they were surprised at how much they had grown spiritually, emotionally, and mentally since their first journal entry. Having read some of their first entries, each is amazed at the person they are now.

Their trip will be over in about two more weeks as they reach San Francisco. But the people I met two-thirds of the way through their journey are now strong individuals who know they can face any challenge that life brings them.

Rich, who had dropped out of college during his drug days, is talking about going into architecture and hopes to attend Harvard.

Jean did not say much about her dreams for the future. But there was no fear in her eyes when she was asked what career she would do next. She had a lot of confidence when saying, "After this, anything will be a cinch."

Just getting to meet these three helped me renew my belief in setting goals to reach dreams and having the faith that I can accomplish anything I put my mind to. This, I, too, learned on a bicycle going up a very large hill as I made my soul journey across Missouri in 1985.

August 17, 1986

Time For New Chapter in My Life

My, how time flies when you are having fun.

I came to Henderson five years ago, expecting to stay two years and then move on. But time seemed to slip by, career opportunities came and went, but nothing seemed to be the right thing to take me away from this friendly town.

At last, I have decided to close this chapter of my life and begin another. As of August 30, there will be a new sports editor here and I will be preparing to move to Albuquerque, NM.

As I have tried to explain to family and friends why I am moving from the security of a successful job to the unknown of a new career and city, I have realized that I, for one, have to keep moving and growing to be happy.

You have to listen to your dream, strive for it and then not be satisfied to rest on your laurels.

Now is the time for me to strive toward a new dream. When I arrived in Henderson, I established some goals, and I have accomplished them. I had some personal dreams that could be obtained from here. But now, the quest for more is making me pull up roots and move.

Every time you accomplish a dream, you need to be looking further ahead to new dreams.

Reaching dreams is like building a wall. The first accomplishment puts one layer of bricks down then the next goal adds another row.

It was said by a philosopher that if the question, "What's your dream?" Cannot be answered immediately, then you are in trouble. You should be setting goals and striving for them continuously.

This philosophy of accomplishing dreams comes from Dr. Robert H. Schuller, who, in the book, "The Peak to Peek Principle," describes how to strive and accomplish dreams.

The basic principle of the book is "a peak experience is an experience that leaves you with an awareness that you are more than you thought you were. It is a self-affirming positive experience that builds your self-esteem. Peak experiences give you a peek (visual insight) experience of what you can amount to."

While working here in Henderson, the friendly people of Rusk County have helped me see what potentials I have in many areas. Unfortunately, these potentials cannot be developed here in East Texas, so I must move on.

I will be leaving, but I will never forget the good times and good people I have experienced here.

There is one point I would like to make to the young people of the area.

Don't fear experiencing new things and places. Go, explore the world. Then if your love for the area remains strong, return and make this area a better place to live because of the different philosophies you have been introduced to elsewhere.

Don't let the fear of the unknown keep you planted in an area. It is not healthy for you or the area.

You, also, cannot keep living on past successes. I have always felt sad to see a middle-aged person living on their glory from high school. Times change and you must change with the times. You must continually strive for new dreams.

I don't know where the highway of life will lead me. But I do know I will always meet interesting, exciting people. I also have learned that people are good. It frustrates me to know people whose only contact with the world is through the tunnel vision of television and they believe the real world outside is evil.

Recently, I wrote this advice to a friend's son in the Navy. The last time he was home on leave, he marveled at how much all of his high school friends had changed. I said, "They have not changed, you have. You have grown by seeing other parts of the world."

Like a locust that outgrows its skin and must shed its exterior, I am stepping forth into a new world.

Yes, I am fearful of what lies ahead. But I have faith that it will only be good. Sure, there will be lonely times when I will wish I was here in the familiar. But the adventure of the new will soon take over the fears. Then the new will become familiar.

When the final dream of life (heaven) is on the horizon, I want to be able to feel that I have faced all of God's challenges that he had planned for me.

The dreams one hears in their mind are those challenges from God. It just takes a lot of faith and self-confidence to strive toward them. Never belittle the little voice in your head. Feel them... build toward them... reach them... and grow.

Henderson Daily News Articles

September 12, 1982

Working to Make a Dream Come True

The hollow sound of a ball hitting leather echoes off the houses. Two boys, standing 20 feet apart, are playing catch on a lazy summer afternoon.

Dreams of playing baseball in the major league are exchanged with every throw.

"When I grow up, I'm going to play for the New York Yankees," the skinny little boy said.

"Well, I'm going to be the major league's leading base stealer," brans the other. "I'm going to beat Ricky Henderson's record."

These two little leaguers are not abnormal. Many boys have visions of being professional baseball players when they grow up. For one Henderson native, the dream is becoming a reality.

Gary Jones is entering an almost dream-like phase of his life. He has signed with the Chicago Cubs farm program, and his future looks bright.

The twenty-two-year-old native of Henderson signed the contract that began putting his dream into action after playing baseball for two years at Paris Junior College and last spring at the University of Arkansas.

Jones, a 1977 graduate of Henderson High School, played catcher and outfielder while on the Lion squad and continued in the outfield during his college days.

What caught the attention of coaches, sportswriters and pro scouts was his batting. Last spring, he came through in the clinches for the Razorbacks and helped his team to victory.

This summer, after not being picked up on the pro spring draft, Jones went to Virginia to play semi-pro ball to keep his skills tuned up.

Jones thought the pros would have to wait one more year, so he planned to return to Arkansas in the fall.

"I was really looking forward to getting drafted," he said. "I felt I needed to get into the pros now; my age is beginning to work against me if I were to wait another year."

What he did not know was that the Cubs scouts were watching him. They finally approached him, offered him a contract, and sent him to Saratoga, Fla.

The door had been opened for him to accomplish his dream of playing in the majors. He played for the farm team until August 31, when the season ended.

Jones had a few changes to go through. The major one was learning to play second base.

"At first, I just warmed up at second, but by the second week, I was playing every day," he said. "At first, I was uncomfortable, but as I got experience, I began to move better and the coaches said they could see improvement."

With the close of the farm league season, most of the players went home to await spring training. Jones, however, was given another opportunity to get a little closer to his dream.

He will report to Instructional League in Arizona on September 14.

"There are only about twenty-five players from the farm league to go to the instructional league," he explained. "It is a real honor to go. When a team sends you there, it tells you they have plans for you.

"The league is to help you to develop your skills. It is not a guarantee for anything. It just says that they like what they see now, but you have to go and develop your skills."

As far as the caliber of play that Jones found in the farm league, he said that there are "better players at each position and more consistent playing overall."

Jones is on his way toward the dream of many little league ballplayers. He is one step closer to his dream, which he says is to reach the major league.

"But you have to be realistic," he added. "Only two members of the Florida team will make it to the majors."

All that Jones knows for sure is it's a matter of getting the right breaks.

"A player works on his skills and waits for those ahead of him to fall on bad times so you can have a shot at the position," he said. "But that is the way it is."

Jones is not dreaming anymore like the little league boys in the backyard. He is working toward his dream as any professional does.

He is getting the training he will need to one day, hopefully, walk out on the field at Wrigley Field.

January 30, 1983

Local Pride in Those 'Killer Bees'

When the 'Killer Bees' of the Miami Dolphins take on the 'Hogs' of the Washington Redskins in the Super Bowl today, the A.P. Mullins' and Henry 'Moon' Mullins' families here in Henderson will be sitting on the edge of their seats.

The current edition of Miami's no-name defense has become known as the Killer Bees because of the prevalence of names beginning with Bs among its members.

Two of the Killer Bees are Glenn and Lyle Blackwood, grandsons of A.P. and nephews of Moon.

In a recent edition of Sports Illustrated, the Dolphin safeties were referred to as the 'baddest brothers' since Frank and Jesse James."

During Miami's game with San Diego, the Blackwoods became prime receivers for Charger quarterback Dan Foust as Glenn made two interceptions and Lyle made one.

The Blackwood brothers were there sliding around in the mud of the Orange Bowl last Sunday as the Killer Bees earned passage to Super Bowl XV! against the Washington Redskins.

Glen intercepted one of Jets quarterback Richard Todd's passes during the AFC championship game.

Can you guess which team the Mullins will be cheering for today?

"You bet I'll have to root for Miami," Moon said with pride. "We are real proud of them."

Granddad A.P. responded with enthusiasm, "You bet ya! We're really proud of them."

The sons of A.P.'s daughter, Jewel, have football in their blood.

Their father, Lyle, was a halfback for Baylor in the mid-forties, and their middle brother played football for TCU.

Lyle, the oldest, is now a 10-year NFL veteran, having played for Denver, Cincinnati, Seattle, and Baltimore before going to Miami.

Finding a college football team to play on was not an easy thing for Lyle. Colleges thought the San Antonio Churchill graduate was too small. But desire makes a player grow.

The trail to the NFL began for Lyle as a walk-on at Blinn Junior College. After sitting on the sideline for the first two games of his freshman year, an injury to a teammate gave Lyle the opportunity to show his stuff.

After two years at Blinn, it was time to go knocking on all those doors that had not wanted him as a high school graduate. He really wanted to follow in his father's footsteps and play at Baylor, but he had to settle for TCU.

At TCU, he was second-team All-Conference his junior year and first-team All-Conference his senior year.

For the younger Blackwood brother, Glen, the trail to the NFL began at The University of Texas and then on to the Dolphins.

Now the brothers are together and are ready to take home two Super Bowl rings.

While the Dolphins' grandparents and uncle sit in Rusk County watching the game on television, the Blackwood clan will be in Pasadena, Calif.

Moon and A.P. say they are going to "just watch the game like any other Dolphin game." But the brothers' parents and brother will be in the stands at the Rose Bowl.

It is still the biggest and the best game of the season because only two teams get to the Super Bowl and of those 90 players working to give their team the cherished trophy this year are the Blackwood brothers.

A.P. doesn't need a Super Bowl to earn him the right to brag about his grandsons. He sums up his feeling by saying, "We think a lot of the boys."

Area Gymnasts Learn from Best Coach In USA

"The only way to win," Bela Karolyi said of world-caliber gymnastics. "Is to show something more difficult and spectacular."

Karolyi should know how to win. He is the best women's gymnastics coach in the world. The more difficult and spectacular won his star gymnast in Romania, Nadia Comaneci, an Olympic gold medal with a perfect 10 in the uneven parallel bars.

That same philosophy of more difficult and spectacular has now earned his American gymnasts Mary Lou Retton the American Cup, which is the most prestigious honor in the United States gymnastics community.

East Texas gymnasts and fans got to see what Karolyi meant as Retton performed on the bars as the grand finale of a clinic and exhibition held here Sunday at the Henderson School of Gymnastics.

The fifteen-year-old West Virginia native, who now lives in Houston, displayed what Karolyi called a unique skill that has been named the Retton leap: to the eighty young gymnasts and parents assembled in J.D. Lowe's building on the Carthage highway.

After leaping on to the top bar by diving over the low bar, Retton began a series of swings that came to a climax as she leaped from the lower bar to the sitting position on the top bar (the Retton Leap) before swinging and twisting her way to her dismount.

The spectators applauded and cheered loudly—they knew they had seen what could possibly be the 1984 Olympic gold medal routine.

Karolyi says the trend in gymnastics is for the "spectacular and difficult skills, but at the same time, the trend is introducing dynamic and exciting movements. Slow and smooth movements are losing ground. The '84 Olympics is going to reflect the style of this generation, just as it (Olympics) has in the past."

After watching Karolyi for a day as his schedule went from working with his world-caliber gymnasts in a Sunday morning practice to working with each of the forty gymnasts participating in the clinic, from using his gymnastic team exhibiting the skills to his talking to each gymnast at their skill level, the one thing that stood out was that Karolyi is an extraordinary person.

"He is truly the best girls' coach in the world," said Paul Spiller of Houston, father of Page Spiller, one of Karolyi's gymnasts.

"It is a sign of a true expert to be able to switch from highly skilled gymnasts to beginners and not get impatient," added Gary Carter of Fort Worth, father of Heather Carter, another one of Karolyi's elite.

The two fathers were in Henderson to support their girls and their coach. Spiller is the director of Karolyi's summer gymnastic camps that are held throughout the United States, including one in Huntsville.

Spiller said that Karolyi and his wife, Marta, are somewhat different from other camp promoters and coaches. "They give each child personal attention and coaching."

The personal touch was apparent throughout Sunday's clinic. Karolyi had something to say to each gymnast, a compliment by saying 'good, very good,' or 'excellent,' or a word of encouragement as he explained what they needed to do to correct their performance.

Karolyi's goal is to develop the gymnastics in Texas and the United States into world caliber that can compete with Russia.

After defecting to the United States during the 1981 Nadia (Comaneci) US Tour, Karolyi and Marta located in Houston and began building their team.

Once the word got out that the Romanian coach, who had trained the 1979 world champion team in Romania, was in Texas, the gymnasts began to flock to him from throughout the United States.

"Some of the other elite coaches in the United States have tried to claim that Bela is stealing their good gymnasts," said Carter. "But that just is not true, these girls are asking him to coach them, not him asking them."

Carter's daughter, Heather, had been in Eugene, Oregon before she and her parents decided to move her to Houston so she could try out for Karolyi's elite team.

Other gymnasts have come from across the country to try out. Kim Hurley came from Florida last year and has not returned home. Hurley is the Texas and Regional Class I Champion in the United States Gymnastics Federation competition.

Jojo Sims came from Virginia. The junior elite gymnast won the USA Championship in Chicago in June. Page Spiller, a Texas native, held state championships and was the champion of the National Junior Olympics in '82 in the vault.

Heather Carter, originally from Fort Worth, holds titles from nationals, and Beth Pope was the 1981 champion of the Sports Festival held by the US Olympic Committee in Colorado Springs, Colo.

Coming to Houston from Indiana is Dianne Durham, who Karolyi says is the best vaulter in the world. She was the national champion in 1982.

Rounding out Karolyi's team is Retton, who has been undefeated in international and national competitions since last July.

Her most recent and most prestigious title is the American Cup. "She has beaten the best in the world," Karolyi said.

Karolyi has stated that he feels that his team has the best gymnasts around. "This team is the most powerful in the country, maybe excepting the Russians, we can beat anybody in the world.

"These girls want to be the best," Karolyi said. "They are willing to make the personal sacrifices and give the hard work to be the best."

The coach added that to be a world-class gymnasts, the teenagers have to be dedicated and be able to prepare a consistent performance.

One of the things Karolyi is also trying to do is get consistency in gymnastic training and coaching. "We are trying to establish a common guideline and establish a specific style of gymnastics," he said.

To do this, he invites coaches to come to his camps to work and attend coaches clinics. This is where Rita Price, owner of Henderson School of Gymnastics and coach of the Henderson Energetics, met Karolyi during a Huntsville camp.

"I like the way Karolyi works with the kids," Price said. "He makes each one feels like his elite gymnast with words of encouragement. Plus, I have learned a lot from him by working at his camp."

Sunday's clinic was a big success. Young gymnasts went away with words of encouragement from Karolyi, autographs from the elite gymnasts and visions of someday performing that difficult and spectacular routine to win the gold.

High Jumper Sails Over New Heights

Jessie Lewis really jumps in over his head.

Or maybe the 5-foot 6-inch and a half senior at Mount Enterprise High School is trying to fly.

Whichever the case may be, he can sail over the high jump bar that he can barely touch when he stands flat-footed beside the high jump stands.

Lewis has sailed over the bar at 6-foot 8-inch once this season. Coach Mike Nix expects him to do it again this weekend in Austin.

There is one more meet in Lewis' high school career. That being his first trip to the state meet. He earned the right to join the top eight high jumpers in Texas by clearing 6-4 at the regional meet in Kilgore on Saturday.

From the beginning of the season, Nix has said that 6-4 would get Lewis to Austin. That proved to be true.

Lewis said he was not nervous until there were only two left in the event. "Once I knew I was going (to state), then I got excited," Lewis said.

He had entered the jumping at 5-8 and had not missed until 6-5 when Lewis and Anthony Vanzandt of Laneville were the only jumpers left.

It's been quite a season for Lewis reaching person-best records. In his first meet of the year at Beckville, he cleared 6-8.

"Jessie beat Vanzandt at Beckville," Nix said of the rivalry that has been building during the season.

"After I bet him (Vanzandt) the first time, he said he would get me back," Lewis said with a smile. Vanzandt made his word good by topping Lewis' 6-2 district jump with a 6-10 1/4 for a new district record.

At regionals, Vanzandt once again topped Lewis' effort with a 6-10 leap, but Lewis said, "I told him I'd get him at state. And that is just what I plan to do."

It is amazing to watch Lewis jump over a bar that is a foot over his head. Coach Nix says that natural spring, good form and determination have made Lewis a jumper.

"I just like to see how high I can jump," said Lewis, who has received an athletic scholarship to Blinn Junior College in football and track. "As a kid, I would jump over just about anything."

He began working on his form in the eighth grade when the decision to beat Mark Ross at high jumping sparked his determination.

"Ever since eighth grade Jessie has wanted to high jump," Nix said. "Mark Ross was first in the high jump that year and it just about killed Jessie. So, he set his goal to beat Ross, and he worked at it and got better. Ross would be a top high jumper too if he was competing this season."

Nix feels that his jumper is capable of jumping 6-10. In the past few weeks, the athlete has been working hard as a runner on the relays and third baseman on the baseball team.

"This week before state, we have just let Jessie rest. Hopefully, the spring will come back in his legs," Nix said. "He has been working them (his legs) a lot."

During practice before regionals, Lewis cleared 6-6, so the coaches are confident that their 'ticket to Austin,' as they call Lewis, will be ready for the biggest meet of his life.

As the days and hours click by, and the Friday meet gets closer, Lewis is preparing himself mentally for the meet.

"Jessie has to stay relaxed and not let the fact that he is in Austin affect his confidence and concentration," Nix said.

"Right now, all I'm thinking about is that I just want to beat Vanzandt again," Lewis said. "If I beat him, I can win."

March 18, 1984

Major League Scouts Search For Future Players

The word is out… Henderson has a strong baseball team with quite a bit of talent.

Lion coach Skip Tamplin has been spreading the word that his squad has got potential, not just for the schoolboy playoffs, but for college and pro ball.

These words of wisdom have reached the right ears. At the Waskom Tournament this past week, 11 pro scouts were taking notes on the Lions and other teams' performances.

"I've been telling as many people as possible for several years about our kids," Tamplin said. "All we can do is get the scouts here and give them the players' names. The rest is up to the kids. They have the opportunity to do something with their baseball skills. It is now up to them."

Scouts have always watched the Waskom Tournament and listened to Waskom coach Mike Daughtry because he is an associate scout with the Phillies. This year there are just a few more scouts around because the Lions are playing.

"The tournament director (Daughtry) said there have never been this many (scouts), usually one or two, but he said these are more this year because of us and what they have heard," Tamplin said.

The pro scouts have seen a product from Henderson and know that the baseball program is a good one. That product is Gary Jones, a Henderson High grad, who is in the Chicago Cubs organization and will be playing Double-A ball this season.

"You go back to good hunting grounds," said Larry Smith, who is with the Cincinnati Reds. "It's a good influence on a program if one of the pros goes back and works with the high school players. The kids in the program realize that the pros are not an untouchable future."

The pros are watching and what they are seeing is several players with potential. None of the scouts would say who they were watching and Tamplin won't say either.

"I will just say they are watching the seniors really close and also eying the juniors," Tamplin said. "I don't want to name names because I don't want to leave anyone out and who knows, one that I don't name may take the opportunity to impress them."

Joe Campise of the Houston Astros said what he looks for are strong bodies, good arms and running speed.

"They have to have speed and be able to throw," Campise said. "The rest we can teach."

Al Heist of San Diego seconds the vote for having "speed and an arm," plus the fundamental tools.

Red Gaskill of Cleveland also likes the speed. "Speed is essential for our system," he said.

Traditionally pros like to draft players right out of high school and put them into their minor league system.

"We like to get them out of high school," Campise said. "We feel we can develop them further in two years than they will develop in the two years of college. They are concentrating their efforts on baseball and are playing against better athletes."

"I like younger kids because they are not set in their ways," said Heist. "It is easier to teach them. Out of college, they are taught one way and it is hard to change that."

Gaskill says that he would rather have high school players. "I like to take those kids before they develop bad habits. Plus, we can develop them quicker."

But things are changing. College teams are getting stronger. College coaching is getting better. The scouts said that if a high school student did not get drafted, going to a good college is a good way to continue to learn and that person can be signed later.

Smith of Cincinnati Reds said some of the better college baseball teams are in the Southwest Conference.

This is the way Henderson's Gary Jones reached the Cubs. After high school Jones went to Paris Junior College. From there, Phillies scout Doug Gassaway directed him to Arkansas so he could get more experience and some exposure to better-skilled athletes.

"Gary went to Arkansas one year," Tamplin said. "When he left there for the Cubs, he left his name in the record books. We had a hard time getting Gary a school because no one knew about Henderson and its program."

Smith of the Cincinnati Reds also added that if a player has any reservations about not going on to college, he should go to school.

"It all boils down to gut feelings," Smith said. "If he wants to play ball more than go to school, he should go pro. If he has any self-doubt about his ability or if he wants an education, he should go to school."

"He must be committed to his decision. If there is any self-doubt, it will eat away at him during the tough times," Smith said.

When a major league club signs a player, it is investing an estimated $1 million into the player's development. The average player takes five years to reach the majors.

Jumping from high school ball to the rookie league is quite an adjustment, says Smith. "A player has to be mentally tough and must have drive. We can only see how hard they hit, how fast they run, and how hard they throw, but we can't open their skin and see what's inside their heart."

Success comes to the player who has a strong self-concept, along with the skills. Smith speaks from experience. He played ball for Arizona State and did one year as a rookie before going into coaching. He coached at the college level before becoming a scout.

"Baseball has been good to me. I got an education from baseball. I have had a very good life, thanks to baseball," he said.

"Those rookie days are tough. An eighteen-year-old has to be ready mentally, emotionally, as well as physically," Smith added. "Sometimes he will need the one, two or three years of college to mature."

An athlete's self-concept has to be sound. "He must be willing to accept adversity. He must be able to take failure and rebound. This star high school player may all of a sudden have three to four off games in a row. He must be able to rebound."

The key to success, according to Smith, is perseverance and patience. "He must have the perseverance to get back up when he is down. And he must have the patience to work day in and day out to develop into a major leaguer."

Once a scout locates a potential player, his organization will invite him to camp and tryouts.

Gassaway says that the Phillies' camp at the University of Texas in Arlington had 180 hopefuls last year.

"At camp, we get a better idea of what they can do," Gassaway said. "Camp is the best way and only way to see what they have. We can't tell how they run realistically in games because of the different field conditions."

Out of the 180 at the Phillies' camp, 106 received college scholarships and 15 were signed to the Phillies organization.

The first step for the Henderson Lions to get an invitation to a camp was made when they played Hemphill at the tournament.

During the Lion's debut before scouts, the players were a little nervous. "They (the players) were a little more nervous than normal," Tamplin said of his team's game with Hemphill. "But once Jason (Brdges) hit his homer, they settled down and began playing ball. The scouts are going to be in the stands for the remainder of our season and with time, these guys will not even think about them being there."

Tamplin feels that this season will be a success not only because of its win-loss record but because the pro scouts know that Henderson has talent.

"I'm real impressed with the Henderson club," Smith said. "They appear to have sound fundamentals."

"Everyone always talks about winning," Tamplin said. "To me, there is more than one type of victory. Sure, I want to go as far as we can in the playoffs, but if the kids get something to help their future, that type of a win is the best. And one you don't forget. If some of our players can get a college education from baseball or even play in the pros, I will feel we have a successful program."

Henderson Coach Two Victories From No. 500

Henderson basketball coach Brooks Dozier's Christmas present from his Lions will be a little delayed this year, but it will come.

The Lions are two victories away from giving their coach his 500th career win.

Opening the season with a career record of 490-411, the Lions are creeping up on that magic milestone. The 8-5 season brings the tally to 498-416.

At times Dozier has joked that earlier in his career, he felt he would reach his 500 losses before 500 wins.

"If I had stayed in Angleton, Ozona and Irving McArthur, I would have reached 500 losses before 500 wins," Dozier said. "Two things happened to prevent that. First of all, I changed my coaching philosophies while coaching at Sul Ross University, and second I came to East Texas."

Dozier had told his wife, Faye, many years ago that it would take moving to East Texas to get a good basketball team.

"If you look at any state tournament, 12 of the 20 teams there will be from East Texas," he said.

Sul Ross was a turning point in Dozier's career. While coaching there for three years, he says he had time to study coaching.

"Sul Ross is where I learned to coach," he said. "It was nothing revolutionary. I guess I just learned that you have to let your athletes' talent determine the team's style of play, not try to force a person to play a role that their natural talents do not produce well in. Before Sul Ross, I thought you couldn't have a good team unless you controlled your guys completely. I had taken away from their individual talent. I tried to mold them into my ideal team. Now I want the guys to do what they do and do it to their best. Some kids have talents that others don't, so you have to put kids where their natural talents work best."

This change in philosophy is apparent in the coach's win-loss record. At Nacogdoches, Dozier had a 66-30 three-year record. Then at Barbers Hill, he went 21-9 in his solo year before coming to Henderson, where he has a 66-20 record coming into this season.

Before Sul Ross, Dozier was closer to a .500 coach. He opened his 35-year career at Round Rock with a 19-6 record. After one year, he moved to Angleton, where four years produced a 43-55 record. Two years at Beeville earned a 29-24 tally before nine years at Ozona produced a 134-110 record.

During his career, Dozier has had seven players advance to college ball.

"I only had one go to a Division I team, that was John Saffle at McArthur. He went to the University of Texas at El Paso," he said.

Joining Henderson's Collin Wade on Dozier's college player, rooster are Jessie Roberts of Beeville, Allen and Kyle Johnston and A.J. Culbreath of Nacogdoches, and one player from Ozona.

Another way of determining a coach's success is how many follow in his footsteps. Of Dozier's players, six went into coaching.

"Three from the Sul Ross teams are coaching, including Jerry Reed at Center," he said. "I don't know if it was something I did or if they were going to coach anyway. I feel that they have incorporated some of the things they learned from me in their coaching. Take Jerry Reed, for instance, he still uses the offense we used at Sul Ross."

One way Dozier rates his coaching skill rather than the win-loss record is how he leaves the school's program compared to how it was when he arrived.

"Every program except Henderson and Ozona were in horrible condition when I got there," he said. "Nacogdoches had only won three district games in five years, and McArthur had only won eight games in three years."

Of those programs, Dozier has taken teams to the playoffs seven times. "It would have been more if we had been taking two teams from each district like we are now," he added.

The furthest he has reached in the playoffs is regional finals while at Ozona. That year the record was 26-6. At Ozona, he went to the playoffs three times, then at McArthur, his team went once. Since his arrival to Henderson three years ago, the Lions have been every year.

This is a special milestone for the Dozier family since Brooks Dozier III, Tres, is on the team. The coach's son has sat on his father's bench since he was a preschooler and has dreamed of the days he would be playing for his father.

"It is really special to be on the team that will give him the 500th win," Tres said. "I remember the 400th win while at Nacogdoches. That was a special year because the Dragons were ranked in the state. Five hundred is a magic number and I'm glad to be on the team and contribute to getting it for him."

Dozier sees the 500 mark as just another milestone. He really is impressed with coaches that have reached 800.

"Now take O.W. Falls at La Mesa. He coached at one place for thirty-five years and won 800 games. That would mean he had several 30-win seasons," Dozier said. "Now that's something. I've never had a 30-win season. That, to me, is impressive."

Another thing that Dozier says is more impressive than 500 wins is a trip to the state final four.

"The 500 milestone is not really a dream. It just means I've been in the business a long time," he added. "Tres and I do have a dream, however, and that's to be on the floor of the "Drum" in Austin."

The elusive trip to the state tournament is something that Dozier's assistant coach Joe Crawford would like to see Dozier get before he retires.

"You see coaches at state that are younger and less experienced than Brooks playing at state, and you wonder," Crawford said. "Brooks has coached thirty-four years and not been down there. You look at all the programs he's turned around but not gone all the way."

Working for Dozier has been a learning experience for Crawford that he says he will never forget. "I feel my coaching career will benefit from what I've learned while working for him."

Crawford says he hates the fact that for the last three years, Henderson did not go to state. "The last two years, we have been as close as anyone. Two years ago, Jacksonville was second in the district behind us and they ended up in the final four. Last year after the team lost to Corsicana, the kids were upset. They said, 'We wanted to win for you, Coach Dozier.'"

Well, this year's Henderson Lions have an opportunity to give their coach a Christmas present that no other team can or will be able to give him, that 500th win.

Before the new year, the Lions will play at Longview on December 28, then in Center on December 30. If the Number 500 does not come in 1985, the Lions will play in Gladewater on January 3 before hosting Carthage on January 7. Anyone of these games could be 'the one.' And who knows, maybe this year's group can also give Dozier that elusive trip to the state finals.

Trains Relaxing, Give Better Views

Air travel has made Americans enjoy arriving at their destination quickly after their departure. But during this time of hurry, some people still enjoy taking the scenic route.

Billy Crawford is one of those who like to see America at a little slower pace—from a train.

"When Betty and I were working, we enjoyed taking the train for vacations because it was relaxing and you could see the country," Crawford said. "Now that I am retired, I still enjoy riding the train."

Crawford's love of trains began fifty-seven years ago when he was five years old and rode the train from Meridian, MS, to Dallas alone. His love of trains was nurtured as a boy every Saturday when the engineer allowed him to ride in the cab from Overton to Henderson.

Through the years, Crawford has been on almost every route in the western part of the United States, as well as many of the eastern routes.

This year he made one of his favorite trips on the Amtrak Zephyr from Longview to Chicago to Reno, NV, through the Rocky Mountains.

"It's just beautiful. The train goes through twenty-eight tunnels between Denver and San Francisco. There are points where the train follows the Colorado River through canyons. It is just breathtaking," he said.

Train travel has been a common thing for the Crawford family. In 1965 the family went from Texas to the West Coast to Canada and across Canada.

"I really think the Rockys are prettier in Canada," he said with a twinkle in his eye. "But I also like the route from Chicago to Los Angeles through the Southwest."

As a long-time traveler of the rail, the Crawfords have seen many changes in the system. Back when each route was independently owned by Santa Fe, Missouri Pacific and others, things were different than now when Amtrak runs all the routes.

"The main difference is in the dining cars. Back then, everything was first class with sterling silverware and excellent food," Mrs. Crawford said.

As the couple traveled yearly to Chicago to the National Selected Morticians annual conference, the Crawford established a friendship with one waiter on the Old Sunshine Special.

"The waiter's name was Magee and he would remember us from trip to trip," Crawford said. "You could ask him what the best thing on the menu and he would know. He never steered you wrong."

Also gone with time are many of the different routes. Amtrak has four main east-west routes. Three routes begin in Chicago, the other in New Orleans.

"I think the prettiest route was through Feather River Canyon in California," Crawford said. "But it is no longer traveled."

Another thing that the Crawfords miss is the five dome cars that were on the Zephyr.

"We always got the sleeping car next to the last dome car," Crawford said. "That way, we were close to the best seat to see the scenery."

One thing that remains is meeting people on the train from all over the United States. With Crawford's outgoing personality, he has established many friendships with fellow train lovers.

One such friend is the Amtrak ticket agent J.C. Hubbard at the Longview station. He is Griff to his friends, which includes Crawford and any other train traveler who frequents his waiting room.

Hubbard is a fifth-generation railroader who says the railroad is his blood.

"To me, rail travel is the most relaxing form of transportation on the face of the earth," Hubbard said.

As the federal government tries to make budget cuts that will eliminate funds to Amtrak, Hubbard points out some interesting things about his company.

"There has been a very noticeable increase in rail-passenger travel," said Hubbard, who has been with Amtrak for twelve years. "The last time I saw such an increase in local rail passenger travel was in 1973, around the time of the oil embargo. You know, when I first went to work for this company, 90 percent of the business was first-time riders, but twelve years later, 90 percent were repeaters. We have patrons, like Billy Crawford, who are on a first-name basis with the engineer and conductor because of the frequency of their travels."

According to Hubbard, the most popular destination from Longview is Chicago, where passengers can connect to other Midwest- and east-bound trains. The second most popular is Los Angeles, while Dallas is third.

"Amtrak has 21 million passengers in a year," Hubbard pointed out. "We average eighteen people per train here in Longview. Of all the American flag carriers such as airlines, buses and commuter trains, Amtrak is the sixth largest."

While Amtrak has needed government funding, it is possibly the only true federally sponsored success story, according to Hubbard. He is a board member of the National Association of Railroad Passengers, Amtrak's only non-profit consumer lobby group.

"Revenues since 1980 have been increasing and covering costs," Hubbard said.

James Miller, head of the federal Office of Management and Budget, has proposed a 'zero' budget for Amtrak and Hubbard said, "If Miller gets his way, there will not be a nationwide rail passenger system in the United States."

But Congress appears supportive of the nation's railway system.

"Congress has already shown its intent to keep Amtrak by funding it for a three-year period, although the exact amount for funding is not known," he said. "Amtrak represents .007 of 1 percent of the federal budget. In other words, the Pentagon could run on Amtrak's subsidy for eighteen hours."

"Amtrak is currently operating at its 1977 federal subsidy level. I can't prove it, but I doubt there is any other government program that can say that," Hubbard said.

For Billy Crawford and Griff Hubbard, the love of railroads runs deep in their veins. Each receives enjoyment from hearing the sound of the train whistle and the clatter of the wheels crossing a rail joint.

Hubbard's interest in the railroad is sparked by the fact of his family's past involvement in the industry.

"I can look out this depot window and know that hundred years ago today, a direct member of my family was working on this same piece of property for the same type of operation," Hubbard said. "I mean, the main line has been in the same location since 1871. They've never relocated it. And in some way, I feel a sense of accomplishment for carrying their (his ancestors) spirit into the present."

August 24, 1986

Hard Work, Frustrating Time Pay Off For Stephanie Hightower

It's been a long, hard road for Stephanie Hightower of Tatum to reach one of her goals. But this June, she reached a goal she never thought she could.

As an outstanding trickster at Tatum High, Hightower had been to the state track meet three times. But a knee injury the week before her senior year district meet put her running career in jeopardy.

Three years of hard work after knee surgery was rewarded this June when Hightower ran the second leg for the Stephen F. Austin State University Ladyjack 1600-meter relay team at the NCAA Division II national track meet in Los Angeles.

"I feel if I have gone through what I've gone through, I can go through anything," the SFA senior criminal law student said.

187

"It was frustrating my sophomore year," she recalls. "I was trying to get back to my high school form after the knee surgery and it seemed like everything I tried made my knee swell. I was in four meets and never got out of the preliminaries."

Hightower had placed fifth in the 200-meter dash at the Texas UIL state meet during her freshman year in high school. She returned in her sophomore and junior year to run in the 800-meter relay and 1600-meter relay.

Doom struck the week before the district met her senior year. She injured her knee during practice while showing a teammate how to run the hurdles. But Hightower was not willing to let her team down. At the district meet, she ran with a heavily taped knee.

"We were in a position that we had to finish at least third in the 1600 relay to win the district title," recalls her Lady Eagle coach Janet Conway. "I wasn't sure if Stephanie was going to make it around the track. But I knew she was not a quitter and if she thought I believed she could make it, she would finish the race."

That was quite a race, Hightower gave it her all and the team finished third, earning the district crown.

Though Hightower's knee was weak, the track coach at SFA knew she had the potential to compete at the college level. Carolyn Barnett offered her a scholarship, which at the time was Hightower's dream come true.

But the old knee just would not cooperate.

"I only ran one meet before it gave out," Hightower said of her freshman year.

The coaching staff at SFA still believed in Hightower and liked her never-say-die attitude, so they encouraged her to have knee surgery.

"After the surgery, I was really frustrated," Hightower recalls. "I was in too big of a rush to get back into competitive form. It seemed like everything I did cause the knee to swell."

But the never-say-die attitude prevailed, and Hightower worked hard in the fall of her junior year. A weight program helped her regain her strength.

Meanwhile, she impressed her new track coach, Cathy Sellers.

"Stephanie's potential is unlimited," the coach said. "It all depends on her training this coming fall. She is a real competitor who runs hard for us every time she is on the track."

Sellers said Hightower was the leader of her national qualifying relay team. "She always gives her all and encourages her teammates to do the same."

As a junior, Hightower said she was in her first 'real' track season. She competed at the Texas Relays, where the Ladyjacks qualified for national in the 1600-meter relay with a 3:47.9. Hightower's contribution was a 56.1-second leg.

During the season, she competed against Carol Lewis in the 200-meter dash at the University of Houston meet.

"I beat Carol Lewis at Houston," Hightower said with a smile. "I knew she was not as fast as she was in the Olympics, but it's still a thrill to run against someone like her and win."

Also, at the Houston meet, Hightower set her personal best time in the 400-meter dash at 57.06.

At nationals, the Ladyjacks finished ninth in the 400- and 1600-meter relay with times of 47.17 and 3:47.82.

"If I accomplish nothing else next year, I will always know I went to nationals," Hightower said.

The Tatum native is realistic about her abilities.

"I really don't dream of the Olympics," she said. "I have seen so many girls that run 52 or 51 (seconds) 400s. I just can't see how I can cut off five seconds from my times."

Coach Sellers believes her times are going to drop this year. And with that coach's belief in her, it will be no surprise if Hightower reaches the lower 50s.

"Each time I run, I wonder if I can run a little bit faster," Hightower said. "If I could get my weight program up to where I need to, it would help me cut down my time. But the old knew is still weak and I have to take it easy in the weight room."

All indicators point toward an exciting season as a senior new year for Hightower.

"I know one thing," Seller said. "We're going to miss her when she graduates. She is so team-oriented. She will run any race you ask of her. In a pinch, if you need it done, she's the one to call on."

Valencia County News-Bulletin Belen, New Mexico 1988-1994, 2000-2006

December 10, 1993

Sports Editor's Brownies

1. Call Mom in Virginia for the recipe. Gossip about relatives while she is digging through her 12x12 recipe box for the recipe that I used for my high school home economics cooking project. Many of these recipes—actually, most of these recipes—have never been tested in Mom's kitchen. She just likes to cut them out of magazines and keep them.

2. After writing down the recipe and concluding the gossip, open the oven and remove the pots and pans that are being stored in it. Go to the cupboard for ingredients. If you can't use cinnamon and sugar, salt and pepper, Tabasco sauce or peanut butter in brownies, then the cupboard is bare.

3. Call Mom back and try to talk her into making the brownies and sending them to you. But she says she's too busy, besides she has not been in her kitchen in decades, so why should she bake for you?

4. Call an old friend you haven't seen in ten years but who made the best brownies you've ever eaten and see if you can con him into making them for you. No luck. Got an answering machine.

5. Go to the store and buy… not the ingredients, but microwave brownie mix. Return home and just add water to the mix in its handy-dandy pan. Put in the microwave, and watch the Dallas Cowboys on television.'

6. What's that smell…? OH! NO! The brownies have been nuked. What should have been chewy morsels of chocolate can now be used to patch the hole in the fence that the dog keeps crawling through.

7. Return to the grocery store… once again, not for ingredients, but a box of delicious bakery brownies.

The time it takes from getting the desire for brownies to taking the first bite—three hours.

Sports Editor's Four Food Groups

Pizza—Pizza Hut
Hamburger—McDonald's
Chicken—Kentucky Fried Chicken
Taco—Taco Bell

Or if you are a sporting event.
Hot dogs
Nachos
Popcorn
Sunflower seeds
Dill pickle

Don't Clean Old Car Out—Buy New One

I didn't really expect it to happen until this summer, but the spring weather we've been experiencing caused me to go out and buy a new car.

Not that I didn't deserve a new car. I've been driving my Toyota since it was new in 1985—just 213,000 miles ago.

Actually, I was just going to look when I went to the dealership, but you know who that goes. A good salesman isn't going to let you walk away when you could be driving one of his cars with neatly folded load papers in your pocket.

The biggest hassle of getting a new car is cleaning out the old one. After all, during eight-and-a-half years and 213,000 miles, you can really build up the trash.

My friends say I bought a new car because I didn't want to have to clean up the quart of orange juice I spilled under the front seat the day before my trip to the dealership.

Well… maybe they're a little right about that. When you have a nice, new shiny car in the driveway, it's hard to get excited about getting all of the OJ out of the carpet of the "Old Blue."

It really is amazing what I found under the car seat. For starters, there was $2.74 in coins, which will go toward my first car payment.

Enough petrified French fries to fill a small order of fries.

At least ten "hand" rocks. You know, those beautiful works of Mother Nature you find while out hiking or riding in the mountains. Since the stones fit in the palm of your hand, they are called hand rocks in lieu of yard rocks or boundary rocks, which are larger in size. Hand rocks also live in the house, not in the rock garden outside. It was amazing the number of cassette tape boxes I found. Most of their tapes have long since worn out and been thrown out.

There were three combs and one brush hiding between the seat and the transmission console. It always seemed like I could never find any of these guys when I needed to comb my hair.

The most unique thing under the front seat was an ankle brace I borrowed from a friend when my foot was hurting a couple of years ago. It had a wonderful orange tine on it from the OJ.

There were also two bottles of hand lotion and two pairs of sunglasses.

Also, one of those handy-dandy suction cup notepad holders are supposed to stick to the dashboard so you can post notes to yourself.

After digging through all this stuff, which was covered with a sticky film of OJ and dirt, I made the new-car owner promise that NO FOOD WILL BE EATEN IN THE NEW CAR.

A new car is like New Year's Day—resolutions are made, then broken weeks, even days, later.

My new car resolution includes the following:

- Throw out trash after arriving at the destination.
- Nightly, remove any books, coats or other objects sued during the day.
- If you eat while driving—BE NEAT. No more petrified French fires.

So now the staff members of the News-Bulletin have established a pool to see how long it is before Jane leaves trash in her car. Or books. Or eats while driving.

I wonder why everyone wants to initiate the first week of February. Doesn't anyone believe I can do these things for more than one week?

Graduation Full Of Memories, Laughs

As I watch Belen and Los Lunas high schools' graduating classes grow in size and people marvel at the classes being 200 and 300, respectively, I remember the night I graduated in a class of 750.

For those of you who have ever organized a group of people in an event, you are probably wondering how do you get 750 kids lined up alphabetically, marched into an arena and across the stage in one evening.

My graduation ceremony was at the Moody Coliseum at Southern Methodist University in Dallas. When we arrived, we were told to find our name tag, which was taped to the wall, and stand in front of it.

The only other instruction we received for the evening was—'follow the guy in front of you.'

These directions were simple and brief. The night before, at Baccalaureate, the class was so big that some were seated on the stage.

Those of us on the stage were told to 'do what the front row does.' As the program progressed, we on the stage couldn't even hear what was going on, nor did we really care.

Then suddenly, the whisper said, 'front row is getting up.' The entire stage rose for what we didn't know. To our surprise, those standing up front were the choir preparing to sing.

Now what! We all looked at each other and then settled back into our seats with a snicker.

Later I asked my parents if they had noticed our mistake. They said, "No, we just thought you were being polite."

Actually, that snafu interrupted many a game of Battleship and cards.

After that, the graduation ceremony was uneventful.

At least until the last guy got his diploma, walked halfway across the stage, and threw his camp Frisbee-style into the graduates and 750 caps went flying into the air.

Four years later, graduation from college was just a little bit better.

Prior to graduation, all fees had to be paid if a senior was going to participate in the ceremony.

One of my classmates fretted that her family was not present since it had cost her $350 to go through the ceremony, which she didn't really care if she did.

As we walked to the stage, we had to go outside from the auditorium, around to the stage door and back in. There were many of us who eyeballed the sandwich shop across the street and threatened to make a run for some food.

As I walked across the stage and shook the college president's hand, I thanked him for the education. He and I were on 'nodding terms. We'd nod our heads at each other when we passed the halls of the administration building.

Through the years, we had disagreed on some issues regarding women's athletics, but I appreciated the work he had done to improve the quality of education provided at the college.

Later, Dad asked what I had said. Because Dr. Ralph Stein turned and watched me go backstage and the next graduates had to wait to shake his hand.

A few years later, I stopped by his dinner table at a restaurant to pay my respects, beginning with, "I doubt if you remember me."

He responded, "Oh, I do. You're the one who thanked me for your education."

December 29, 2001

New Year's Resolutions: Truth Or Consequences

It's that time of the year when we take stock of ourselves and make New Year's resolutions.

Usually, the grim reality comes while standing in front of the mirror, which produces the most common resolution—weight loss.

I am among those who make this annual promise to eat correctly and get more exercise. This promise is made with a good intention.

On New Year's Day, between football games, when I'm not going to the refrigerator for more refreshments, I move my exercise bicycle in from the garage.

All is well the first few weeks. I peddle for fifteen minutes first thing in the morning and compliment myself for my renewed commitment to better health while eating a donut as I drive to work.

To break up the boredom of bicycling to nowhere, I add a mile walk during the second week. Usually, the walk takes me by the donut shop, so of course, I have to help the economy.

Because I don't want to put my body into complete shock, I decide to cut the donuts out slowly. It's kind of like cutting back on cigarettes when you are a pack-a-day smoker.

I cut back to one for breakfast, with the good intention of eliminating them completely tomorrow.

While breakfast is far off the healthy eating scale, my other meals have improved to include salads and vegetables.

By the fourth week, the scales have moved slightly to the left. I have discovered if you stand sideways on the scales, you can cut a couple of pounds off and standing on one foot can knock off at least five pounds.

Entering the second month, I begin finding reasons not to ride the bicycle, and, of course, it's too cold to walk.

Soon the bicycle becomes a great clothes rack, where clean clothing hangs from the handlebars and folded items balance on the seat.

On a serious note, I do like to set some goals for the upcoming year.

When I'm pondering the next year, I like to divide my goals for the next twelve months into five categories. Besides health, there is education, travel, home improvement and finance.

The education category can be general knowledge or spiritual. This year I want to learn about the Dead Sea Scrolls. The books have been on my bookshelf for many years collecting dust. Hopefully, this year I'll get them read.

Financially, my resolution usually is to improve my investments by at least 10 percent.

Travel usually means a destination such as Vegas to see the Blue Man Group, a goal I accomplished in 2001.

Home improvement means a project I want to complete. This year, it was to extend my patio by 210 square feet. I think 2002's will be to plant bushes along my north fence.

Once I have decided what my five goals are, I write them on a piece of paper and fold them to fit in my billfold. There they will reside until December 31, when I review them to see if they were accomplished.

Hopefully, 2002 will be the year I get past February on my fitness plan. And I learned what was learned from the Dead Sea Scrolls. And not only do I plant the bushes, but they live.

February 16, 2002

Birthday Cake More Than Meets The Eyes

Birthday celebrations are usually fun events where people gather to honor a friend or family member's special day.

Last weekend, in honor of a friend's 60th birthday, another friend made a gourmet meal and invited several people over for an evening of fine dining and good conversation.

As the honoree arrived, she noticed through the dining room window one of the hostess' dogs eating something off a sideboard cabinet.

"Stay away from the hors d' oeuvres," she said to the guests arriving with her. "The dog is sampling the goodies."

After the greetings, the birthday gal and friends discovered what the dog had been sampling was actually the chocolate birthday cake. He had devoured half of it—including the birthday greeting.

"I was late to work this morning because I stopped and ordered the cake special for you," the mortified hostess said while her guest laughed.

Always the investigator, I bent down and greeted the three dogs while searching for the one with chocolate breath. Pumpkin was the culprit.

The hostess offered to send someone to get another cake, but we all said, "Don't worry about it. We'll just eat the other half."

So, after the gourmet dinner, the rose-adored chocolate cake was brought forth, servings were sliced, ice cream was scooped, and we all ate the cake while telling birthday cake disaster tales.

In college, the dorm gang planned to celebrate Stella's birthday with a German chocolate cake.

When it came time to light the candles, Stella was downstairs watching television. Various people went down to get her, but she refused to leave the show.

Unbeknownst to her, the gang opted to use her cigarettes for candles. They had lit them when the first of three people went to get her. By the time she arrived back at her room, the makeshift candles were columns of ash.

By the time we got the cigarette butts off the cake, the ashes had fallen into the coconut caramel frosting, making the cake far from appetizing.

To top it off, we all discovered there is only one type of cake Stella didn't like—German chocolate, with or without ashes.

Prior to last week, my funniest birthday party involved the blowing out of the candle with the honoree's nose.

When the cake appeared with one large candle, it just seemed natural for the dare to be made—"bet you can blow it out with your nose."

For health reasons and the desire not to wreck the cake, the candle was removed from it, and the cake was moved away from the trajectory of the honoree's snout.

With a candle located below her nostrils, the birthday gal gave one good puff of air from her nose and the flame disappeared.

It took us a good two minutes to stop laughing enough to breathe, let alone talk. As tears of laughter still streamed down our cheeks, we cut the cake and marveled at our friend's truly hidden skill.

Easter Means Family Traditions Of Spirituality

Easter is a time for family traditions.

In Valencia County, it may mean the family comes together for the annual walk to Tome Hill.

The Good Friday walk is a wonderful way for people to take time to reflect on their spiritual existence.

Family members make the pilgrimage to the top of the county landmark in an act of faith and remembrance of the events in Jesus' life.

Easter is also a time to rejoice at the return of spring and the renewal of life in the form of blooms on trees and flowers and the greening of plants.

When I was growing up in the 1950s and '60s, Easter had its own traditions in our family.

The morning began with a family Easter egg hunt. What child would not wake in anticipation, knowing that there were massive quantities of candying awaiting them?

One year, my mother decided to just buy jellybeans for Easter candy. It was an early Easter, so the weather did not permit an outdoor hunt, thus, she had to be creative on how to 'hide' piles of jellybeans around the house.

She created a memorable event when she linked the piles of candy together with kite string, causing a web effect throughout the house.

When my brother, Dave, and I walked into the living room, Mom and Dad handed each of us an end to the kite string and said, "Start rolling it up, and when you get to a pile of candy, it's yours."

This was one of Mom's many ways to extend an event and make it unusual and fun.

We laughed as we crisscrossed the living room and dining room to find piles of jellybeans everywhere, from behind the easy chair to on top of the piano.

Mom and Dad must have had their own fun the evening before as they created the string maze.

After the annual candy haul, it was time to dress in our new Easter outfits—Dave in his new suit and me in a new dress, with accessories of hat, purse and gloves.

For some reason, these annual new clothes remained in the memory more than other new clothes. It could be because of the events which followed on the way to church.

As we headed to the car for the drive to church, Dad insisted he takes the annual Easter morning photo.

Some years it was of Dave and Jane, standing on either side of Mom, who was holding an Easter lily.

Other times it was posed more artistically, with the three of us sitting on the front porch steps.

But, in all of them, we had a look of agony on our faces.

As we waited for Dad to focus his new 35mm camera, our frozen smiles became looks of aggravation as we said between clenched teeth, "Come on and take it."

The final Easter tradition in my family is purchasing an Easter lily to help decorate the church. To this day, I donate money to my church for a lily in memory of my loved ones who have passed on.

I have started a new tradition for these plants. They are brought home from church and decorate my home until their blossoms die.

Then they are planted in my garden's lily area in hopes that they will return next year as the earth awakens from its winter sleep.

May 11, 2002

Senior Prom Adventure is a Memory Of Lifetime

High school memories seem to fade with time. With 30-plus years gone by, I find I can remember the faces, but the names escape me.

But one memory will never leave me, for it was my great adventure, the only time I walked on the 'wild side.'

Entering my senior year, I was determined to go to the prom. So, I checked out the prospects for dates and staked my claim on Phil.

Phil was a nice guy; he just didn't have much of a backbone when it came to his mother. She ruled the house with an iron fist.

When it came time to plan for prom, Phil asked his mother if he could go to the dance. She said no.

Now I don't know how much he pushed the issue, but he was left without his mother's blessing.

War was declared between two strong-willed women, and poor old Phil was in the middle. He had a girlfriend who wasn't going to accept defeat, much less accept not going to the prom.

So we put our teenage heads together and came up with our version of defying parental rules.

Phil saved his lunch money each day while I provided his meal, and he rented his tuxedo for our clandestine rendezvous.

Meanwhile, my mother went to work sewing my prom dress. The dress, she declared, she would not start making until I had one foot in the car.

Prom Saturday finally arrived. Phil came by in the afternoon to report in. I tactfully asked about the corsage, which only brought a blank look to his face.

"Mom, Phil didn't get me a corsage," I told my mother, who is a resourceful soul.

She went into the backyard and picked roses from the bush and proceeded to make a boutonniere and corsage.

It was a monstrous flower thing that went from my shoulder halfway down my front, but, by God, it was a corsage.

Meanwhile, Phil was securing the keys to his mother's car by telling her we were going for a hamburger and then to a John Wayne double-feature at the neighborhood theater.

The night went without a hitch. Phil went to a friend's house to change into his tux, they picked me up and we went to the Sheraton for the dance.

The thrill of victory came when I got home and I realized we had pulled off the conspiracy.

The next week, we talked about the "what ifs" of his mother finding out about our going to the prom. The scene would go something like this on the night of graduation:

Jane's mother meets Phil's mother and says, "Jane really enjoyed the prom."

"Oh. Who did she go with?" Phil's mother would respond.

"Phil."

"Phil. PHIL!"

Phil would be racing out of the building with Jane on his heels.

The Saturday after the prom, I was awakened by my mother saying, "I'm going to Phil's house to give his mother one of the candles I made."

As I sat up in bed, I said, "Wait! I must tell you something! Phil's mom doesn't know we went to the prom."

After hearing the story, Mom said, "Good for you kids. That was awful for her not giving him permission to go to his senior prom. Now it makes sense about the corsage. I wish you had told me; I would have helped more."

With that, she left for Phil's, and I went back to sleep, never thinking about calling him and informing him that I had told Mom.

Instead, Phil answered the door and began to live the longest 30 minutes of his life.

Mom could see he was sweating bullets while staying within earshot so he could jump in and divert the conversation if the prom came up.

She messed with him a little by letting him think the prom might pop up in conversation at any moment. Later, she tries to cop out of causing Phil so much stress by saying, "The devil made me do it."

But all went well, and Mom kept the secret of the "Great Prom Adventure."

Time has passed. I lost track of Phil after our first two years of college together. He married someone else, and we went on our merry ways.

But the memory of the Great Prom Adventure still brings a smile to my face.

Amazing Woman Wrote 59 Juvenile History Books

As a little girl growing up in Kansas, reading was not one of my favorite things to do. After all, it was inside and sitting down. I'd rather be outside playing, especially playing baseball.

But there was one series of books that I liked, centered around the activities of the Button family—Mr. Button, Mrs. Button, Bucky, Candy, Eddy, Dotty, and baby Freddy.

The Button family came back to mind recently when a group of friends were talking about books they liked to read as youths.

When I was introduced to the dinner guest, one was Edie, a ninety-year-old lady who, I was told, had authored books for juvenile readers.

I had not thought of the Button family until that conversation, and I said, "I liked the Button family series."

Edie quietly said, "I think that was one of mine."

I was so surprised that I said, "Well, your books got me to read."

She was surprised and didn't know what to say, so I said, "I guess you did your job."

And she responded, "I guess I did."

The reporter in me started working the next day. I called Beverly McFarland, the librarian at the Belen Public Library. She used the Internet and verified that my Edie was indeed Edith S. McCall, author of the Button family books.

I had Beverly track down a few of the books in the Inter-Library system, and within a week, I returned to my childhood as I read the Button family's adventures at a pet parade.

I also got a copy of "Butternut Bill."

Next, I used the Internet to visit the Library of Congress website to search for more books written by Edie. To my surprise, during a forty-six-year career, which ended in 1999, Edie had authored or co-authored fifty-nine books.

The next time I visited with her, we talked about her career.

In 1953, she left the classroom as a fourth and fifth-grade teacher to become a reading consultant for the La Grange School District in La Grange, IL.

"I knew what children like to read about," she said. "The subject has to be something they can relate to or something they want to learn about to get them interested in reading."

With that formula, Edie wrote about what interested her as well—history.

Her book titles include "Abe and the wild river," "Stalwart men of early Texas," "Biography of a river, the living Mississippi," "Cowboys and cattle drives," "Cumberland Gap and trails west," "Hunters blaze the trails," "Log fort adventures," "Men on iron horses," "Pioneer show folks," "Pioneering on the Plains," "Pioneers on early waterways," "Heroes of the western outposts," "Settlers on a strange shore," and "Wagons over the mountains," to name a few.

The other night, while visiting with Edie, she said she had just re-read one of her books and was thinking of ways she could modernize the book.

Her bookshelves are filled with copies of her books. She even showed me one from Japan.

One thing I have learned from this encounter is that you never know who you are going to influence with your work. Thanks, Edie, for introducing me to the Button family and reading.

School Supplies Used For August Birthday Gifts

As a child, I looked forward to August almost all year long. Not because it meant school was going to begin soon but because it was my birthday month.

My brother's birthday is January 1, so, as a kid, he always said I had a better deal because I got gifts twice a year, while he only got gifts during Christmas week.

His birthday gifts were placed under the Christmas tree and were not opened until his birthday. Written in big, bold letters on the wrapping paper was HAPPY BIRTHDAY, OPEN NEW YEAR'S DAY.

Like any good big brother, Dave liked to mess with his little sister's head. He told me that Dad loved him more because he closed the feed store for his birthday, but not Mike. He failed to tell me that all stores closed on New Year's Day.

It wasn't until I was older that I figured it out.

Another aspect of my birthday that I didn't figure out until I was older—say thirty-five or so—was that most of my birthday gifts were actually my school supplies, and if it hadn't been my birthday, I would have gotten them anyway.

Each year I got excited about my new pencil box, complete set of crayons and new white blouse and other clothes.

It really wasn't until I was working at newspapers and publishing the school supply lists that I figured out that all kids get those things in August.

I took control of my birthday gifts the summer before fifth grade when I accumulated all my gift money and purchased my first transistor radio.

This was a big thing since transistor radios had just been invented. Unlike the wonderful miniature AM-FM radios we have now, it was three inches by five inches in size and only played AM.

It came in a genuine leather case and had an earphone, not a headset—just a single earplug.

My best friend, Tomisha, and I thought we were hot stuff that year because we could listen to the World Series while walking to the store.

The next year I bought a junior archery set with a fiberglass bow and three REAL target arrows.

Right off the bat, Tomisha and I shouted our first arrow and it went into the neighbor's yard. We had to sneak in and get it.

It wasn't long until we were down to one arrow because we couldn't find the stray ones.

I'm here to report that we did not kill anyone with our archery skills, not even ourselves, even though we gave it our best shot with a game we liked to play.

We'd shoot the arrow straight up in the air and stand watching it come straight back down. The game was a form of chicken—who had nerves of steel to stand there and see how close the arrow would land on them.

It wasn't long before we learned to angle the shot slightly so it wouldn't land on our heads.

Maybe it was a good thing that August also marked the end of summer and we kids were corralled back into school—or else our own exploration into the laws of science might have done some serious damage and I wouldn't have reached my 50th birthday this year.

October 5, 2002

Visitor's Lasting Memory Makes National Magazine

Valencia County has made the national media this month, and it's good news!

Cheryl Solimini wrote a story appearing in Family Circle magazine about her quest to find her late father's 'piece of the Southwest.'

Her father was like many owners of land on the county's east mesa. He purchased a lot from the Horizon Land Corporation in a moment of whimsy, Solimini said in the article.

Solimini's story is like so many stories we hear regarding the many people who purchased land after seeing an ad promising 'one full acre of sunny enchantment in booming New Mexico' as the one appearing in Time magazine on March 24, 1961, which enticed Solimini's father.

Solimini visited our fair county during Labor Day weekend of 2001 to locate her father's lot.

The magazine story tells of her quest and the many friendly people she met here, including Paul Mondragon and his wife, Yolanda, at Casitas at Mountain View in Belen, Odie Otero at Whiteway Café, Marilyn Silva at the county clerk's office, Val Tabor at the Valley Improvement Association and Boyce Edens at Altura Realty.

The article caused me to recall my own father's desire to find the piece of land his minister in Virginia owned out there on the east mesa.

We didn't have the patience to pursue the quest like Solimini to find the actual piece of land. Instead, we went out and took a photo from the highway. Dad told Rev. Regan that it was his land. After all, we figured that one lot out there looks just like any other.

The other thought that came from the article was that we never know what an encounter with a stranger is going to produce.

One day, while in the drive-through at Kentucky Fried Chicken, I noticed a man standing in the shade, looking at a map. His wife walked pasted my car, and we exchanged a smile and a hello.

I figured they were travelers, so I asked where they were headed. She said White Sands, and they were trying to figure out which way to go—by the Interstate to Las Cruces or through Alamogordo.

I said how about the real scenic way and showed them the route through Mountainair, Corona and Carrizozo to Alamogordo. I also suggested they stop at Gran Quivira to see the Salinas Pueblo Missions National Monument.

As I went on my way, I wasn't sure which way they were going to go, but I knew they would remember the lady who had given them directions.

The county's chambers of commerce are always promoting our county, but it is every citizen's job to share our love and enjoyment of the area with visitors.

One person's action can leave a lasting impression on a place. A friendly smile or helpful directions can make a traveler return to their home and recall the wonderful experience they had in New Mexico, especially the friendly area south of Albuquerque, better known as Valencia County.

Keep up the good work, neighbors. You never know when it's going to show up in a national magazine.

October 26, 2002

Everyone Can Make a Difference If They Try

Today is "Make a Difference Day." This national day of helping others is a celebration of neighbors helping neighbors. Some people got an early start.

In 2002, 2.2 million people cared enough about their communities to volunteer, tackling thousands of projects in hundreds of towns and helping an estimated 25 million people.

In Valencia County, members of the Belen High School Student Council participated in the effort sponsored locally by the Retired Senior Volunteer Program.

This year, the students painted fences to cover gang graffiti. The youth worked two hours after school for two days to make their community look better.

Members of Belen USA Down Under will be working with the New Mexico Youth and Family Services' child protective services volunteers program to raise funds for the state program.

They will be washing cars at Reliable Chevrolet in Albuquerque. The group will also be helping at the Run For Adoption on November 10.

I'm sure there are other groups working on projects on this special day, but I have not heard about them.

Having a day set aside to make a difference is an interesting concept. It teaches the younger generation to help their neighbors and, hopefully, it will carry over to other days of the year.

It's good to keep an eye out for someone who could use a little help.

One day, driving in Albuquerque, I saw a man running on the city bus. It pulled out and left him behind. I reacted by pulling over and giving the guy a ride to the bus stop ahead of the bus so he could make his connection.

It really felt good to help that guy out. That's the neat thing about helping people—it makes a difference inside of you.

There's a second grader at Rio Grande Elementary School in Belen who is already enjoying that feeling.

Josh Vallejos keeps an eye out for his classmates and helps them whenever possible.

One day, on the playground, a classmate fell and broke an arm. Josh helped her to the nurse's office.

Another day, when a classmate didn't feel good and was napping at her desk, Josh offered his coat to cover her up and keep her warm.

Because he is so considerate, the son of Cindy Cordova and Jonathan Vallejos was honored at a school assembly, receiving the Commonsense Award from his teacher, Delfin Baca.

"Josh takes care of everyone," Baca said. "He knows to do the right thing without having to be asked."

All of us can think of someone who has made a difference in our lives. For a brief moment in time, that person helped us out.

Making a difference should be second nature for all of us. We should be watching the world around us, looking for opportunities to help.

We are lucky to live in Valencia County, where there are a lot of very caring, nice people helping others and teaching the next generation to be helpful.

I think I'm going to follow Josh's lead and keep a better eye out for others. I help others will join me.

November 23, 2002

What's For Dinner?

The season of eating is upon us.

From Thanksgiving to Christmas and on to the New Year's Eve party, food—from turkey to cookies—is a key part of the celebration.

Most people have turkey on Thanksgiving, but that's not necessarily true for the Moorman clan.

One year Mom didn't want to have to mess with the whole turkey thing, so she decided to bake a chicken.

But, when asked what we were having, she told us, "The old barn owl that's in the barn."

Our family is famous for pulling people's legs with stories. As a child, it was fun to go along with the tales.

I got the last laugh on the owl menu. At school, the teacher asked what we were going to eat for Thanksgiving. She expected the usual answers of turkey and dressing, but Little Janie piped up that her family was going to eat owls.

Needless to say, the word got back to Mom.

A strange thing happened that "Owl Thanksgiving" —the real owl disappeared after the holiday. To this day, no one in our family is sure if we did or did not eat him.

Only Mom knows for sure, and she's determined to keep us on our toes when she tells us a tale, so she's not revealing the true identity of that Thanksgiving dish.

It was a good thing my brother married Sheri; she could cook the Christmas goodies. Her divinity is to die for, not to mention her fudge and cinnamon rolls. But, one Christmas, her efforts to bake a turkey went awry, and it started a new tradition for our family.

About the time you should be smelling the turkey baking, Sheri discovered the bird was stone cold in the oven. The stove was broken. When the amateur mechanics could get no heat out of the oven, we bundled up the grandkid, parents, aunt and grandparents and went looking for a place to eat.

It's not easy finding a restaurant open on Christmas Day, but several miles of driving found Denny's ready to serve a nice meal.

The following year, the attitude was, why cook when we've got a Denny's nearby?

The only problem with eating out on these 'traditional food days' is no leftovers for snacks during the afternoon and evening.

The solution—bake a turkey before the big day and have it ready for leftovers.

I must admit this seems to be a little much; I personally would rather cook a turkey roast that has both white and dark meat pressed together or get a smoked turkey breast to slice for sandwiches.

Then there was the year of the green stuffing. Mom made cornmeal stuffing with sage for flavoring. She got a little heavy-handed on the sage and the dish came out green.

Or the year I postponed Thanksgiving dinner with a friend so I could go to the Dallas Cowboys game. I tried to assure him that eating the meal on Saturday would be just as good as Thursday.

While he ate the entire pumpkin pie with an entire tub of whipped cream, I was in the stands at Texas Stadium, freezing my toes off. By the third quarter, it was apparent that the Cowboys were going to win, so my friend and I headed to the car, which was parked in the furthest parking lot from the stadium.

By the time we got there, a cold was brewing, so it was time for Thanksgiving liquid cheer at Friday's Restaurant.

The following Saturday, my dining friend had no sympathy for my runny nose since he burnt his hand while baking another pumpkin pie for our meal.

Yes, the holidays are all about food, friends, football and memories.

December 24, 2002

Boxing Day is No Match

Looking at the calendar the other day, I realized there is a holiday listed for England that piques the imagination: Boxing Day on December 26.

One's first thought is that boxing refers to the slamming of one's fists onto another person's body with velocity and force.

Or maybe, since it follows Christmas Day, the throwing away of boxes in which the DVD-Play, PlayStation, microwave or other gifts were packaged.

There is a little digression of thought in this area when I remember the time a friend threw away a $100 bill in the Christmas trash—fortunately, her loss was recovered before the boxes and wrapping paper was burned.

Back to Boxing Day—it is an English holiday that is celebrated in the United Kingdom, Australia, New Zealand and Canada.

Like any holiday, there are many stories as to why it began and what one is to do on that day.

The tradition I like is the honoring of those that serve others with gifts.

Ronnie McComb, a native of England who now lives in the county, said it is a day of giving tradesmen and the postman monetary gifts.

"Milk is still delivered to the door in some towns, as well as the mail. Those men look out for your property when you are gone and they hold your mail, so we thank them with an annual Boxing Day gift," she said.

The holiday may date from the Middle Ages, but the exact origin is unknown.

Christmas celebrations in the old days entailed bringing everyone together from all over a large estate, thus creating one of the rare instances when everyone could be found in one place at one time. This gathering of his extended family, so to speak, presented the lord of the manor with a ready-made opportunity to easily hand out that year's stipend of necessities.

In 800 AD, servants were required to work on Christmas and were responsible for making the holiday run smoothly for wealthy landowners. They were allowed to leave on December 26 and visit their families. The employer gave each servant a box containing gifts and bonuses.

Around the ninth century, churches opened their alms boxes, where people placed monetary donations and distributed the content to the poor of the parish. In the Church of England, December 26 is known as the Feast of St. Stephen.

In the English Colonies, this day was when people would box up their unwanted clothes and other things for the poor.

These traditions are about as much as anyone can definitively say about the origin of Boxing Day.

Today, it's a national holiday that allows some British citizens one more day off work.

The day is filled with visiting family, shopping and, for the sports fan, watching "football" —better known as soccer to Americans.

Few people have servants, but the custom of giving gifts or money to those who provide service continues.

Whatever the tradition, the concept of giving to those who have served you during the year is nice. I have a very nice mechanic who fixes little things on the car for no charge. So, this year, I bought him a gift as a thank you.

The other aspect of Boxing Day carries on with them by helping those less fortunate, whether it is by giving toys to needy children, food baskets to hungry families, or coats for children. Sounds familiar—maybe we do celebrate Boxing Day and just don't know it.

Domino Theory 2003: Keep It Friendly, It's All For Fun

Okay, I have a confession. I'm addicted to playing dominos, specifically Mexican Train. Never in all my years did I think I'd say such a thing.

When I was a child growing up in a little town in Kansas, there was a domino parlor where the old men spent their day.

I'm not sure what game of dominos they were playing, but now I understand the attraction.

Every other Saturday night, we gather at a friend's house. There may be five or ten players ready for an evening of visiting and nibbling on snacks while trying to be the first person to play all their dominos.

First of all, you have to understand that Mexican Train is played with a set of 12 double dominos. It begins with the 12s and works its way to the double blank, taking about four hours to be played.

We have learned that each box of dominos seems to have different rules for this game. This causes some confusion if you forget to declare which rules you are using before the game starts.

Our group plays a rule called the Faulkner Shuffle, named after Perry Faulkner, who taught it to us. Perry has been playing for so long that none of us are going to doubt his rules. However, we haven't been able to find the Faulkner Shuffle in any of the written rules.

Another standing rule for our group is that we stop for dessert at the Sixes. And there is always a question of "Is it before we play the sixes or after?" It all depends on the dessert selection and our level of hunger.

One evening, 10 of us were playing with eight of us were women (not that it makes a difference) when Steve said, "What are my options?" while trying to decide where to play.

Suddenly, the room filled with a sound similar to a flock of snow geese taking flight as all eight of us answered, but in different order of options.

About a second into the response, Steve had the biggest grin on his face. "Got ya!" he said.

I must admit that we have played our fair share of jokes on Steve as well.

One night, he was away from the table when we drew our dominos, so we placed the required number in front of his place.

When he returned, he said, "Maybe I don't want these Dominos."

I was sitting next to him, and I didn't like what I had drawn, so I said, "Okay, you can draw from these," as I turned my tiles over and mixed them into his pile.

We play with very lax rules at times, especially when a beginner realizes he or she played the wrong domino. We allow takebacks or replays if no more than one player has played after your move.

Once, when teaching the game to a ninety-one-year-old friend who had never played any form of Dominos, I asked her if she had a seven. She answered, "This one has seven," as she held up a four-three combination tile. She was adding up all of the dots while trying to find a tile to play.

The majority of our Domino buddies just happen to go to the same church. This can be good and this can be bad.

First of all, we play on Saturday night and sometimes don't get finished until 11 p.m. So, getting to church the next day can be hard when you are tired, but we feel that if they can do it, so should I.

Secondly, it's not nice to be a bad sport toward your church friends. They have a tendency to remind you about your spiritual values.

One must never forget the object of the evening—to relax at the end of a busy week and have fun.

The game is simple enough that you can visit and tell stories and jokes. You can even break into a song when an old favorite is playing on the stereo.

Going To The Dogs

Statistics show that a slight majority of Americans are dog people, while the remaining are cat people.

I must admit that I'm more of a cat person than a dog person. I like the way cats are independent. You give them a clean kitty-litter box and bowls of dry food and water—they're happy.

Sure, they like a warm lap to nap on, and if it's cold, a blanket would be nice. And if you are trying to read something, they will be right there trying to get between you and the reading material, be it paper or on the computer.

At my house, we know who's in charge and who rules the roost. We named the cats, Princess and Duke. But our kingdom went to the dogs this week.

A friend, who has six dachshunds, went out of town for three weeks, and I was among the platoon of dog sitters.

Saturday, while making our weekly visit, I noticed one of the 'girls,' Sarah, had a raw wound. So, off to the vet we went, and she became a house guest since medicine had to be administered.

With one dog in the house, the cats felt like they had a fighting chance or at least one of the felines did. Duke, while he is 16 pounds, is basically a chicken at heart, so he hid out.

Princess and Sarah were both curious but cautious toward one another. Sara did communicate loudly but without malice.

After one night, it was decided a second dog would help Sarah not be so homesick, so we added Kala to our guest list.

While Sarah's lower back is paralyzed, causing her not to get around easily, Kala runs on all four paws. So, we quickly closed off all rooms to keep the dogs in the main part of the house.

For the cats, two-on-two was not good odds, so I put their food, water and lavatory in my bedroom and captured them there for the duration.

Kala has a unique skill—smiling. She wrinkles her nose and lifts her upper lip to produce a toothy grin.

The first night the two girls were there, I was awakened at 3:30 a.m. by barking. I went out to see what was happening and all I saw was Kala's teeth glowing in the soft light from my room. She was glad to see me. Her wagging tail exclaimed, "Oh since you're up, do you want to play?"

By the time the dogs' human picked them up on Wednesday, Kala had explored all parts of the house available to her.

She spent Tuesday evening sitting by my room's entrance, watching Princess through the space under the door. Every once in a while, there would be a bumping sound—I'm not sure which one was trying to open the door.

I must admit that I did enjoy having them visit. I liked having them curled up with me in the recliner.

It was neat when Kala nuzzled her head under my chin, but I still do not like doggie kisses.

I discovered the joy of treats. To dogs, it's heaven on earth just thinking about the morsel of food. So, when a human produces the treat, it is just seconds before it is devoured.

The two dogs discovered our neighbor's dog, Grace, while in the backyard. After their first visit with Grace, each time they went outside, they gave a bark of welcome to their new best friend.

I was a little sad Wednesday when I realized that their joyfully wagging trails would not be there when I got home from work.

Watching television would be a little lonely without two dogs curled up under the lap blanket. It almost made me think about getting a dog.

But then the cats gave me "the look," which told me if a dog moved in, someone would have to move out, and it wasn't going to be them.

Just when I was getting over missing the pups, we got a call from their human. She's going out of town for two weeks—would we consider having a houseguest again?

I'd better not act too excited when I ask the cats if they mind being captive in one room for two weeks.

Leavenworth Joke Lives On At Tax Time

There are three sure things in life—birth, death and paying taxes.

As I was growing up, there was one rule in our house that was observed, hard and true. When my parents were working on the taxes, stay clear and don't bother them.

Each year, Mother would get the tax guide from the Internal Revenue Service and read it from cover to cover. She wanted to be sure they were getting all the credits possible.

Mother was the family bookkeeper, so it was up to her to gather the check stubs, receipts, and other paperwork in preparation for an evening of filling out the forms.

Before copy machines and computers, my parents would sit facing each other at the dining room table, each with a typewriter in front of them. They would go line-by-line, each filling in the information.

When Mom told Dad of a deduction they could take, he'd say, "Are you trying to get me sent to Leavenworth?"

The year after my father passed away, I was faced with the task of doing my mother's taxes. All went well, and I got them sent off on time. But, on April 15, I couldn't resist continuing the Leavenworth joke.

"Mom, I've been looking at your finances, and I've decided you will have to move to a more affordable retirement home."

"Oh," she said with caution in her voice.

"And I've found you the perfect place at the right price. You will have a private room and your clothing will be provided."

There was no response from the other end of the phone line, so I continued with my best imitation of a salesperson promoting a deal.

There are three square meals a day, an exercise yard and there are even arts and crafts. And, if you're lucky, you might get to learn how to make license plates."

"Oh?"

"But there is bad news. You're going to have to move out of Albuquerque—to Kansas."

"This new home wouldn't happen to be in Leavenworth, would it?" Mom asked.

Well, the jock was not over. Mom called my brother and told him the news. After learning where her new home would be, my brother Dave laughed so hard that his wife wondered who was on the phone and what was going on.

The next day, I called Dave to let him tell me what a great jokester I am, but the last laugh was on me.

"There's just one thing you forgot," Dave said, laughing. "You do her taxes, right? Well, if she goes to the federal pen in Leavenworth, you're going to have the cell next to her."

Since I don't think an orange jumpsuit is the fashion statement I want to make, I guess I'd better be extra careful when I'm doing her taxes.

The joke turned a little sour when Mother and I had to visit the IRS office because of a slight mistake I made the next year.

With a little explanation from the government representative, I was able to get the glitch straightened out so we didn't have to go home and pack Mom's suitcases for the Kansas journey.

On a less humorous note:

Taxes are necessary for a government to serve its people. Each year, we wish our government leaders could reduce our taxes, but we also want the service provided by them to increase.

I learned this week from the Valencia County state legislators that it is estimated the state's revenue will be reduced by $90 million in the first year, and a total of $380 million in five years, because of the tax cut signed by Gov. Bill Richardson this year.

Yet citizens want more money for very important programs, such as education and correction, as well as special appropriations and capital outlay projects for various government entities.

Any manager of a budget, be it a family's home budget or a corporation, knows revenue has to be there before expenses can be made, or else you are walking on thin ice above the abyss of financial problems. Only time will tell the impact of the tax cut, but many feel it will not be good.

May 24, 2003

Memorial Day Means Family, School Reunions

Memorial Day marks the annual trip to Kansas for the Moorman clan.

Through the years, it was time for my parents to go back to their school reunions and see their former classmates. It is also time to pay tribute to our ancestors with the Memorial Day visit to the cemetery.

I joined them in 1990, my 20th class reunion, to see what all the hubbub was about.

I hooked up with them in my mother's hometown, Minneapolis—population 2,000 or so.

It is here that I spent my summers as a child, visiting my grandparents and helping my grandmother prepare meals for the harvest crew.

The farm is what I think of when I envision going home. It is your typical midwestern farm, with a two-story white house, a barn, a corral and outbuildings.

Grandmother had an amazing iris garden and most of it remains—all except the part Granddad fenced for his cattle back in the '70s.

The highlight of visiting my grandparents was getting to sleep on the sleeping porch with my grandmother. When they added indoor plumbing to the house back in the '40s, an open-air, screened-in area was created on the second floor.

To reach this porch, you had to go through Granddad's room, which proved to be a problem one night when it was raining, and I had to go to the bathroom because I was afraid I'd awaken him.

Spending time at the farm, where television waves were impossible to get back in the '60s, taught us how to entertain ourselves without the TV. We played Monopoly, read old National Geographic magazines, and explored the barn and outbuildings.

As an adult, I still walk the property and hear the ghostly voices of kids calling to each other from their hiding places.

In 1990, several cousins also came home for the weekend, and we had a nice reunion.

On Memorial Day, while placing fresh-cut peonies on the graves of at least four generations of ancestors, I got an idea.

"Mom, Dad, Aunt Margaret, Uncle John. Come and lie down beside Grandma and Granddad's grave, so I can see how it's going to look when you're dead," I joked as my cousin, Roger, looked at me with an appalled look on his face.

Humor has always been a part of our family's creed. Mom was the only one who almost lay down.

The next stop on our tour of Kansas was my hometown – Nickerson. This is where my father's people settle at the turn of the century (1900, that is).

This town was a hopping place before the Santa Fe Railroad moved the roundhouse to Newton. Now the mile-long and half-mile-wide town has a population of 1,100 people.

The school reunion is always the Saturday after Memorial Day. It was interesting to attend the event.

The class of honor is celebrating its 50th anniversary. That class sits at the head table, while the other classes sit at designated tables grouped on the gymnasium floor.

At one point, the emcee said, "Let's see which family has the most graduates present." As I looked around and counted the heads of Moormans, I realized we had seven. But another family had the same number.

As the Moormans and Cavanaughs stood, the emcee said, "Well, of course, they tied. They're all related."

But the main reason there were so many Moormans and Cavanaughs present was the family reunion the next day.

This is one of those 100-plus attendee events where I had no clue who anyone was, except for those aunts and uncles who were my father's siblings.

This event used to be held at someone's house, but now it is held in the meeting room at the Farmer's Co-op Elevator. We gather and try to figure out who is related to whom.

The one thing that was interesting about the school reunion was that people my age were not there. I figure as long as our parents are alive and going to the reunion, my generation will not make an effort to go.

Only when we get older and realized how precious those friendships of youth were and will we make the annual trip back home to see how things have changed.

July 5, 2003

Pranks? On July 4th? It Certainly Wasn't Us!

The Fourth of July is a red-letter day for any red-blooded American kid.

It's the day we get to play with fire and gunpowder—better known as firecrackers.

As a kid, I was a little afraid that firecrackers would blow up in my face.

A classmate, Donald Jones, had the misfortune of looking down a pipe to see why a firecracker had not fired just as it blew up. He was lucky he didn't lose his eye.

I had my own up-close and personal experience with fireworks when a spark from a sparkler got into my eye.

That was the year of the great firework display. My parents' friends gathered each Fourth of July and pooled their small clutch of fireworks for one great display.

One year, the display went on and on and on. As the evening progressed, one mother said, "Wasn't it nice what John did?" she said this to John's wife.

She replied, "What did John do?"

"He bought all of the leftover fireworks from the dime store last year at a discount. That's why we have so many."

"HE DID! JOHN!"

It turned out that John, the town's insurance man, had stored the fireworks in the attic of his garage, unbeknownst to his wife.

Upon her discovery, she said, "What if we had had a fire in the garage? How would it have looked, him being an insurance man?"

While I wasn't big on the explosive side of firecrackers, my brother loved the thrill of working with gunpowder. He took the Fourth of July to a higher level.

Dave's first extravaganza was a cannon built from scrap parts at my grandparent's farm. He used an old stove pipe for the cannon—which even had wheels.

He placed firecrackers at the closed end and when they exploded, the stove pipe amplified the bang.

Dave's dream since he was little was to work in the movies. He explored the world of special effects one Fourth of July with the help of cousin Roger.

The guys build a war scene with plastic army men and vehicles. The scene came alive with the strike of a match.

They connected buried firecrackers with fuses that had been removed from other firecrackers. It was all timed out, so the firecrackers exploded at different times, blowing up and knocking over men and vehicles to represent a war scene.

Dave always saved a shoebox of firecrackers for other times during the year, such as Halloween.

One year, he had a group of guys spend the night enjoying Halloween pranks and trick-or-treating around the neighborhood and town.

The next day at church, one boy's mother commented, "We had fun last night. We parked downtown and watched the town marshal drive back and forth from one end of town to the other as firecrackers were fired. First, we'd hear firecrackers at the north end and, when he'd drive that direction, we'd hear firecrackers at the south end. He was kept busy all night. We commented that we were glad Chuck was at your house because we knew he wouldn't be involved in this type of stuff."

My mother responded, "I hate to tell you this, but your son was among the kids on the north end of town."

Dave and his friends were sleeping in the basement, and Mom and Dad would hear them plotting their next venture out. Then the guys would leave through the basement door, some firecrackers would be heard exploding and pretty soon, the guys would be back inside, laughing and talking.

"We knew what they were doing," Mom said. "We knew they were being safe and they were having fun."

I guess it was a better activity than the group of older guys who were putting a toilet on the roof of the elementary school gym.

Why Do You Do Things The Way You Do?

Have you ever watched someone do a task and thought, "They're doing that wrong" or "Why do they do it that way?"

It happens at my house quite frequently because you can't have two people from different upbringings and expect them to do everything the same way. Better yet, you can't expect siblings to do things the same.

One area of discussion at my house is ironing. I've discovered the routine I use is not a universally taught method.

So how do you iron a shirt? Do you iron the front and back first, then do the yoke, collar and sleeves? Or do you do the yoke, collar and sleeves first, then the front and back?

I was led to believe the front-and-back first order was incorrect until, one day I asked a friend which method she used. It turns out she's a front-and-back first person, not a sleeves-first person.

The sleeves-first person informed me that this technique was taught to her when you had to sprinkle clothes before ironing. "You did the collar and cuffs first because it was thicker and held more moisture. If they weren't dry when you finished the shirt, you would go back and iron them again," she said.

Another area of difference is how you eat a plate of food. Are you a one-item-at-a-time person? Or do you move around the plate, taking a bite of this and that?

I've been told by a one-item-at-a-time person that she doesn't like to mix the flavors. I personally like to mix the flavors, and as I come to the last bites, I decide which flavor I want to be my last.

What order do you use when putting on socks and shoes? Do you put sock and shoe on one foot and then go to the other? Or do you put the socks on both feet first, then the shoes?

I've discovered I always start with my right foot and put both sock and shoe on before going to my left foot.

Maybe I started this after my brother, while still in a sleep stupor, put two socks on one foot.

How do you fold bath towels? Do you fold them in half longwise first or across the middle?

Most people, including myself—at least in the past—fold then across the middle, then longwise.

I discovered if I fold them longwise first, I don't have to refold them before hanging them on the towel rack.

How do you read a magazine? Do you start from the front cover and work your way to the back? Or do you use the random flip-through method of selecting the story to read?

When I was a kid, I would crawl onto my dad's lap, and we'd look at the Saturday Evening Post together. We'd start at the back and read the Hazel cartoon first, then flip through to the front cover. Since I was mainly looking at the pictures, this seemed to be an acceptable method of reading a magazine.

When you draw a circle, do you start at the top, bottom or side? Where do you start when writing letters and numbers—top or bottom?

When I was learning cursive writing, I would start my capital J at the top of the circle, then make a tail. The teacher kept telling me my name was not Gane.

It took my big brothers to show me what I was doing wrong: I needed to start at the bottom and move the pen to the left, circle around and extend the line past the circle intersection to create the tail.

A co-worker tells me her brother writes his number from the bottom up. Try it—it's difficult to do. It's almost as hard as writing upside-down and backward, which is one of my lesser-known skills.

I'm not sure what the psychological analysis is for these various acts, but I know we all do things differently. But I guess that's what makes life interesting—getting to watch someone do it the wrong way and wonder, "Why do they do it that way?"

December 27, 2003

Shopping Trip Snowballs Into a Complete Re-Do

How can a simple trip to the store to buy drapes turn into a major decorating project?

This is the question that comes to my mind every time I shop for a single piece of furniture. It always seems to snowball into a complete home makeover.

It was a perfectly innocent trip to the store to purchase drapes for my living room to brighten the room when I sighted the most unique and wonderful sofa. Of course, I fell in love with it and had to have it.

As I hung the drapes and awaited the delivery of the sofa, I realized the color of the upholstery just would not go with the old, gold-shag carpet. So, off to the store we went to look at new carpeting.

Meanwhile, the recliner, which had seen better days and listed to the right, now did not go with the new carpet. So, off to the store, we went to look for a new recliner. While looking for the perfect chair, we found a wonderful platform rocker as well.

Before all was said and done, we had wallpapered two walls to brighten the room and had a room full of new furniture. Once the living room had new drapes, carpeting, a sofa, a recliner and a rocker, the dining room now looked drab.

The next thing I knew, we were off to the store to find a new dining room table.

This little remodeling in 1995 was duplicated this year when it was time to replace the recliner. But, this year, women's logic came into play when good deals just seemed to make it impossible for us not to redecorate the dining room.

When the ideal recliner was found, it was $500 more than I wanted to pay, so we decided to shop around. As we were leaving the store, to our delighted surprise, the ideal curio cabinet, which we had been dreaming of getting, was right there waiting for us to purchase it and have it delivered the next day.

A quick turn-around and the salesman found himself earning a commission with the greatest of ease.

However, the woodwork of the cabinet did not match our dining room table.

So, off we went the next day to find a table. We didn't find a table, but we did find the same recliner for $260 less and the same cabinet for $400 less.

We ordered the chair because, after all, it was a great saving.

Now—how to get the saving for the curio cabinet? We made a quick trip back to the first store to tell them we had decided we liked the cabinet but not the antique silver wood stain.

"Could we order it in natural wood? And, by the way, we found the exact same cabinet elsewhere for $400 less. Can we make a deal, so the salesman won't lose his commission?"

With a yes from the store manager, we were ecstatic. We had saved $660 in just one day of shopping, but we still needed a new table.

One more furniture store, just to see what they have. Oh, my, there is the perfect table—and it has a leaf.

The nice salesperson told us that the table was a stock item and there was going to be a sale in a couple of days that would get the table and six chairs for $660. This was a great deal because we were getting a dining room set with a value of $860 for the amount we had saved on our other two purchases.

Men, any woman will tell you that this is definitely good shopping. Who cares about how much we had to spend for these great savings? We got three things for the price of two. But, as in any remodeling, once the furniture was placed in the house, it became apparent that there were just a few things that needed to be replaced—such as the microwave stand in the kitchen and a chair in the living room. They just don't seem to go with the new things.

Super Bowl VI: What a Memory

Super Bowl Sunday. It's an unofficial national holiday. While the banks don't close early on Friday, the event is as great as any traditional holiday.

People gather in front of the television with mass quantities of junk food and canned liquid consumables to ward off hunger during the closing minutes of the last football game of the year.

The next best thing to a good Super Bowl party is attending the actual event. I must admit I have made the pilgrimage to the Mecca of football.

The year was 1972—Super Bowl VI. I was a sophomore in college in East Texas, just a six-hour drive to New Orleans, where the Dallas Cowboys faced Miami at Tulane University's stadium.

Yes, this was in the days of outdoor games. When huge men didn't just face off against other huge men over a pigskin ball, but fans had to survive the effects of the weather—in our case, cold feet. But I'm getting ahead of my story.

What does one say when your boyfriend's father offers you extra Super Bowl tickets? The word that comes to mind is YES! Especially if you live in Texas and America's Team—the Dallas Cowboys—is playing.

But first, let's digress to the divisional playoffs. A friend working at a Dallas suburban grocery store tells the story of a conversation the head cashier had with Roger Staubach during the playoffs.

"Roger! Did your team win?" she asked, yelling across three checkout lines.

"Yes, ma'am," Staubach said shyly.

"Now, when do you play again?" she asked.

"Next week in New Orleans."

"Well, are they going to let you go with them?" she continued.

Roger Staubach lived in the same suburb of Dallas that I did and frequently, you would see him in the store or post office.

Getting to go to the Super Bowl was one of the highlights of my life. But the lesson I learned was free tickets are not necessarily better than watching the game at home on television.

Super Bowl Sunday began with our group of four 100 miles from New Orleans. The car owner had a phobia of driving on Interstate highways, so we worked our way to the city through the bayou country.

When we arrived in New Orleans, we had no idea where we were in relation to the stadium. So, we took a stab at finding it, only to discover we were going away from New Orleans instead of into the heart of the Crescent City.

As we raced to find the stadium, then found a parking lot, the car owner was threatening that if we missed the kickoff, we might as well go home.

Thank God we got to our seats in the nosebleed section of the endzone just as the ball was kicked.

From where we sat, we saw a bunch of 'six-inch-tall' men playing on a green field with white lines on it. The game was good—after all, Dallas won 24-3, but it was hard to keep your focus on the game when the various drunks around you were more fun to watch.

Our section seemed to yell more at the Goodyear Blimp when it passed between us and the sun, causing our body temperatures to drop another few degrees. And then we would cheer when it would move on and the sun would shine on us again.

Today, the halftime show is a huge extravaganza with hundreds of dancers performing on the field at one time. Through the years, many great entertainers have performed, including the memorable "Heal the World" featuring Michael Jackson at Super Bowl XXVII or rockin' country with Clint Black, Tanya Tucker, Travis Tritt and Wynonna and Naomi Judd.

Each year seems to be an opportunity to see if the halftime show producer can outdo the guy from the year before.

Back in 1972, it was very simple, so simple we could hardly see it from the nosebleed section.

The theme was a Salute to Louis Armstrong, with performances by Ella Fitzgerald, Carol Channing, Al Hirt and the U.S. Marine Corps Drill Team.

From where I was sitting, all we saw were these six-inch-tall performers on a float going around the field on the running track. I guess it was entertaining, but I was more worried about the drunk sitting next to me spilling his beer on me.

Meanwhile, back in Dallas, my parents were at a Super Bowl party where all the guests were watching the television intently, looking for Jane.

At one point, a woman said, "I'm looking for Jane and I don't even know what Jane looks like."

Mother swears she did see me during a shot of people leaving the stadium.

"Were you wearing that ugly plaid coat and goofy knit hat?" she asked me the next time we visited by phone.

"Yes."

"Well, I think I saw you on television. It was the coat that stood out."

That was my first experience of attending a national sporting event. Since then, I attended the 1984 Olympics and various professional basketball and baseball games, and even a track and field event.

Through the years, I've thought that if you aren't on the sideline or in the expensive seats, it's better to be home watching the game on the television with mass quantities of junk food and canned liquid consumables.

Also, while at the game, you don't get to see the great, newly-released television commercials. So have a fun Sunday and celebrate the 38th Super Bowl and know that you're really not missing much not being there in person.

March 13, 2004

Quest for Perfection in Donuts Ends

I have been in pursuit of the perfect donut for most of my life.

But unlike what most people think, my quest did not end when Krispy Kreme came to the Southwest. If anything, it has put me on a donut-free diet.

As a donut-aholic, I have come up with many justifications for the consumption of deep-fat-fried pastry. Did you know that if you are on a diet, it's all right to eat a donut because all of the calories were in the middle, and the making of the hole took those calories away?

Also, if you eat a donut with a diet drink, the remaining calories are negated.

Okay, so my waistline says otherwise.

Have you ever had a Spudnut? This is a donut in which dehydrated potato flakes have been used instead of flowers. It's been many years since I had one of these. In the '60s, when I lived in Columbia, MO., there was a Spudnut shop by our church.

That was when I discovered the joy of a good donut.

As life continued, donuts were my saving grace. Once, during the lean monetary years, two friends and I held off starvation with a dozen donuts.

When we combined our pennies, we had enough for a dozen, which were to keep us going while we earned money for supper by officiating a softball game.

As my friends umpired the game, I sat at the scorer's table and ate the freshly baked donuts. The first base umpire called time out, and when the home plate umpire went to see what her concern was, she said, "Someone stop Jane from eating all of the donuts, or I'm going to have to kill her."

She had been standing out there at first base, watching me devour more than my share of the food.

There is a new name in Albuquerque for donut connoisseurs— Shipley's. This is an old friend of mine since the donuts that were melting in my mouth during that ball game were from Shipley's.

In recent years, I have been trying to find that special taste that I remember from my youth.

Dunkin Donuts comes close with its batter, but the flavoring in the icing is not as strong as I like. Shipley's has a great maple frosting, but the batter does not have the flavor of Dunkin Donuts.

It seems as if every time I find the perfect donut, the business closes. I have a routine of stopping at Furr's Supermarket each morning for a strawberry donut for breakfast.

That was almost the perfect donut. It was big and fluffy, with distinct flavoring in its icing.

When Furr's went away, it took the freshly baked donuts. The John Brooks and Smiths that have purchased the two Furr's near my house produce a donut that is heavy for my taste.

Meanwhile, I found the next best thing—Dunkin Donuts.

I have had a Sunday morning ritual for many years of stopping on the way to church at the Dunkin Donuts near my house to get one for the road, but at the first of the year, the shop closed. This could be because I had stopped going to church and thus had not been in to see the Donut Ladies. I'm sure my weekly donation to their business was a factor in the owner's decision.

For whatever reason, the shop closed for remodel and, when it reopened, not only was it an espresso bar, but now it serves Krispy Kremes.

Sorry folks, I'm not crazy about the sugar-drenched, oily, small donuts that everyone is raving about. Plus, they are twice the price of other brands.

Prior to the changeover at my local bakery, I'd confess my sins to the Donut Ladies by saying, "Forgive me, for I ate a Krispy Kreme this week." Now they are peddling their former competitor's creations with smiles on their faces.

Maybe this is an act of God. Since I have been unable to find the perfect donut, I've actually gone on a real diet.

But the other day, a co-worker brought nourishment to a staff meeting and, to my delight, it was—you guessed it—donuts. Her offerings ranked a '9' on my donut meter.

"Where did you get these?" I asked with a full mouth.

"Lowe's Supermarket in Belen."

With that discovery and the exploration of other bakeries in Valencia County, my quest is revived.

Even though I'm dieting, I must admit I can be found sneaking into Donut King in Belen or stopping at Manny's Bakery in Los Lunas for 'just one.'

These guys know how to make the donut the old-fashioned way—not automated. You can tell they have added that secret ingredient—the human touch.

May 22, 2004

Santa Fe Railroad Runs Through My Life

This is a special time in my hometown. The residents of Nickerson, KS, are preparing to celebrate the town's 125th anniversary.

Now, in New Mexico time, 125 years is no big deal, but in Kansas, that's about the time the land was being settled.

Nickerson is in central Kansas, along the Arkansas River. As I think about the town's history and my growing up there, I can't help but see correlations with Belen and Valencia County.

Both towns experienced boom times because of the Atchison, Topeka and Santa Fe Railway. And both have experienced the economic impact of changes made by the railroad.

Nickerson was named in 1875 in honor of Thomas Nickerson, then president of the railway.

The town was located at the end of the second division of the ATSF railway and the company's site of the larger and more extensive machine and repair shop of the railroad. Doesn't that sound familiar, ATSF families?

Nickerson was a hopping place at the end of the 19th century, with a population topping 2,000.

In History of the State of Kansas by William G. Cutler, published in 1883, the author declared about Nickerson: "The future of the place is assured, as it is surrounded by rich and fertile country, and, within its limits, about \$200,000 is paid out annual by the railroad company."

Then, at the turn of the century, ATSF moved the roundhouse to Newton, KS.

At the time, Newton was regrouping after having been a cattle boomtown when ATSF was first laying rail west. After the railhead moved on west, Newton's population dwindled to 250 before the company began growing again.

With the roundhouse being moved to Newton, hundreds of people followed, leaving Nickerson to remain at about 1,300 people.

My ancestors came to Nickerson because of the railroad and stayed to eke out a living by farming and to own the livery stable, icehouse, and feed store.

As a child, I heard stories of when the roundhouse was there. In fact, we could still see the embankments of the rails at the old location.

We also learned that the first self-propelled threshing machine, a forerunner to the combine, was built just south of town.

We were also amazed that there had once been a cheese factory of some size. But by the time I was a kid, the town was a skeleton of its former self. We still had a depot and a station master. Those remnants of the past are gone today.

One of the most amazing memories of my childhood was of the evening I got to go up into a train's engine cab.

My family was eating at the café when the station master came in and told the cook a crew would be there in 15 minutes. "Have something ready," he said.

When the men came into the café, my brother, Dave, and I went to look at the train. We were examining all the mechanisms that drive the great wheels when a man stuck his head out of the cab window.

"What are you kids doing?"

"Just looking."

"Want to come up and see inside?"

We didn't have to be asked twice. We climbed up the ladder to a world few kids got to see. The man was the fireman, and he told us the train was a mile long. That was pretty impressive to us because we knew what a mile looked like since Nickerson is a mile long and a half-mile wide.

One summer, while I lived in Nickerson, I got a letter from a Girl Scout in Chicago who wanted to be a pen pal. I lost interest very fast when, after she asked me to send a postcard of my town, I discovered there were no postcards of Nickerson, Kansas. I thought, *What would I possibly have in common with a city girl? We don't even have postcards.*

The only modern-day claim to fame for Nickerson is that it was the location for the movie Picnic, starting Kim Novack in the 1950s. And in the 1970s, a movie starring William Holden was filmed in the area. Holden played a World War I ace pilot who was traveling around the country as a barn-stormer.

Another similarity between Nickerson and Belen is how the towns in the area have grown. When Nickerson was at its heyday, 10 miles down the road, Hutchinson, while the county seat was smaller.

After the roundhouse moved, Hutchinson came into its own with salt mines and other industries, and today, Nickerson is a bedroom community to Hutchinson.

This is similar to Belen and Los Lunas. During the heyday of rail, Belen was the boomtown while Los Lunas was the farming village. Now those roles have changed as Los Lunas experiences a boom as a bedroom community for Albuquerque.

During my years here in Valencia County, I have met many people whose families have a tie to Newton, including Sandy Battin, whose grandfather was from Newton, as well as the Trembly family and others.

When I meet someone with a tie to Newton, it almost feels like meeting people from home. It has made me aware of what a great impact the railroad has had in moving people west.

August 21, 2004

Golden Or Platinum, Each Birthday is Special

Another birthday came around this week for me, and I must say I do like my special day.

This year marked a special moment in my life—my age is the same number of the year I was born. No, I'm not 1952 years old, but I am the last two numbers.

The question came up about whether this is the golden birthday. So, I went surfing on the Internet to see just what a golden birthday is.

It turns out that the golden birthday is the one in which the day's date coincides with the age of the person. My golden birthday was nineteen, and I didn't even know it back then.

The concept of the golden birthday was conceived by Joan Bramsch as recognition for the special birthday of each of her five children.

This tradition has spread across the land to friends and relatives, and yet not one greeting card company has agreed with her that this birthday is truly special.

I've been wondering: If the date and age matching marks the golden, what is it when the year and age coincide? Platinum?

The more I thought about this, I realized people born in the latter part of the century would have a harder time reaching their platinum birthday. *Those born in 1985 will have to be eighty-five. The odds are against the majority of people living that long.*

Whether golden or platinum, birthdays should be special, it is a day for friends and family to celebrate a person's life.

My mother called me on Wednesday to wish me a happy birthday and I had to tell her she was a day early. She said, "Really? Are you sure? After all, I was there too."

Birthdays can be a tough issue for some people. Comedian Jack Benny dealt with the issue by claiming to be perennial thirty-nine. My father took this strategy and my mother, who was two years younger, followed suit by saying she was thirty-seven. This worked until her children became older than thirty-seven, and there was a question about miracles of birth and such.

I've come up with my own unique age. This year I turned two. I don't worry about the decade, I let others figure it out.

Some days I might want to act like I'm in the Terrible Twos. When was the last time we were allowed to have a temper tantrum when things didn't go our way? Or I might feel like being twelve, twenty-two, thirty-two or even forty-two—age is a state of mind anyway.

Besides, if you only claim birthdays up to 10, you get many opportunities to get good at being an age. Take 2. This is my sixth time being at this age, so I'm getting really good at it.

It's always fun to find out who else was born on your date. My mother was born on the same date and year as Former First Lady Barbara Bush.

My father shares his day with Martin Luther King Jr., so Dad has a national holiday on his birthday, and the date is highlighted on all of the calendars in red, which is handy for his kids to remember it.

I also have some pretty impressive people, including President Bill Clinton and Tipper Gore, the wife of Former Vice President Al Gore.

Wealth and success seem to shine on those born on Aug. 19. Some that have benefited are Malcom Forbes, multimillionaire publisher of Forbes magazine, and Willie Shoemaker, a legendary jockey who won 8,833 horse races in a forty-year career.

On a sci-fi note, the creator of the original Star Trek, Gene Roddenberry, and Star Trek: The Next Generation's Commander William Riker, Jonathon Frakes, also share this birthday. In the realm of flying, Orville Wright of the famous Wright Brothers at Kitty Hawk share this fabulous day.

From the world of arts, some of the many are Matthew Perry, LeAnn Womack, Li'l Romero, Adam Arkin and John Stamos.

As far as famous events happening on this day, in 1995, one of the most famous weddings in television history is reported as frequent Tonight Show guest Tiny Tim got married.

Genes Count But, You're Also on Your Own

Family genetics can be a blessing and a curse.

I'm blessed by coming from a gene pool that has strong hearts, low blood pressure and low cholesterol and is free of disease—mental as well as physical.

But the Moorman curse comes in two forms, prostate cancer for men and obesity for all of us.

I'd always considered myself overweight but never obese until recently when I did a story about Compulsive Eaters Anonymous, and I did research about the nation's second leading cause of preventable death.

That's when I learned about the body mass index and found that I was, indeed, considered obese since I weighed in at 205 pounds.

I decided it was time to quit kidding myself about why I was allowing myself to slowly expand out of one size of clothes and into the next larger one. It was time to take control of my physical condition.

Besides, with the diet world becoming low-carb crazy, it has become easier for me to eat healthy.

During my life, I have topped 200 pounds three times and each time, I have been able to lose the 50 pounds health providers told me I carried over my preferred weight. I have used a low-carb diet.

Since everyone is claiming the ideal dieting methods, I might as well get on board and proclaim that my successful diet is to stay at or below 60 carbs a day.

This task is easier now as restaurants are offering special menu items and nutritional drinks that have low-carb versions that have less than ten carbs. But I have learned over the years that counting carbs is not enough to cut the inches off the waist and thighs. That only comes with hard work and sweat.

One thing that is great about being a newspaper reporter is that you meet people who are inspiring.

One of these for me is Leona Chavez, who beat her weight problem and was featured in Shape magazine. Besides changing her entire eating habit, Leona dedicated herself to walking four miles each day.

This spring, I took to the track and began walking. At first, I would just walk for a half hour and didn't worry about the distance. I was just trying to get my muscles to stop complaining since they had been forced to go from sedentary to active.

I read articles about walking and learned that the greatest benefit comes with distance. So, I pushed myself to walk three miles each day and then worked to get it done in an hour.

Meanwhile, I read about cardiovascular workouts and the use of a heart rate monitor. From the literature I have read, if a person maintains a heart rate of 60 to 75 percent of their maximum heart rate for an hour, their body will use its fat storage for 50 percent of the energy needed during the exercise.

You determine your maximum heart rate by taking your resting heart rate after you have lain perfectly still for at least twenty minutes. Then there is a formula for determining your maximum heart rate. I found a website that calculated it for me. My ideal exercise heart rate ranges from 130 to 146 beats per minute.

So, four evenings a week, I mount my bicycle trainer and pedal until my heart rate is at 150 beats per minute. I find that, over an hour's time, I average about 144 beats per minute since I do stop pedaling when I drink water.

This brings up another thing I've worked on—drinking water. A co-worker learned from her doctor that a person should drink a quart of water for every 50 pounds they weigh. I've been drinking a quart during my three-mile walk in the morning and a quart while bicycling in the evening.

Now, you are thinking, *okay Jane, what's this all leading to?*

I've become the shrinking lady of our office. After four months, I have lost 25 to 30 pounds, depending on how I stand on the scales. I'm just 10 pounds away from my target weight to be considered no longer overweight.

However, I want to get down to 160 pounds since I know I will probably rebound with some weight gain after I cut my exercise routine to just walking.

The greatest thing about all of this weight loss stuff is that I get to go shopping. I have dropped from a loose size 22 to a loose size 18 and, hopefully, will even get down to a 16.

As all women know, when you talk about weight loss, you actually are hoping to be able to get into those smaller jeans someday.

Nov. 13, 2004

If I Only Had Thumbs, Life Would Be Grand

By Princess Moorman

Humans! You can't live with them, and you can't eat without them. All they are good for are their thumbs.

If we felines only had thumbs, then we could open our own cans of tuna and life would be grand.

My human, Jane, was starting to write this column, but she got a telephone call, so I decided to help her out.

I always like to help her when she is sitting at that little television and making a tapping noise on that button pad.

It is especially fun when she has all those envelopes open and paper spread all over the desk—I just love the smell of the glue on the envelopes... it's also great to lick, but not as great as the emulsion on photographs.

That really gets Jane's dander up. She puts the photos up where she thinks I can't reach them. I let her believe she's in charge, even though I am the Princess of the house.

Let me introduce myself—I'm Princess. I live with Jane and her other cat, Duke. He's twice as big as me, so I have to scream at him to keep him in line. He's really easy to bully. But I must remember to be just nice enough to him so he will let me curl up beside him during nap time.

I think I'm the smartest cat Jane has ever had; she may not agree. I hear her tell stories about my predecessor, Nacle, as in Moorman's Tabernacle. Jane thinks that's a funny joke. When I hear her tell it, I just lie down and clean my undercarriage to let her know how I feel.

Jane says Nacle thought she was French. Now how could she tell that? And better yet, what is a French?

She says Nacle would come running when she whistled the French national anthem. Any cat that would lower itself to respond to a whistle, let alone run to the human, is not so smart in my book.

I prefer to just saunter into the room after she has called my name at least ten times. And I refuse to answer that "Kitty, kitty, kitty" stuff. *How belittling!* I'm not a kitty. I'm a Cateople—you know, a cat that thinks it's people.

Jane also tells me about her favorite cat ever, which I thought I was, but whatever! The other favorite cat was Domino.

Now what type of name is that for a cat? Jane said the white cat had a black spot between her ears when she was born, and Jane didn't think it was right to call a cat Spot, so she went with Domino. But the feline's wisdom ruled. The spot fell out when she was six months old, leaving Jane with a double-blank domino. Ha!

I've been informed that Domino would walk with Jane in the woods. That must have been a lot of fun. I'm not allowed outside because there are big mean animals out there that could eat me, like dogs and COYOTES!

Domino also got to eat pizza! I'm never allowed to have human food, except if it's ice cream, then I get to lick traces of cream from the bowl when Jane is done.

Just to keep Jane on her toes, I will check out any food she is eating in her easy chair. I figure it's fair game if she is breaking the house rules and eating in the living room.

You, humans, eat some really strange stuff, such as chips with spicy stuff on them. It really burns my tongue when I sneak a lick.

My favorite thing to do with Jane is lie between her legs, either when she's sitting in her chair that she makes raise up under her legs or when she is asleep in bed. She really grumbles when she wants to roll over at night and I've got her pinned under the blanket. That's what I call CAT POWER!

Oh, she's getting off the phone and coming this way. I'd better get down and go see if I can torment Duke. He's been acting like he rules the house, but everyone knows a Princess outranks a Duke any day.

Meow!

(Editor's note: Princes Moorman lives with News-Bulletin reporter Jane Moorman)

New Kitten Causing Terror in the Moorman Household

By Princess Moorman

Well, Jane went and did it again. She dared to bring another cat into my home. It's bad enough that I have to deal with Duke; now I have to put up with a kitten.

They named her Scooter, but Duke and I call her Brat. She should be called Feline Intimidator, the way she terrorizes us. Life definitely has gotten livelier since she showed up.

She just arrived one day when she was nine weeks old. She told us her humans threw her out and she spent all day trying to get Jane's neighbor to let her move in. She cried at the top of her lungs, but they said they were allergic to cats.

They thought maybe she belonged to us. Well, she didn't. Not until she ran straight into my lady's arms. What could our humans do—she was just a baby and if she stayed outdoors overnight, the coyotes would eat her.

When I expressed my feeling about her arrival, Jane said, "Be nice. You didn't have a home either when we brought you home from the animal shelter. What is it about a baby—cat or otherwise—that makes humans go goofy?

They start talking in a high-pitched voice and they let the "little darling" do just about anything it wants. It doesn't matter that she was abandoned. There are rules, you know.

Our humans find themselves sitting and watching Brat play, and they laugh at the predicaments she gets herself into. No cat with any self-respect would do some of the things she's done.

One night, she got herself up inside the arm of the sofa. Jane had to open the hide-a-bed and sweet-talk her out. Finally, I jumped in and told her to get her furry behind out of there.

At first, I wouldn't have anything to do with her. I told Duke if he dared play with Brat, he'd be in big trouble with me.

But he was the first to break. I caught him playing with her one day, and he said, "But she was attacking my tail and I just couldn't let that go unanswered."

Now the two of them are wrestling and romping through the house, especially first thing in the morning when I'm trying to sleep.

The other day, Duke was watching a bird outdoors and his tail was quivering and twitching. That was just too much for Brat to ignore. She attacked his tail—causing Duke to lose concentration on the bird. He bopped her on top of the head. Ha!

Brat just doesn't know her place. She's been playing with all our toys.

Granted, we haven't played with the toys since we grew up. But really, it's our stuff and she should keep her grubby paws off— especially the balls that rattle; everyone knows those are mine.

Jane was so excited when Brat fell in love with the new contraption we got for Christmas. It has dangling things from a wand, which is supposed to drive us wild. Only when you start playing they spring away and you have to chase them.

Brat almost kills herself playing with that stupid thing. She plays so hard that she finally has to lie down and catch her breath.

Brat also has no respect for her elders. When Duke and I walk into the room, she comes running and jumps on us. I give her a look and she flops down on the floor. Duke just turns and walks away.

One day, she was playing on my sofa, and everyone—or at least Duke knows that's my territory and he stays off. I jumped up on the cushion and swatted her. She thought I was playing, and, I guess, I was, but don't tell her that.

I must admit it was fun chasing her and keeping her captured between the sofa and the wall.

It was bad enough having to share my sofa with her, but then she explored the closet, which is my safe house. I told her what I thought about that in no uncertain terms. She just looked at me with those big yellow eyes and sashayed away with her tail straight up in the air.

I caught Duke laughing and I gave him a piece of my mind. But he who laughs last laughs best.

The other day she finally got strong enough to get up on the bathroom counter and then onto the window shelf, which is Duke's special spot.

It really makes him mad when I get up there with him and force him to move. He was not pleased seeing Brat up there. He said, "Is no place sacred?"

I finally figured out why the humans called her Scooter. She races through the house and is just a streak of color. She'll run, bounce off the back of the sofa and fly halfway across the room before she lands.

I thought I was going to get her the other day by lying in the hallway, so she couldn't get by. But that didn't stop her.

She had the nerve to run right up and over me. "Man, did that make me mad?" I yelled at her, and Jane scolded me for being such a grumpy old woman.

"Well, what do you expect? I have been the Princess of the House for seven years."

Editor's note: This is Princess's second column about life at reporter Jane Moorman's house. She says she will keep everyone posted on any breaking news or lamps.

Top Cat—Finally! What a Great Life!

By Duke Moorman

There's a new cat in charge at the Moorman house.

I'm the top cat, finally. I've waited almost nine years to be able to say that and now the girls are doubting my authority.

Princess, whom you have heard from in the past, got sick in January and gave up the ghost. She had been losing weight for some time and just got to the place where all she did was sleep—she didn't even want to eat. Imagine not wanting to eat—I can't since I weigh in at 18 pounds.

In Princess' last will and testament, she said I could become the News-Bulletin correspondent from our house.

But before she made that last trip to the vet, our humans brought in a new kitten to live with us. They always said they had a two-cat limit house rule, but then they allowed Scooter to move in. Then we were four.

Jane said they could modify the rule to be two cats per person. Will it ever stop? There is such a thing as too many cats. After all, there are only two laps available for naps.

The Scotter isn't that bad. She finally got big enough not to be a brat, but now she thinks she's the top cat. Women, you give them a little authority and they want to take over.

The newest member of the family is a cutie. After we heard the story—over and over and over again—we decided to let her join our clan.

They named her Lucy, even though we thought Scarface was more apropos. When our humans found her at the animal shelter, Lucy was recovering from a horrible fate.

Someone had placed a rubber band around her neck and it had slipped over one ear before it became embedded in her skin.

Imagine the human that would be that stupide or cruel. Jane says maybe the rubber band was holding a bow and the people didn't see it in the cat's fur. Whatever! It was still mean!

So, Scarface is now the one everyone dotes over. She is kind of scary, actually. When you look at her straight-on, she had two faces—half is pure black in which her eye disappears, and the other is butterscotch with black freckles. Thank goodness they didn't call her Freckles.

She's not like Scooter was when she was itty bitty. Lucy's calmer and quieter. But she is still a pest, especially when she wants the window bed.

Now Scooter has someone to play with, so she leaves me alone. They chase each other through the kitty cubes and wrestle on the bed.

Scooter says she's trying to clean the little one, but I think she's just using that as an excuse to be able to put a full nelson on her.

One thing that's different is the energy around the house since Princess left. She was such a grump and would screech at us if we did anything.

Scooter was daring and would play with toys, especially a mouse that was so enticing with the aroma of catnip. But I wouldn't dare play with the toys because Princes would scream at me.

It only took me about an hour to realize she wasn't coming back from the vet, and the coast was clear for playing.

Now I get my turn to sit on Jane's lap. And I take a swipe or two at a toy when no one's looking.

My favorite thing to do is to lay square on Jane's chest, all 18 pounds of me. It stops her dead in her tracks. She can't read or do Sudoku puzzles. She can't even see the television very well because I'm lying right in front of her face. She just has to lie there in her easy chair and pet me.

Petting is the greatest thing a human can do. They can rub my ears and that spot between my shoulder blades that I can't get at. I just love it. It's so addictive. I can't get enough.

To me, it's on top of my list, even above a full bowl of food or lying in the sun.

Editor's note: Duke, a flame-point Siamese who was rescued from the animal shelter nine years ago, may periodically be reporting on life with Jane.

September 24, 2005

She's Dressed in Purple and Has Her Red Hat On

Red hats and purple outfits for as far as the eye can see.

No, this isn't a dream. I was awake. I was at the fourth annual Branson Fall Fling, which was organized by Red Hat Society members from clubs in Missouri.

It was my first trip to a Red Hat Society regional event. Just the thought of 400 women wearing red hats covered with every type of feather imaginable is kind of scary. To see it is unbelievable.

When the hotel elevator doors opened, a man waiting to ride the lift gasped and took a step back. He had the look of a deer caught in the headlights when he saw that the compartment was packed with women—all wearing purple topped with red hats.

I joined thirteen other women from New Mexico to make the pilgrimage to the entertainment capitol in the Ozark Mountains of southern Missouri.

If you ever need a shot of American patriotism, go to Branson, where every show is family entertainment focused on God and country. Besides music and humor, every show ends with the audience standing while "God Bless America" is sung.

Besides seeing three shows each day, we enjoyed the humor of our sisters in purple and red at the traditional Pajama Breakfast, where prizes were awarded for the longest feather, most feathers, best slippers and best group outfits.

Our group's outfit received the Popular Choice Award. We wore red hats shaped like volcanoes with flowers erupting from the top since our club is the Las Ladies from Los Volcano Senior Center in Albuquerque.

We were clad in purple bloomers and t-shirts that were adorned with breaded fringe and red lace.

A talent show was also held and, as they say, "What happens in Branson, stays in Branson." So, I can't report on the hilarious skits that were performed, especially by our very own Dingbats.

As one lady said, "Wearing purple outfits and red hats gives us a license to do silly things that we would otherwise not be able to do."

When you are attending programs with 400 other women, funny things happen.

During Tony Roi's performance as Elvis, he received the ultimate compliment when a Red Hatter gave up her cherished purple scarf.

In every performance, the Presley family's chosen Elvis impersonator receives women's undergarments. But, this time, he was caught off guard by the triple-X size briefs that were thrown to him on stage.

He was a good sport, having given a special after-hours performance for the Red Hatters. He also took time in the show for each woman or group of women to be photographed with him. Yes, I have proof that Elvis lives. I'm standing there in the photo with my head next to his.

At the Legends Theater, Marilyn Monroe had a hard time finding a man to join her on the stage. While searching for just the right guy, she said to the Red Hatters in the audience, "My, there's a lot of you out there."

The funniest showstopper came the final night on the Branson Bell Showboat, where we had a dinner cruise on Table Rock Lake.

A frisky Red Hat sister was selected by ventriloquist Todd Oliver for his audience participation segment of the show. When she took the stage, she did a soft-shoe step that let him know he was about to be upstaged.

While he tried to make her a live puppet, she actually mouthed the words to the song he was singing.

Oliver has a unique twist to the old puppet act by using live dogs as his hilarious cast of characters.

It was especially fun to be in the audience, no matter if there were a handful of Red Hatters or 400. We always received a comment from those on the state.

My favorite shows were put on by Russian comedian Yakov Smimoff and Japanese violinist Shoji Tabuchi.

They both make you proud to be an American as they talk about why they became naturalized citizens.

"What makes Americans great is their kindness and giving," Yakov said as he recalled his first impression of the United States. "Our apartment house neighbors learned that we had nothing and they came bringing us furniture, appliances and food."

We laughed as he shared his insights into life, family and the United States.

As an accomplished artist and former art teacher, he uses his paintbrush now as a means to further his philosophy. Yakov's mural "America's Heart," which hung at Ground Zero in New York City for the first anniversary of 9/11, illustrates his love for Americans.

Tabuchi played every type of music imaginable, from traditional Japanese to classical, modern and country of her new homeland.

A much when going to Shoji's theater is to visit the restrooms. The women's facilities are decorated in gold leaf mirrors and fresh orchids, while the men's room has a billiard table available for a gentleman's game.

Finally, our trip was made special with the reunion of one of our gals with a high school boyfriend. Known as Grizzly to his Branson friends and as Charlie Daniels to the Legends Theater audience, we know him by his given name of David Lafferty.

David is the official look-alike of country musician Charlie Daniels. He was selected by Daniels to perform in the Legends program. We received quite a few looks from our Red Hat Sisters when he dropped us off at the hotel after a day of seeing the sights around Branson.

Besides being silly and enjoying the shows, the Red Hatters also did a lot of their other favorite activity—shopping.

Successful Relationships Come Down To Four Basic Things

Valentine's Day is when we take stock of our relationships and tell those who mean the most to us that we love them.

As I look at the various relationships in my life, I realize that they have gotten better during the past few years. I attribute that state of affairs to my practicing and preaching the Four Cs of Successful Relationships.

I've been a student of inter-relationships for most of my life, and I finally found some basic things that seem to be the foundation for people being able to work well with each other.

I first aired my findings in a wedding letter to my nephew as a gift I hoped he and his wife would learn to appreciate.

I have shared them with my friends and anyone who will take the time to listen, and I know they, too, have had good results when practicing the Four Cs.

Now I want to share the Four Cs with you, our readers, in hopes that you, too, will find joy that can grow from having successful relations with the people in your life.

Commitment

The foundation of a relationship is a commitment to accomplish a common goal, be it a marriage or a business. The commitment must be so strong that the concept of quitting is not an option.

I kiddingly say my personal relationship has survived the hard times because I own heavy furniture and I can't move out easily. That heavy furniture has stopped me from giving up on my commitment when I'm in the heat of anger.

Communication

Communication is a two-way street—talking and listening. People have to share their thoughts and ideas, their desires and their fears.

While some people may have the power of mind reading, the average person does not. You can't expect someone to know how you feel about a situation unless you tell them. And they usually listen better if you are not sharing your thoughts, yelling at the top of your lungs.

I have noticed that communication is the brick that can take down the wall if it is missing. Life runs smoothly at my house when we are communicating. But let one of us not share our thoughts, it doesn't take long for the train to run off the track.

Compromise

With communication comes compromise. It's fun to see how much better a project can become when you are working together and compromise.

Many times each person thinks their idea or way is the best, but usually, when you begin to build on an idea and receive input from others, the final results are greater than you could have come up with by yourselves.

I love to brainstorm and solve problems, especially when they are win-win situations. Being so strong-headed that you cannot compromise only sets you up to be left out of the fun.

The key questions are "How can we do this?" or "How can we make this better?"

Compassion

Recently, while interviewing couples who have been married for more than 50 years, one wife described compassion as wanting happiness for the other person more than they do and you are willing to work hard to accomplish it for them.

If both parties in a relationship are striving to make the other person's life as pleasant as possible, each will find ways to help the other through the day's challenges, so it makes it a little easier for both of them.

I warned my nephew that verbal arrows spoken in times of anger are non-retrievable—once a mean thing is said, it can't be taken back. And the impact of the comment will leave a wound that will never be heeled. So, the old saying "think before you speak" is part of the framework of compassion.

Following the Golden Rule of "do unto others as you'd want others to do unto you" is also a solid foundation for interpersonal relationships.

March 26, 2005

Honorary Citizenship? She Thinks She's Ready

The time has come for me to apply to be an adopted New Mexican.

I have lived in New Mexico longer than anywhere else. In the past, when I lived in Texas longer than I had in Kansas—twelve years—I became an adopted Texan.

Now, don't hold that I'm an adopted Texan against me. At the time, I had not discovered the wonderful Land of Enchantment. I am ready to mend my evil ways and become a New Mexican.

Also, it's not my fault that the stork was directionally challenged and he got the Arkansas River in Kansas confused with the Rio Grande in New Mexico. Both rivers are more sand than water, so it is understandable when he dropped me in Hutchinson instead of Los Lunas.

One nice thing about being a wandering soul is that when you find a better place to live, you move there. That's why I moved to New Mexico.

Being an adopted native is not just about living somewhere longer than elsewhere. You also have to develop the personality traits of those born there.

I realized during last week's snow that I have done just that. When it was snowing Monday night, I knew I was going to stay home the next day.

In the past, I would say, "I learned to drive in snow. I can go to work in this little bit of white stuff." This time around, when the roads cleared by 10 a.m., I called in to volunteer to come to work but didn't argue when it was suggested that I just work out of the house that day.

The other thing I've noticed in my lifestyle that was not present eighteen years ago is mañana. I've learned that there is plenty of time to do things – even when I wait until tomorrow.

I discovered I had this trait when it bothered me how fast Gov. Bill Richardson was making things happen. I was shocked when I realized he was operating at normal national speed, and I had adapted to New Mexico's speed. I had gotten to the point that a few more studies on an issue would be just fine.

Another thing I've noticed that has changed is that, during this year's wet winter, I got grumpy because we didn't have blue skies every day. I got tired of gray skies, which were normal in my past life.

You know you are becoming a New Mexican when you have to search for your heavy winter coat on one of the few very cold days. Two years ago, I even had to go out and buy a coat and ended up wearing it only that day.

So here are some other things I've discovered that indicate I'm eligible to become an adopted New Mexican.

You are a New Mexican if:

You have three jackets of different weights in your car. Chances are you are going to wear each one of them as the day progresses.

You don't own a snow shovel, snow chains or snow tires, but have bricks in your trunk so the car won't slide on the ice. Or at least not if you live in the Middle Rio Grande Valley.

You fight the mice for their stash of pinon nuts.

When you get to a gathering, you hug everyone you meet.

You put green chile on your green chile.

Your idea of a day trip is a four-hour ride.

You faint at the sight of water in the Rio Grande.

You cultivate your tumbleweeds as yard shrubs.

You are walking to the top of Tome Hill on Good Friday. And your hidden Easter Eggs have sand on them.

You go to a different town and see several distant cousins. Or you go to the grocery store and everyone you see is your cousin.

Your favorite cookie is a bizcochito—and you know which grandma in your neighborhood makes the best.

Is It a Bird, A Plane? No, It's Just Jane

A recent hike to the top of Tome Hill gave me a bird's eye view of Valencia County that I hadn't noticed on other such trips.

I've been up there in the fall when the trees have turned golden and the bosque almost glows as it snakes through the valley.

But, this time, it was the patchwork of the farmland that caught my eye. The trees had not leafed out, so I was able to see the fields as I watched a farmer working his land in preparation for planting.

Sometimes I wish I was a bird and could observe life on Earth from above. That desire has not driven me to learn to fly a plane, but it does make me enjoy looking out the window of commercial airliners during trips.

In 2000, when I was making frequent trips to Washington, D.C., to see my father, I became very adept at identifying the rivers and cities we flew over.

It was a big thrill to see my hometown and my family's farm from above. It is very tricky to find familiar places from the air because you have to know the lay of the land and large landmarks such as rivers and highways.

During one trip, a group of Japanese businessmen were sitting behind me and I could tell from the tones of their voices that they were excited about something they were seeing.

I looked over the seat and saw they had an atlas open and they were trying to compare a map to the view out the window. When I asked what they were looking for, they said in broken English, "Mississippi River."

We were flying over the Ohio River at the time, and they thought it was the Mighty Miss. I had to tell them that the Mississippi was a much bigger river, but when we would see it while landing in St. Louis, it would be hard to tell how big it really was.

How many non-pilots do you know who own a pilot's map? I have one of the United States. I thought it would be fun to take it on commercial flights so I could keep track of where we were, but I never seem to remember it when I'm packing for a trip.

A humorous marking on the pilot's New Mexico map is a flying saucer in the Roswell area.

This love of looking at the earth from above caused me to acquire "Orbit: NASA Astronauts Photograph The Earth," published by the National Geographic Society.

It is a collection of photos taken from the space shuttle. I wanted the book because I had read that the Great Wall of China is the only man-made structure visible from space, and I wanted to see what it looked like, but, unfortunately, there is no photo of it in the book.

Despite that fact, the book is one of my prized possessions and I spend many hours looking at the photos.

Seeing how the air currents around an island cause a spiral cloud formation and how a river delta reflects the erosion upstream are fascinating to me.

This week, I purchased a satellite imagery map of the state from the geology department at New Mexico Tech. It is a composite of satellite photos.

You can see the land formations, highways, cities and the green of the bosque and fields. On the east side of the map, you can even see the difference in traditional acreage compared to the circular fields watered by sprinkler irrigation.

When I walked into the house with the map, I was not sure where I was going to hang it since my map wall already had a United States highway map, as well as state maps from New Mexico and Kansas.

As I laid the map on the dining room table to look at it, we realized it would be neat to just leave it there. Since our wooden table has a piece of clear vinyl as a cloth, we decided to place the map under the protective surface.

Now, as we eat, we are able to look at New Mexico and see the salt flats near Estancia or the lava flow near Grants. The most amazing thing about this view of New Mexico is the beautiful red-brown colors that are highlighted by green, blue and black.

August 13, 2005

She's Gone, But Not Forgotten

Have you ever had a friend's death reported in the New York Times? It happened to me this week.

E-mails began coming in on Friday regarding the fate of my former coach and college professor. So, I took a little time this week to reflect on this person and what having our life paths crossed has meant to me.

Sue Gunter has been proclaimed one of the pioneers of women's college basketball. As an inductee into the Women's Basketball Hall of Fame in 2000 and the Basketball Hall of Fame in 2005, she has won nearly every individual women's sports coaching award in existence—maybe even a few that don't exist.

She holds the title of most seasons coached at 40. Her career record was 708-308, including a 442-221 mark in 22 seasons at Louisiana State University. With that record, she is ranked third in wins and games coached and fourth in more than 20 winning seasons, with 21.

Among women's college coaches, only Tennessee's Pat Summitt and Texas' Jody Conradt have more victories than Sue Gunter.

For any coach building a program to become a national champion is a dream. Sue Gunter neared that dream in 2004 when her team reached the NCAA Final Four. But Sue's health had already begun to fail, and she was forced to watch her assistant coach and protégé Pokey Chatman take the helm and try to bring home the crown. The Lady Tigers had to settle for the semifinalist role that year.

But I remember Sue Gunter from way before the NCAA included women's sports or even before there were athletic scholarships for women athletes.

I was a junior at Stephen F. Austin State University in 1972 when she returned to her coaching and teaching assignments after a leave of absence to complete her doctorate.

We affectionately referred to her as Coach Gunter, Coach, or—if talking about her out of earshot—Gunter. That was back when women came to Stephen F. Austin just hoping to be selected for Gunter's team. There was no recruiting with promises of playing. You had to try out.

My interaction with her was not as a player but as a physical education major who supported her team as a video technician.

This was even before videotaping was common practice. I had taken a class in educational television and was asked by the physical education department chair to operate the newly purchased reel-to-reel video system.

Gunter saw the value of taping her teams during practice so the women could see the plays that she had drawn on the chalkboard come alive.

We also had to modify the newly completed coliseum to have a platform installed for the camera and video machine to tape games.

Gunter was always a visionary and knew that things were going to change for women's athletics. She knew if we just kept working in our own organization, the Association of Intercollegiate Athletics for Women, eventually, the sports world would wake up.

As a player on the 1960-62 U.S. teams that competed against the Soviet Union, Gunter knew the importance of having athletics available to young girls. She was there fighting for Title IX, from which today's girls and women athletes have benefited. They can't even imagine a day when their predecessors had to provide their own way to out-of-town games or meals on the road.

When I was in my twenties, Gunter served as coach of the U.S. National Team in 1976, 1978 and 1980. She was assistant coach to the 1976 U.S. Olympic team that brought home silver medals during the first Games in which women's basketball was an event.

She was asked to coach the 1980 U.S. Olympic team in Moscow and the team had qualified, but she had to accept the fact that President Jimmy Carter felt that our athletes should boycott the Games because of Russia's war with Afghanistan.

Because of her involvement with the U.S. National Teams, our campus hosted several international squads, including the Russians.

I'll never forget the night the Russians came to East Texas. It was the winter of 1980 and the U.S.A. hockey team had just defeated U.S.S.R. for the gold in the Lake Placid Games.

The Stephen F. Austin fans knew that our Ladyjacks were no match to the nearly 7-foot-tall Russian center, who, in fact, scored 23 points individually—the margin by which her team defeated us.

But we knew we had national spirit, so when the national anthem was sung, we did so loudly and proudly. It was like we were saying, "We might not be able to beat the Soviet sports machine, but we will show them we love our country."

Gunter's vision impacted me personally when she realized we needed to wake up the local sportswriters to the fact that the women's program was worth covering.

She asked me to see what I could do. I got a job with the college sports information director with the understanding that I would take the game and tournament results from the coaches to him to be written into press releases. In the end, he let me try my hand at writing, and I caught the bug when my stories appeared in the local newspaper.

Yes, I attribute my eventual entrance into the field of journalism to this woman, who died from emphysema on Aug. 4 at her home in Baton Rouge, LA.

Many words have been written since Thursday about this legend in newspapers across the country. Many coaches and current and former basketball players have expounded on this great woman's contribution to the sport of women's basketball and their lives.

Now head coach of the LSU women's basketball program, Pokey Chatman has been quoted as saying, "I am who I am in no small part because of the role she has played in my life—both as a coach and as a person. In one way, I lost someone very special today—but, in a more important way, I know she will always be a part of me."

You encounter very few people such as Sue Gunter in your life, and I was blessed to have known her.

October 29, 2005

You Don't Have To Be Born Here To Call It Home

When does a community become your hometown?

For me Valencia County took on that role when I returned to the News-Bulletin in 2000. The last half of 1999 had been probably the worst year of my life, and I was pretty far down emotionally when I came back.

It did my heart good when people seemed to be happy that I was back. Their hugs and greetings made me realize that you don't have to be born somewhere to call it home.

The song "I'll Be Home for Christmas" always makes me sad because having moved several times while growing up, I don't have access to my childhood homes. And my grandparents' farm and house are now my aunt's home, so it's not really my place either.

Through the years, I've learned that home is where the heart is—and, as far as I'm concerned, Valencia County's residents constantly demonstrate that they have big enough hearts that I proudly consider the Middle Rio Grande Valley my home.

Working with people from all areas of the county, I have observed that there is a definite Valencia County personality.

It comes in the form of a hug when greeted. Congressional delegates' staffers have commented that they can tell when Washington, D.C., visitors are from Valencia County because of the hugs. And there are also homemade traditional New Mexico treats that are hand-delivered.

There is an underlying love for rural life and the sounds of that environment, such as geese and sandhill cranes on an autumn day or the motor of a tractor working a field, or horses, cows or sheep calling to each other.

That love also extends to our fellow residents in their times of need. I can't tell you how many times a story in the News-Bulletin about a person or family being down on their luck has generated an amazing level of generosity. This is a community that reaches out and helps one another.

This is also a community that cries together when one of your young or old dies. One aspect of being a reporter is that you get to know many community members, so I am not ashamed that my tears flow when one of these new friends perishes.

The News-Bulletin's Unsung Heroes and Citizen of the Year are examples of what makes this county such a great place to live.

Each year, while working on this special edition, I can't help but think of all the other individuals in our community who do truly wonderful things but whom no one nominated.

There are also a lot of good-hearted people who, because the sharing of their kindness is part of their occupation, are not considered for Unsung Hero honors.

So, I'd like to say thank you to everyone who makes this county a special place to call home. People touch my heart daily with their kind acts, whether it is as simple as a kind word or smile or as big as giving a helping hand.

The acts of kindness that make this county so special are also being passed on to our children. Each year, young people get involved in food drives to help make the holidays special for needy families or coat drives to give their classmates warm garnets.

Philosopher Arthur Schopenhauer wrote that "the experiences and illuminations of childhood and early youth become, in later life, the standards and patterns of all subsequent knowledge and experiences. So it is that time, in our childhood years, that the foundation is laid for our later view of the world. It will be in later years unfolded and fulfilled, not essentially changed."

Because of the passing along of values that makes Valencia County a special place, I know that, in generations to come, others will venture into the Rio Abajo and discover that they have come to a place they choose to call home.

December 17, 2005

Journeys in Cars Make Best Christmas Memories

"Over the river and through the woods.
To grandfather's g house, we go…"

My father had only one request of his children when they left home—to do everything possible to spend Christmas together as a family. For thirty years, I traveled to wherever the family gathered.

So, for my family, the holiday song's verse above should be "Over the river and through the woods to my brother's house we go."

My brother is a Methodist minister, and since Jesus is the reason for the season, our family's annual Christmas reunion has had to be at his house no matter where he might be.

This has allowed us to celebrate the holiday in Salt Lake City, Kansas City and various small towns in Colorado. One year, it was in a motel in Columbia, MO, because my sister-in-law's father was in the hospital.

We also met at my parent's house as well, where ever that might be—Mississippi or Virginia. We have also gathered at the family farm in Kansas before and after my grandparents' death.

And then there was the year of my grandparent's 50th anniversary when we went to Florida.

Celebrating Christmas in different cities and states has really been a joy. The cultures of each community influence events of the season and each city has wonderful light decorations.

Family reunions are interesting events. For our family, because we only see each other once a year, we use our company manners or personalities. In other words, we keep it positive and don't dive into those various personality issues that drive us crazy about our family members.

One thing that I have discovered about our group is that we usually end up in a car going somewhere. And that seems to be when the most interesting interactions occur.

My brother announced he was getting married while we were en route to Florida in 1970. He was in his second year of college, and all that I can say is that I tried to squeeze into the corner of the back seat and become invisible to avoid the wrath that ensued.

I, too, had my moment of truth with my parents while traveling at 55 mph through western Kansas. The question arose, "Was there anything we should have done differently as parents while raising you?"

First, I must say that after hearing about other people's childhoods, I was blessed with a very wonderful childhood even though finances were tight.

So how do you answer such a question when you know your parents did the best they could with what they had?

At age twenty-five, my response was to joke with my father that I had really wanted that pony and that I have permanent emotional scars because of it.

One year we learned that my grandmother was having a heart incident and we needed to drive about five hours from the middle of Missouri to the middle of Kansas in the wee hours of Dec. 23.

To help Dad stay awake, and because we were all worried about Grandma, we visited about our philosophies on life. I can't remember the details of the conversation, but I do remember it was the closest I had very felt to my parents. While that event could have tarnished the holiday, it actually made it one of the best for me.

One thing that I did learn over the years is: timing is everything for flying during the holidays. Some of the things I learned:

Planes are usually not full on Christmas morning, but they are packed in the evening.

Fly before New Year's Eve, when winter storms seem to bring in the new year.

Have faith that your gift box will reach the destination with you. Don't think you have to carry the five-pound ham and 10 pounds of Ruby Red grapefruit with you—been there and done that.

Meet your family at the baggage claim. Just sit there on your suitcase and wait.

March 25, 2006

A Modification or Two Never Hurt Any Project

Tim Allen, move over. There's a new home improvement klutz in the house.

I love to do projects around the house, but sometimes they just don't go the way I expected.

When I moved from my mobile home and everything was out of the house. I realized the furniture had covered all of the projects that didn't get quite done or weren't quite right.

With each project, you learn something that you can use in a future endeavor. This can be good, or it can be bad, which was the case with my latest task.

It seemed like a simple project—a microwave hutch kit. You know, one of those easy-to-assemble pieces of furniture where all you need is a screwdriver.

All was going well. We had only had one oops because I didn't read the next step in the directions, but it was not hazardous to humans or furniture.

Then a good idea turned it into the project from hell.

Drawers! Wouldn't it be great to have a roller track on them to make them easier to use? Sounded easy. I've put those on other drawers, so, sure, let's do it.

Maybe the first sign of trouble was when we were removing the wooden, or should I say fiberboard, tracks from the cabinet. They broke into pieces.

After installing the metal roller tracks, we decided to test the drawers in the cabinet before we glued everything together. Good thing we did! The drawers were now too wide for the cabinet opening.

Needless to say, words were uttered that cannot be published or they would be a bunch of Xs.

Now what do we do? We have destroyed the manufacturer's draw system.

Idea one: Take the kit back to Walmart and tell them Piece Q was missing.

Idea two: Call the manufacturer and have the pieces we destroyed replaced.

Idea three: Adapt the drawer to make the roller work. This, of course, is handyman code for "Get a hammer and beat it to death."

The second misthinking occurred about this time. "Let's chisel the top edge of the track wider because then there will be a level edge for the roller to run on."

Wrong!! But of course, I didn't realize this until we were nearly done with the chiselling and had hit my hand with the hammer.

Any engineer or even a person with clear common sense will tell you when there is a track on a drawer, the bottom edge will run along the roller, not the top.

So, when we got the drawers to finally fit into the cabinet, they worked. Or at least they can be pulled out. It's a little bumpy and hard to pull at times. "So don't put anything in the drawers that you need to get often," was the response.

The easy-to-do Saturday project just took us nine hours, three bandages, and only a few drops of blood and was finished at 10 p.m. on Sunday.

Once the hutch was completed, we immediately put the microwave on it. And then we held our breath until we knew it wasn't going to fall apart.

Building furniture is fun. We have assembled a wardrobe cabinet, filing cabinets, and a television stand.

We modified the TV stand that has a nice open space for a VCR. We wanted the TV to be lower, so after completing the project, we got the circular saw out and cut off the side panels to eliminate the VCR space.

One wonders how the people designing the furniture and developing the kit's instruction would react if they knew a home improvement klutz thought she could make a piece better with just a few simple modifications.

Maybe someday I will be able to declare I have a Ph.D. in kit building, as I proudly say about toilet repair.

Or it could be like installing doorbells, which I flunked when I tried to enlarge the hole in the door frame with a drill and broke the wire off. Nine years later, the doorbell still doesn't work, but that's another story.

Editor's note: Got a project you want to be done? Maybe you don't want to call Jane.

Who's Who in Movies? Only Hollywood Knows

To an untrained eye, watching a movie set is confusing. This week, I spent a little time on location in Highland Meadows for the pilot of the TV series *In Plain Sight*.

Fortunately, I had an experienced hand by my side to help decipher what I was watching.

Don Mason is an EMT from Pecos Valley Rescue, who, among many other roles, was the medic for the *In Plain Sight* production crew.

Don admitted that his many duties included handing out aspirins and being sure everyone had sunscreen on, but his presence was also needed in case a stunt went wrong.

I watched the activity outside of the Wild Horse Mesa Bar near the intersection of NM 6 and Interstate-40 from Don's van, which serves as a rolling first-aid room.

Thanks to Don, I knew when the director Mark Pizmarski and leading actor Mary McCormack arrived on the set.

He also pointed out the producer, Randi Richmond, and the director of cinematography, as well as various assistant directors.

The most amazing thing about the film industry is the number of people it takes to create a movie. There were 100 crew members on this project.

Also, the amount of time it takes to set up a scene is phenomenal. The crew expected to be working twelve hours to get approximately four minutes of action.

But sitting there in Don's van brought back memories of other film locations I have visited.

My first was in 1972 when Hollywood came to my hometown in Kansas. It was the second time that the quiet little town of 1,100 people was invaded by a movie crew.

The first time was in 1955 when the movie *Picnic* with Kim Novak was filmed there. Outside shots of the home were done in Nickerson.

The high point in the film for me is the actual picnic that was held at the community lake in Sterling, a town 10 miles away. That's where I spent many a summer day swimming and playing.

The other moment in the movie that we await with bated breath is the final scene when the characters catch a bus to leave town. The bus passes the old high school, which burned down a few years after the movie was filmed. Seeing the building is always fun.

The second time Hollywood came to town was for a movie that didn't make it to the theaters—*Ace Eli and Rodger of the Skies* starring Cliff Robertson.

That summer, my friends got to ferry the film crew back and forth at the town's lake during a scene filmed out on an island. They also got to befriend the props man, Greg Jensen; among his many claims to fame was building the miniature airplanes for *Tora, Tora, Tora*, one of the first movies about Pearl Harbor. He also worked on *Hello, Dolly*.

While working at my first newspaper in Nacogdoches, Texas, I got to spend time on the set of a James Garner movie, *The Long Summer of George Adams*. The storyline was about a train station manager during the 1950s when diesel engines were eliminating the need for water stops.

That time around, I hung out with the makeup man. His first movie was White Christmas. Being there by his chair as he made up the actors gave me time to visit with various stars, including David Graf, one of the guys who was in all of the *Police Academy* movies.

As I was leaving the set one day, I saw two gals walking toward the location with cameras in hand. I said, "If you hurry, James Garner is coming out to give autographs."

One of the gals had a look on her face that told me I had just put my foot in my mouth. She said, "Actually, I've seen a lot of his autograph. My boyfriend is his personal driver."

It turned out that while the townspeople were excited about taking photos of the stars, the crew members were enjoying taking photos of our town. Because of that incident, we became friends.

As I said, it takes a trained eye to know who's who on a movie location.

Rains Invited to County by Convertible Driver

Okay, folks, I'm going out on a limb here, but I'm going to take full responsibility for the recent rain.

No, I haven't developed a new rain dance or sinned to the point that God is warming up to a 40-day and 40-night storm. What I have done is drive my convertible, which doesn't have a back window, this entire week.

Now this may seem to be a very silly thing to do when there are rain clouds in the sky, especially in a state that normally is cloudless. But I resorted to driving my fair-weather car because out-of-town guests have been using my other vehicle.

You are probably wondering why someone would have a car without a back window, and all I can say is it had one when I bought it. But a couple of springs ago, high winds blew it out one day when I was driving through Los Lunas.

The advantage of not having a vinyl window is that the view is clear. And there is a constant breeze.

But there are some negatives, such as the constant roar of road sounds, which is no different than when the top is down.

And sandstorms. During a recent sandstorm that was blowing a tailwind, I found that as long as I drove faster than the wind, I was all right, but the minute I slowed down or stopped, gritty sand filled my car and swirled into my eyes.

The other downside of no back window is the time it takes to install the rain protection on cloudy days.

This week whenever I have parked somewhere, I have had to secure a large black trash bag over the window. With trial and error, I can now do this quickly and effortlessly.

But this little inconvenience does not offset the enjoyment I get driving the convertible.

Having a convertible has always been my dream. New Mexico, where it is clear and sunny 350 days out of the year, is a perfect place for such a vehicle.

I love driving with the top down, letting my hair blow in the wind. It's like riding a motorcycle, only with more vehicle comforts, such as radio and air conditioning, which also makes as much sense as driving with the windows up while the top is down.

There are many things you have to learn when first driving or riding in a convertible.

First is trash control. Eating fast food is fine, as long as you put the trash between your legs and the car seat. Otherwise, it will blow out.

The second is the road sound. Earplugs cut out the wind and roar of other vehicles and allow you to hear the conversation with passengers and the radio.

Third is sun protection. A good, tight hat and sunscreen are a must.

I must admit in the wee hours of Thursday morning, when I was awakened by the sound of heavy rain, I was not looking forward to coming to work.

Because I had driven home Wednesday evening with the top down, now, before heading to work, I had to put it back up. This, too, can be a pain because of the idiosyncrasy of the framework.

So, on Thursday, I headed out of the house with the top down. I'd like to think that the other commuters were envious of my free spirit.

However, this week, I think they have viewed me with disbelief. Why would anyone be driving a convertible with the top down while there are rain clouds still hovering over the mountain?

I wondered this myself as the cool morning air was chilling me. Finally, I pulled to the side of the road to put the top up.

When I got to the office, I asked myself if I wanted to test fate and not put the black plastic bag over the back window, but I decided I should do it then rather than when it started to rain.

So, farmers, I hope you appreciate my efforts to bring rain to our area. And, yes, I will be glad when my guest leaves and I get my other car back.

September 23, 2006
Universe Conspires to Change Your Life

There's an old saying, "Be careful of what you ask for because it might come true." It's proven true in my life recently.

The last week of June, while taking a morning walk at my family's farm in Kansas, I proclaimed that I really wanted to do something with agriculture. I really wanted to be connected to agriculture, more than just being the business manager for our family's farm.

I really didn't think anything more about it as I got back into the routine of working after my vacation—at least not until I got a phone call the second week of July from a former boss.

Darrell Pehr, former editor of the News-Bulletin, and current assistant editor for New Mexico State University's Communication Services called to tell me a position with NMSU stationed out of Albuquerque was opening and he'd thought of me.

After talking to him about the position that includes writing stories about the work being done at NMSU research farms and the Extension Service, I sent my resume, with examples of my work, to Las Cruces.

He had warned that it took about three to four months before he was hired, so I expected it to take a while before I would know if I was starting a new chapter in my life.

Low and behold, the director of news and media relations called and set up a meeting the first week of August and before I knew it, I accepted a position with NMSU the last week of August.

On Friday, I packed all of the trinkets I've accumulated during the six years I've been with the News-Bulletin and walked out the door of a very special place and time in my life.

When I came back to the News-Bulletin in 2000, I thought, "You know you could make this your final stop until retirement." My career goal was to reach retirement a sane Jane.

I've never worked anywhere longer than six years, that being at the News-Bulletin when I was writing sports and education news. I really thought I would stay here for the duration of my working life.

Through the years, my family has gotten used to me changing jobs. It seems as though I like new challenges on a regular basis.

I've worked for 11 different places during my thirty-two years of being a responsible adult. I've been everything, including a self-service gas station cashier, a florist, a factory production scheduler, a factory production line assembler and quality control inspector, a public school information officer, and a risk management consultant. I've only been without a job for a total of five months in all those years.

As I once said to my father, "I always seem to come up smelling like a rose."

It's hard to think about not seeing the many friends I've made in Valencia County on a regular basis. I consider Belen and Los Lunas to be my home.

As I leave the News-Bulletin, I must tell you, the reader, how lucky you are to have the quality of journalists who keep you informed through their stories. Any one of these people could be working elsewhere, but they choose to be here in Valencia County.

While I'm excited about starting a new chapter in my life, I'm sad that I am leaving this group of people who have been there as my friends as I faced the challenges of my life.

I never thought when I proclaimed that I wanted to work in agriculture that it would evolve without my having to work at it.

I have a quote from Goethe taped to my computer monitor that says, "At the moment of commitment, the Universe conspires to assist you."

So, take heed and know the power of your words when they are spoken with a belief in the ability of God.

Valencia County News-Bulletin Book Reviews

Isn't Economics Boring?

Who would have thought a book about an economist would be interesting?

Aren't economists stuffy old men who track the world's finances and tell us whether we are in inflation or depression?

Well, needless to say, with that type of attitude, I was pleasantly surprised when I received "Freakonomics: A rogue economist explores the hidden side of everything" by Steven D. Levitt and Stephen J. Dubner and discovered that economics is not just about money.

It's about how we humans are motivated to do what we do.

Dubner met Levitt, who has been proclaimed the "most brilliant young economist in America" by a jury of his elders, when Dubner wrote a story about the University of Chicago economics professor for The New York Times Magazine and the encounter was expanded into this book.

Levitt, through devilishly clever and clear-eyed thinking, shows how to see through all the clutter to view in a new light the correlation between events.

Freakonomics establishes an unconventional premise: If morality represents how we would like the world to work, then economics represents how it really does work.

As Levitt sees it, economics is a science with excellent tools for gaining answers, but it has a serious shortage of interesting questions. His particular gift is the ability to use the tools on everyday issues such as cheating and parenting.

His questions explored in the book include: If drug dealers make so much money, why do they still live with their mothers? Which is more dangerous, a gun or a swimming pool? What really caused crime rates to plunge during the past decade?

Dubner says many people, including a fair number of his peers, might not recognize Levitt's work as economics at all.

But when you realize that the underlying thinking in all human action is incentive or motive, then the economist, who says everything is driven by incentive, has the key to unraveling the data to find the truths.

So why do drug dealers still live with their mothers? Because, when it all comes down to it, the guy on the street corner selling the drugs is only making $3 per hour. But the reason he's there is because of the prestige of being in the gang, which is a greater incentive than the money he is earning.

Beware, parent—more children die each year from swimming pool drownings than are shot because they are playing with a loaded gun.

And Levitt decrees that what really caused the national crime rate to plunge during the 1990s was not a better economic environment nor some of the crime-fighting activities but rather the legalization of abortion in 1970.

Now I'm not taking a stand on which is correct, pro-life or pro-choice. What I'm about to tell you is what this man says in the book, so don't shoot the messenger.

His premise is that a percentage of the population who are at risk of becoming criminals when they reach their twenties were not born in the 1970s because their mother was able to obtain abortions.

I must admit this seems like a stretch, but I invite you to read the book to see how he reached this conclusion.

So how did this book impact me? It has caused me to realize that, sometimes, conventional wisdom is not necessarily true; there may be other factors involved.

Levitt writes about the impact of the book on his reader by saying, "You might become more skeptical of the conventional wisdom, or you may begin looking for hints as to how things aren't quite what they seem. You may find yourself asking a lot of questions. Many of them will lead to nothing. But some will produce answers that are interesting, even surprising."

So how did one man's action cause the Ku Klux Klan to lose its stronghold in America? Inquiring minds want to know. Read "Freakonomics." Levitt and Dubner will give you the answer.

Novel About Harvey Girl Occurs Partly in Belen

Many families in Valencia County have a connection to the railroad and the former Fred Harvey restaurant chain that brought quality meals to rail travelers during the first half of the 20th Century.

I must admit that my mental picture of the Harvey Girls was only that provided by Hollywood in Judy Garland's *Harvey Girl* movie.

So, when a copy of Sheila Wood Foard's new book Harvey Girl came to the office from Texas Tech University Press, I was eager to read it.

I have visited the Harvey House Museum in Belen many times for work and personal pleasure, and I've even taken my turn writing about the museum for our annual Visitor's Guide, so I have some idea about the women who worked in Fred Harvey's restaurants.

But Foard brings the life of a Harvey Girl alive in this historical fiction about a feisty Ozark girl, Clara Fern Massie, who ran away from home on her 14th birthday after standing up to her harsh father.

She follows the lead of her cousin, Opal, and strives to become a Harvey Girl, despite the fact that she is under the required age of eighteen.

Massie's first assignment after being accepted as a Harvey Girl is in Belen. Having been to the museum, I could imagine and feel the effects of the train passing by the restaurant and dormitory those many years ago as I read of Clara's adventure.

Foard developed her research for the book while serving as a docent at the Belen Museum for three years.

In the book, she wrote of her visits to various Harvey Houses, those still standing and the vacant lots of those demolished, "I loved them all. My favorite, however, will always be the Belen Harvey House, which the citizens of Belen saved from demolition, the fate of many other Harvey Houses. The Belen Harvey House is listed on the National Register of Historic Buildings and continues to be restored."

303

While she served as a docent, she conducted her research by using the museum's archives as well as interviewing other docents who had studied the history of the Harvey Girls and former Harvey Girls who dropped by to reminisce.

In the acknowledgement of the book, she also cites the Belen Harvey House's docents, Maurine McMillan and Richard Melzer, who befriended her and helped her.

From the story, I learned of the expectation and high standards to which Harvey Girls were held. It doesn't sound like it was a bunch of singing and dancing, as Judy Garland's movie depicted. It sounds like it was a lot of hard work.

The girls had to serve travelers meals quickly and efficiently and never miss a step. One strict rule was the girl's appearance. If a spot of food fell on their starched white aprons, they had to immediately go to their rooms upstairs and change them.

Foard developed a story that left me feeling proud of the character. She faced personal danger when her father didn't want her to get "above her rearin'."

From the example of suffragists Susan B. Anthony, Elizabeth Cady Stanton, Alice Paul and Carrie Chapman Catt, Clara learned that she could be more than a girl in the Ozark Mountains of Missouri.

The book also talked about the medical care given to the tuberculosis patients who came out west to a climate and treatment that saved many lives.

Finally, the book draws a picture of the Grand Canyon and El Tovar, Fred Harvey's South Rim hotel and restaurant that has been called the "most expensive log house in America."

This book is a must-read if you want to go back in time and travel on a steam engine. Go and Harvey Houses along the Atchison, Topeka and Santa Fe Railway, where the Harvey Girls are waiting to serve a hungry traveler a gourmet meal for that day.

Valencia County News-Bulletin Articles

National Geographic documents Barb horses

The nation and the world will know about the New Mexico Horse Project when National Geographic Explorer televises a half-hour documentary on the project early next year.

A Geographic crew was in Valencia County last week filming the roundup and taming of a herd of wild horses and the drawing of their blood for a DNA test.

This is the second roundup of wild horses conducted since the project was begun by historian Carlos LoPopolo after tests of blood samples from wild horses proved they were direct descendants of the original horses brought into North America by the Spanish explorers.

The blood drawn in the first roundup proved to be the purest of the Spanish Barbs found so far in the United States.

LoPopolo and experts at the Equine Blood Typing Research Lab at the University of Kentucky have named the line of horses New Mexican because its traits are unique.

"The DNA markers of these horses are so distinct that Dr. Gus Cothran in Kentucky said we got to name them," LoPopolo said. "These DNA markers are nowhere else in the world, so we are calling them New Mexicans."

The goal of the New Mexico Horse Project is to capture horses from the wild to record their markings and estimated age while drawing blood for typing.

"We are hoping to find 150 horses out there who have the blood identification of Barbs," LoPopolo told the film crew. "When they have been found, we want to place 30 to 40 on a 6,000-acre preserve where they will."

LoPopolo's plans for the project called for the preserve's herds to be left untouched for five years. "We want them to reproduce naturally to see if the Barb traits strengthen," he said. "Then we want to offer the horses for breeding with other horses to strengthen the Barb bloodline in the animals where they will run wild."

The historian expects the project to take 10 to 15 roundups before all horses are blood-typed.

National Geographic television and magazine crews documented the second roundup and blood drawing by Los Lunas veterinary Jerry Cosper of Arrow Animal Clinic.

"I'm excited about this group of horses," LoPopolo said. "The stallion has a warbonnet marking over his ears which only appears in horses from the Santo Domino breed."

Among the herd of paint horses, he saw a buckskin which he thinks is from the southern county herds. "I can't wait to see the results of the blood tests," he said. "Even if only a few of these horses have the Barb traits, we will have typed one more herd."

Along with the veterinarian's work, Geographic photographer Jim Sugar and the film crew of West and Jerome Aston, under the direction of producer Brian Armstrong and assistant producer Grenda Norris filmed the taming of the wild animals by horse whisper Pat Parelli of Pagosa Springs, CO.

When Cosper arrived at the corral on Sunday to draw the blood, he was impressed with how calm the horses were.

Parelli and his wranglers worked two days with the horses after capturing them on Thursday to get the animals used to the touch of humans.

"We just kept moving into their personal space and let them see that we weren't going to hurt them," the nationally renown horse trainer said. "We then used fishing poles to touch them from a distance. As they got used to being touched, we moved in to touch them with our hands."

During the process, the horses went from panicking when touched to standing calmly as wranglers scratched the animal's rumps.

One mare's effort to get away from the wranglers caused her to cut the bridge of her nose on a seven-foot fence, causing her face to swell and bleed. By Sunday, the swelling was down and the animals were calm enough to be held while the veterinarian drew blood.

By the end of the two days, the wranglers were able to put halters on the animals.

"I am surprised how easy they are dealing with all this. They are not as suspicious as the first herd we did (which was not captured or tamed by Parelli)," said Cosper. "These guys are cautious but not stupid. They've got a level head on them and are not a flighty breed. This herd is much calmer, I'm impressed."

Prior to Cosper drawing blood from the horses, his four children interacted with the herd, stroking and petting them. His son Tyson and daughter Alyssa gently approached a colt. Tyson drapes his arms across the animal's back. Three-year-old son Derek hand-fed grass to the stallion and several mares. Brad pet the horses through the fence.

Cosper said the most important aspect of retraining the horses while he is drawing blood is for the horse to feel secure. "These horses tend to be easier to handle. Once you get past the pricking part of putting the needle into the skin, it's pretty easy to draw blood."

To prepare the horses for the sudden sharp pain, Parelli pinched the area around the horse's jugular blood vein and poked the horse with a toothpick. "Our pinching is actually harder than the needle prick, so the horse will not flinch when the vet draws the blood," said Parelli.

Stallion Leads Stand On Mesa, 'Whisperer' Traps Wild Horse Band

(Editor's note: National Geographic television and magazine crews were in Valencia County last week documenting the capture of while horses believed to be descendants of the Spanish barb breed lost by Onate's expedition in 1599.}

The moment of truth is upon them. The wild stallion standing between his herd of 11 and a band of seven wranglers looks for a way to escape the approaching net of capture.

His band is cornered on the tops of the red-and-tan striated sandstone mesa on the Laguna Reservation. A helicopter circles overhead as a film crew from National Geographic television captures the moment.

It is a battle of wills. The stallion with a brown warbonnet mark cresting his head stares down the cowboys. Two charges to break past them had failed. Nationally renowned "horse whisper" Pat Parelli's Wranglers had turned the herd back each time.

From their location at a sheepherder's cabin a mile away, the supporters of the New Mexico Horse Project watch the standoff through binoculars. "I can see the horses," says Bernie Trujillo, an Isleta Pueblo representative. "They're standing there at the edge of the mesa."

Six sets of binoculars peer to where he points. "You can see the guys surrounding them," adds Carlos LoPopolo, the Valencia County historian who organized the project, as he watches the scene, which is too small to be seen with the naked eye.

With nowhere else to go, the lead mare steps off the edge of the mesa onto a narrow path down the side. Each mare and young colts follow her as the stallion stands guard between the herd and the wranglers.

"Look—they're going down the side of the mesa," exclaimed Trujillo as he watched through his binoculars. "I can't believe it—they're going down the side."

Once the mares and colts are on the path, the stallion follows with the wranglers close behind. The horses—wild and domesticated—pick their way along a path of loose flat rocks lying in disarray.

The helicopter pulls away, heading to the sheepherder's cabin to retrieve another pack of film from a four-wheel-drive truck driven by National Geographic associate producer Grenda Norris.

As the helicopter touches down, soundman Jerome Ashton jumps from the aircraft and runs to the truck saying, "They were pinned on the mesa edge, then they got freaky and went down the side of the mesa."

He races back to the aircraft to return to the bird's-eye view of the roundup. Geographic magazine photographer Jim Sugar also climbs into the helicopter to join in capturing the action on film.

The film crew had been airborne for an hour, capturing the first stage of the roundup.

"We had a handle on them up there on the mesa," said Parelli an hour later when the horses were captured in a corral. "Then it came unzipped."

Parelli and his wranglers had systematically moved the horses to the edge of the mesa by turning them back and forth across the plateau as the riders raced to stay in position.

"They adjusted to fit the situation, and we adjusted with them," the Pagosa Springs, CO, horse trainer said. "Coming into this, we knew they are faster and more cunning than we are, and they know the country, but we had a plan."

Earlier, as Thursday's sun rose over the horizon, Parelli told the wranglers before heading out to gather the horses: "We have to do this as gently as possible to not upset them. Think about being a sheepdog, not a roper. Turning the horses is how we get them under control. Every time we get more than a three-degree, we're getting control. Every time we turn them, they have to think."

"It was really interesting watching them," said helicopter pilot Gary Spidell of AeroWest Helicopters based at Albuquerque's Double Eagle Airport. "They just kept compressing and compressing, tightening their line around them until the horses were stuck at the edge of the mesa. Then they went over the edge."

The wild horses work their way along a path, dropping at a 15 percent grade. They know what is ahead; it could be their opportunity to get away from the cowboys.

Once the horses reach the bottom of the upper plateau of the mesa, they pick up the pace and gallop to the path leading to the bottom. They haven't gained much distance on the pursuers, but their chance to get away is coming.

The second path proves to be an adrenaline rush for both horses and riders as its incline increases to a 45-degree angle. It became a real challenge for the domesticated animals as they picked their way along the loose rock footing.

"It was so steep that my saddle slid down onto my horse's front shoulders and neck. We came to a flat spot, so I slid back on my horse's rump and pulled the saddle back in place," Linda Parelli recalled as she demonstrated her moves. "My adrenaline was pumping. So was my horse's.

That was the first part of the hair-raising ride. "The path dropped off again. This time I just jumped off my horse and let her find her way. When I hit the ground, my legs were shaking so badly I could hardly walk. My horse jumped up to a ledge above the trail, then she jumped down to a spot below the trail and worked her way down the slope and waited for me."

"The rocks were really hard to walk on. I'm amazed we didn't have any injuries," Linda said as her horse cocks its back legs and hung its head in exhaustion after drinking its fill of water.

When Parelli was asked about the thrill ride, he said, "It got pretty exciting up there. When we were on the trail, I had to close *my shirt collar, so my horse's manure wouldn't go down the back of my neck."*

Once the horses are off the mesa, the race is on. The wild horses explode into a full run and distance themselves from the wranglers as the thunder of their hooves echoes off the red sandstone rock formations of the mesa.

As the riders spur their horses into a run, they crouch in the saddle and whip their mounts with their reins to get maximum effort from them.

National Geographic producer Brian Armstrong's favorite hat blows off his head and falls to the ground to be left behind as he charges after the horses. The wranglers with the fastest horses take the lead and race after the wild stampede. His horse flies past a cholla cactus, causing the rider's chaps to be pierced with needles.

Outriders Rich Johnson and Leroy Garcia of the local Back Country Horsemen Club keep up with the others, maintaining a parallel path to prevent the wild horse from cutting out into the wide-open terrain.

There is one more chance for the horses to escape. Ahead is a path that works its way over the sandstone ridges of the foothills.

But unbeknownst to them, the wild horses are racing directly into the trap set for them. The gathering corral is waiting in a cove where the sandstone bluffs form walls on three sides. Two days earlier, Parelli had chosen the spot because of the large amount of horse manure in the area.

Just two hours after the wranglers began the roundup, it came to an end when the horses ran directly into the gathering corrals.

"You usually only get one chance when wild horses see a corral," Parelli said while watering his horses after capturing the band. "We got two chances."

The horses reached the corral, which blocked them from taking the path over the rock formations, with just one rider with them.

"I was the only one here," Parelli said as he shifted his weight in his saddle and rested his hands on the saddle horn. "We weren't

ready to put them in the corral. The helicopter and film crew were not here to film it. When they got in place, we ran them right in."

The horses turn away from the corral and circle out into the open, but Parelli and his wranglers quickly adjust and contain them. With the help of waving plastic bag flags attached to poles, the wranglers turn the horses back to the corral as the camera crew films the capture for a half-hour television documentary.

"I knew if we didn't get these horses captured in two hours, we wouldn't be able to do it. Wild horses are so cunning you have to take them out of their game fast if you are going to control them," Parelli said. *"The turning point was actually back up there on top of the mesa when they charged us and could not break through."*

The stallion faces defeat as he leads his herd around the interior of the corral, looking for a way out. After several trips around, he gives up and grazes on clumps of dried grass.

The wild animals' encounter with humans has just begun. During the next three days, they will find the two-legged animals working in their personal space and causing them to learn not to fear them.

Parelli and his wranglers worked with the horses for two days to tame them so the veterinarian could draw blood for DNA testing.

New Mexico State University University Communications and Marketing 2006-2021

While working for New Mexico State University's University Communications and Marketing Department, I wrote more than 1,000 press releases for the College of Agriculture regarding Cooperative Extension Service programs and research at its agricultural research farms in northern New Mexico.

NMSU Tribal Extension Agent Jesse Jim Lives the Life of Her People

CROWNPOINT, N.M.—Navajo Jesse Jim is working to improve the lives of her people as they live the Diné culture and traditions.

As a lifelong resident of the eastern Navajo Nation region, the New Mexico State University graduate and Tribal Extension agent deals personally each day with many of the same issues experienced by her neighbors.

She lives on her family's 5,287-acre ranch 25 miles north of Crownpoint in the Standing Rock Chapter, the Navajo governance area equivalent to a county.

"My grandfather, Willie Jim, built the sandstone house that I live in," Jim said of the three-room structure that is reached by a 5-mile dirt road. "We have a typical rural Navajo homestead."

In the 1970s, when the Navajo Nation was making capital improvements to provide water, electricity and telephone lines to tribal members in remote areas, Jim said her grandfather only asked for electricity.

"I have to haul 500 to 600 gallons of water each week from Crownpoint to fill a cistern so I can have running water in the house," she said. "You really appreciate something when it's limited. You learn to conserve it because you have to."

While there are no telephone lines to her house, Jim is not out of touch because of modern technology—a satellite dish on her roof. "I have access to the Internet and cell phone service, so it's not as remote as when my grandparents and parents lived out here."

Like many Extension agents, Jim raises livestock and manages the rangeland in addition to her assignment with the university.

"My brothers, sister and I are continuing the ranching tradition of our elders, which includes raising sheep, cattle, horses and chickens," she said. "Unlike many of our neighbors who run their livestock on the open range, we have fenced our land into ten 430-

acre pastures. We move the cattle from pasture to pasture to protect the grass from over-grazing."

As an NMSU College of Agricultural, Consumer and Environmental Sciences faculty member working through the Cooperative Extension Service, Jim's duties include providing youth development, nutrition and agricultural programs for the people of the Navajo Nation's eastern region.

"The Tribal Extension job is to find the balance between living in a Western society and traditional culture," she said. "There is a balance in everything. Coming from the Navajo culture, the only balance is agriculture. I'm demonstrating that we can teach the youth critical thinking through other projects, such as Lego robotics and rocketry."

Besides providing STEM programs to the youth, Jim teaches many Navajo traditions, such as cooking, finger weaving and braiding.

She is also working with the tribal members to show them how they can have healthier diets by raising a garden using a low-pressure, gravity-driven drip irrigation system designed for well-less areas where water has to be hauled in.

"We've had a demonstration garden at the Office of Diné Youth Center in Crownpoint for several years," she said of the Yeego Gardening project. "Yeego" means "go" in the Navajo language.

"A lot of people have stopped to see what we are doing and raising," she said. "I've seen more small gardens beside people's houses since the project began."

Agriculture, especially raising sheep, is the backbone of Navajo tradition.

"Traditionally, we used all of the sheep. We ate the meat and used the wool to protect ourselves from the cold with garments and blankets," she said. "Sheep are still part of our cultural activities."

Through the years, the way the tribal members manage their sheep has changed.

"When I was a child, I helped herd my grandfather's sheep in the summertime," Jim said. "We'd move them from the winter camp to the summer camp and back. In the evenings, grandfather would teach us aspects of our culture while speaking Navajo and limited English."

It is from those lessons that Jim understands why the sheep growers lack an understanding of modern agricultural practices.

"When the sheep were herded from camp to camp, they grazed on the native plants, including those with medicinal properties," she said. "Our elders never gave vaccinations to their sheep. But now, many sheep herds do not graze the open range but are kept in pens where they can contract diseases."

Because vaccinations are not administered, the annual shearing of the sheep is not practiced by many herdsmen.

"There are many reasons why people are not shearing their sheep," she said. "Two main reasons are that blanket weaving is becoming a lost art, and the money received for the wool at the trading posts does not equal the cost of hiring someone to shear the sheep."

Jim is working with Felix Nez, the agricultural agent at Dine College in Tsaile, Arizona, to improve the Navajo sheep herd. They host an annual conference in the spring at the Navajo Technical University in Crownpoint. During the conference, many topics related to the care of the sheep and the marketing of the wool were covered to help inform the tribal members.

"People need to know there are information resources out here to help them," she said. "I want to provide the information on how to manage the livestock and rangeland to my community. I want to tell them, 'I've been there, and I'm here to help you. What you are doing is not wrong, but here is a better way to approach it to make it better.'"

NMSU Studying Thirty Chinese Varieties of Jujube Fruit Trees New To United States

Late frosts in northern New Mexico have a significant financial impact on fruit growers in the area. The problem is not just with apple trees, which may only set fruit 50 to 60 percent of the time, but also the stone fruits, such as apricot and peach. These fruits are all early bloomers that might bloom every year but not set fruit because of late frosts.

Fruit specialists at New Mexico State University's Sustainable Agriculture Science Center at Alcalde have explored alternative crops that will thrive in the shorter growing season.

One possibility is an ancient fruit from China, the jujube or Chinese date, that blooms later in the spring, thus missing the last dip in the thermometer for the season.

Current fruit specialist Shengrui Yao was inspired by the existing jujube trees at Alcalde, which were planted by former fruit specialist Ron Walser and agricultural specialist Charles Martin in 2006.

Yao has surveyed the state for existing jujube trees and has found many situations where the property owners did not know the fruit was eatable and are high in Vitamin C nutrients.

"I have found jujube trees throughout New Mexico from Las Cruces and Silver City to Tucumcari, Tome and Alcalde," she said. "Some were planted by Chinese immigrants who came to this area with the railroads. Others have been planted more recently by homeowners."

Because of what she has seen during her survey and from her background of working with fruit in China, Yao predicts its potential in New Mexico.

"This climate is really good for jujube fruit to grow, and it is a nice alternative crop for the growers," Yao said. "We just need to find a wider selection of cultivars that ripen at different times and can be used for different purposes such as fresh eating, drying or both."

One issue Yao is addressing is that commercial nurseries are offering the same few cultivars—Li, Lang, Sherwood, Sugarcane, Contorted, and GA866.

"The Li and Lang cultivars are the most prominent ones today. For commercial growers, this is limiting because they ripen and are available for the market at the same time," she said. "To extend the availability of the fruit in markets, the growers need a variety of cultivars that ripen at different times and are for different uses."

The question is which of the 800 known cultivars in China will prosper in New Mexico. In 2011, Yao contacted her peer scientists in China and imported 30 cultivars under a U.S. Department of Agriculture importation permit.

"I picked some popular and famous varieties from the major growing areas in China, some traditional fresh eating, drying, and multipurpose varieties, and newer selections, plus several ornamentals," she said. "Hopefully, we can select some good ones for growers to extend their market season and meet the different uses for consumers."

After a two-year USDA quarantine to ensure no pests or disease accompanied the plants into the country, Yao is now propagating the imported cultivars along with other varieties existing in the U.S. to conduct replicated variety trials to see which will thrive in northern New Mexico.

Yao is seeing success in her first season of grafting, with eatable fruit forming during the second year of growth.

"I am very hopeful that we will find a nice selection of cultivars that will thrive here, allowing the commercial growers an alternative crop to offset their losses when the traditional fruit does not produce, as well as provide a good nutrient source for consumers."

NMSU Introduces Junk Drawer Robotics to Albuquerque Youth

ALBUQUERQUE—Have you ever tried to build an air-powered robotic arm that can pick an item up and place it somewhere else? Now imagine doing this task with re-purposed items found in a typical junk drawer or garage.

That was the challenge facing a group of youth this summer during a 4-H Junk Drawer Robotics program hosted by New Mexico State University's Bernalillo County Cooperative Extension Service.

"The goal of this program is to make science, engineering and technology engaging and meaningful in the lives of young people," said Brittany Grube, Bernalillo County 4-H agent of the 4-H Robotics curriculum developed by the University of Nebraska.

"The activities do this by encouraging them to use the processes and approaches of science, the planning and conceptual design of engineering, and the application of technical skills and abilities they possess.

Mark Howard, a mechanical engineer at Sandia National Laboratories who volunteers with the 4-H program, as well as the FIRST Lego League and FIRST Tech Challenge robotic competition, led the youth through six meetings where various aspects of engineering and physics were introduced.

The program began with the youth learning to think like a scientist, communicate like an engineer and build like a technician.

"The kids learned the steps we engineers use daily," Howard said. "As we do, they came up with an idea, drew it on paper, created it, tested it and returned to the drawing board to improve the design or start over with a new idea."

The youth, ages seven to nine, worked in groups of three to create a marshmallow catapult, a robotic arm that bent at an elbow, and a gripper from re-purposed items, such as paint stirrers, egg cartons, plastic tubes, wooden sticks and various other items.

Along the way, they learned several laws of physics—like the Law of the Lever—and aspects of mechanical engineering.

"They learned about balance and how the fulcrum point helps balance items of different weights or how you use that point to catapult a lighter item," Howard said.

They learned the terminology of the movement of the robotic arms: vertical, radial and rotational—and wrist: yaw, bend and swivel.

When it came to moving their robotic arm, the youth learned about pneumatics, the use of air to perform mechanical tasks by either wind power or pumping air through tubing and cylinders.

"They created several designs of grippers after working with chopsticks to pick up a ping-pong ball," Howard said. "They also learned how clothes pins and pliers pinch to grip. And how reversing air flow can cause a vacuum that will pick up the ping-pong ball."

At the final meeting, the culminating activity combined all that they learned during the previous three build projects.

"It's just plain fun to take a pile of unrelated items, put them together with duct tape, glue and wooden dowels, add a little air power from one's own lungs or a hand pump, and have the robotic 'arm' grip a ball, bend its 'elbow' and then let go of the ball." Howard said.

"This was the first time we've offered this enrichment class," Grube said of the class that met every two weeks, March through July. "The kids really enjoyed it, so next summer, we plan on offering a repeat of the first level and the opportunity for this year's youth to do the next level of the curriculum, "Robots on the Move.""

NMSU, Dine College Help Navajo Sheep Producers Improve Wool, Meat Marketability

From the time Churro sheep were introduced to the indigenous people of the Southwest by Spanish explorer Francisco Vazquez de Coronado in 1540, sheep have been an important part of Navajo cultural tradition.

More than 47 percent of the 89,745 sheep raised in New Mexico are in Navajo herds in McKinley and San Juan counties, while 83 percent of Arizona's state herd is raised on Navajo land in the northeast region of the state, according to the U.S. Department of Agriculture 2012 Census of Agriculture.

New Mexico State University and Dine College Cooperative Extension Service agents are combining efforts to help the next generation of sheep producers not just carry on the tradition of raising a herd but to improve their monetary profit.

"Traditionally, all of the sheep is used. Our ancestors ate the meat and used the wool to protect themselves from the cold with garments and blankets," said Jesse Jim, NMSU Tribal Extension agent for the Navajo Nation's eastern region. "Sheep are still part of our cultural activities."

Felix Nez, the Extension agent at Dine College in Tsaile, Arizona, and Jim are helping sheep herdsmen to produce fine wools and carcass characteristics through educational workshops and a breeding program that can increase economic returns.

"What they are doing is not wrong, but there are better ways to approach raising a herd to make it better," said Jim, who is working with producers, teaching them about the need for vaccinations and how to efficiently shear the sheep. "We partnered with Navajo Technical University's Spring Sheep conference, held in Crownpoint, to introduce the various resources available to the producers."

Some sheep producers have a mixture of breeds. As Nez began working with the producers, he realized that many producers did not know about different breed types or the difference between commercial and value-added wool markets.

"To be profitable in the commercial market, sheep will need to produce fine wool and have a good meat carcass when butchered," Nez said.

To accomplish that, Nez is trying to improve the genetics of Navajo sheep for producers who are willing to look into the commercial markets. He turned to NMSU's Corona Range and Livestock Research Center for help.

Optimal lamb growth without compromising the marketability of the wool is an important objective for range sheep producers in the Southwest. NMSU is conducting a crossbreeding program to combine the South African Meat Merino breed genetics with the Rambouillet breed.

"New Mexico is known worldwide for our wool," said Shad Cox, superintendent at the Corona facility. "It's a clean, long fiber that is ideal for fine weaving. We don't want to lose those traits as we worked to improve the meat quality."

SAMM has been used successfully in Australia and South Africa as a terminal sire on merino-based ewes as a means to increase lamb growth and improve carcass characteristics. These traits are being seen in the Corona crossbreeding program.

In 2013, Nez purchased six Corona rams that are one-fourth SAMM. They are being leased to Navajo sheep producers who want to provide for the preferences of commercial wool and meat buyers by introducing SAMM genetics into their herd.

Another area in which Jim and Nez have helped the Navajo wool producers is by capitalizing on the quality of wool they are producing.

"Our producers were only getting 5 to 10 cents a pound from local buyers," Jim said. "Felix is working with Stanley Strode, Mid-State Wool Growers Association out of Ohio, to provide a better market for the wool."

Since 2005, Alex McClure, of the same wool growers association, has worked through NMSU Cooperative Extension Service specialists to purchase wool from Native Americans in New Mexico and eastern Arizona.

"The wool produced here is outstanding," McClure said. "We are able to get at least a dollar a pound for the wool."

NMSU Extension Teams With State Corrections Department for Prison Vocational Training

SANTA FE—Thirteen men dressed in orange prison uniforms work under the hot September sun, building four greenhouse structures at the Penitentiary of New Mexico in Santa Fe. They are the inaugural team in the Corrections Industry's latest project, in which state inmates will grow vegetables to supplement the prisons' cafeteria menu.

New Mexico State University and New Mexico Corrections Department are collaborating on the project to provide horticultural vocational training to the inmates.

The College of Agricultural, Consumer and Environmental Sciences' Cooperative Extension Service is providing technical advice and guidance in building the hoop houses.

The men were selected from 80 applicants to participate in the Roots of Success program. The Level II inmates have completed an environmental literacy course as part of the program.

"The corrections department approached NMSU in August to provide training to the inmates on the construction of the hoop houses on the state penitentiary grounds in Santa Fe," said Del Jimenez, Extension agricultural agent with NMSU's Rural Agricultural Improvement and Public Affairs Project, who is conducting the training for the project that has the potential to spread to all of the state's correctional facilities.

After receiving instruction while building the first 32-foot-by-14-foot structure, the inmates were divided into groups to construct the three remaining hoop houses.

Once the structures were completed, nine 4-foot-by-10-foot raised planting beds were constructed for each house.

Then the dirty work began, as the inmates filled the planters with wheelbarrows full of dirt and organic material, installed a drip irrigation system in each house, and planted winter greens seeds.

"The first harvest was in early November and has continued weekly," Jimenez said. "The fresh greens are supplementing the Level II unit's cafeteria menu."

"It's a privilege to participate in this pilot program," inmate Waylon Robinson said as he echoed the thoughts of the other men in the program. "It gives us a chance to learn new things and to perfect some things that some of us knew already. It's giving us a sense of pride."

Inmate David Maez, who has been assigned to teach the environmental literacy curriculum, said he has seen "the men become a cohesive group with an enthusiastic, positive attitude."

Many of the men envision using the skills they are learning once they are released from prison.

"The hoop house extends the growing season that allows a grower to have fresh produce earlier and later in the season," said inmate Charles Martinez. "My family has a ranch in the Mount Taylor area, where the growing season is short. I am hoping to build a greenhouse there once I am released in twenty months."

Learning the vocational skill is just one aspect of the program. Secretary of Corrections Gregg Marcantel said the program is designed to also provide life skills training and a sense of accomplishing a task that is bigger than just the selfish behavior that brought most of these men to prison.

"We want to teach our inmates to become entrepreneurs who can provide for themselves and their families upon release," Marcantel said. "It's not enough to just teach someone a new skill; we have to change hearts, to make them feel part of a bigger purpose in life. These hoop houses do just that; these inmates have had to nurture these plants to provide food to feed other inmates. This program has really shown them that if you work hard, focus on your goals, and pay attention to detail, you can harvest meaningful and plentiful bounties."

"What really attracted me to this program was the educational part," said inmate Ronny Garcia. "I'm learning how to be productive with my life instead of keep coming back to prison. This is teaching me a lot that I will be able to take home with me."

July 31, 2015

NMSU Valencia County Extension Office Establishing Seed Library

LOS LUNAS—Some libraries house books. Other libraries are home to seeds. Seed-saving libraries, a place to literally check out and return seeds, are increasing in popularity as more and more growers and farmers gain interest in producing the best-tasting vegetables that you can get.

Historically, saving seeds from the annual harvest was practiced to provide seeds for the following year's planting. Through the years, growers collected seeds of plants that had specific traits they wished to maintain, such as flavor of the fruit, yield rate, disease resistance or plant characteristics.

Today, a seed library is a way for community members to share their favorite plants' seeds. These libraries assist with this by providing a central location where growers can exchange seeds that can improve plant production or preferred characteristics of a vegetable.

New Mexico State University's Cooperative Extension Service office in Valencia County is establishing a seed library for gardeners in the county.

"Saving and sharing seeds is a tradition that we've lost to some degree," said Newt McCarty, Extension agricultural agent in the county, who is developing the Valencia County Heritage Seed Library. "It's a tradition gaining in popularity and practice, especially for small-scale growers."

To reduce the risk of non-viable or diseased seeds, the library organizers require that seed donations come from individuals who have attended seed-saving training.

The next training will be from 6 to 8 p.m. Thursday, August 20, at the Valencia County Extension located at 404 Courthouse Road in Los Lunas.

"It's a way for people to take gardening to the next level, where they select plant traits they wish to build upon," said McCarty. "They become more aware of the plant's characteristics and the taste of the product as they determine which cultivar they want to save and share."

During several years of a selection process, a gardener can develop plants that become more and more conditioned to the micro-climates of an area.

"You save the best of the best and eventually, you have a plant that thrives in your specific soil or environment," McCarty said. "It would be exciting to share with your family, friends and community a variety of vegetables with all of the finest qualities."

A seed library maintains its collection through donations from community members who have completed seed-saving training. A common attribute of many seed libraries is to preserve agricultural biodiversity by focusing on rare, local and heirloom seed varieties.

Seed libraries exist in the Albuquerque area through the city's library system and in Sandoval County through the Cooperative Extension Service Master Gardener Program.

For more information about seed saving or the seed-saving workshop, contact McCarty at 505-565-3002.

Nov. 30, 2015

NMSU Social Work Faculty Researching Equine-Assisted Psychotherapy Model

ALBUQUERQUE—Equine-assisted psychotherapy is known to help people address mental and behavioral health issues, but there remains little evidence-based research to prove it.

New Mexico State University School of Social Work associate professor Wanda Whittlesey-Jerome is dedicating her academic career to establishing and promoting scientific standards for gathering such information.

"Horses are prey animals, so they are constantly scanning their environments," Whittlesey-Jerome said. "When we enter the arena, they sense if we are calm and balanced—or troubled and on edge—and react accordingly. When they meet us on their own terms, horses become mirrors. They react to our inner feelings that we may not show outwardly. They teach us so much about ourselves and can give us insight into what it means to be human."

Whittlesey-Jerome has conducted several studies with at-risk charter high school students and adult female survivors of interpersonal violence. The findings indicate the Equine Assisted Growth and Learning Association's equine-assisted psychotherapy model has had positive impacts on resilience, general self-efficacy, depression, anxiety and global functioning among human participants.

These pilot studies of the model focused on using EAP as an add-on to existing conventional treatments. The first study was with at-risk charter high school students attending Los Puentes Charter School in Albuquerque in 2009.

"There were positive results among the students receiving EAP compared to the students just receiving the psycho-educational component of the study," she said.

A second study was done with women receiving services from the Domestic Violence Resource Center in Albuquerque in 2013.

"These were women already in the process of trying to manage their abusive relationships," she said. "While the women received individual counseling and group therapy from the center's staff, we added EAP to approximately one-half of the overall women studied."

The results of this study have been published in The Practitioner Scholar: Journal of Counseling and Professional Psychology.

"The data showed an improvement in the women in the equine group; their self-esteem increased as depression and anxiety decreased," she said. "But what really intrigued the reviewers of the manuscript was the richness and depth of the qualitative data from the women's journals. After the groups were over, several of the women were willing to take the next step to walk away from their abusive relationships and move on with their lives because of the self-realizations they gained by participating in the eight EAP sessions."

A third study is currently being planned for future implementation.

The Behavioral Health Services Division of the New Mexico Department of Health and Human Services is in the process of providing funds to two non-profit equine therapy organizations to provide free EAGALA-informed equine groups to military families, including warriors and veterans. In addition to funds to pay for the groups, funds are available for gas cards, healthy food and snacks, and healthy beverages, as well as recruitment supplies.

"The Family Fun with Horses Program is an add-on to conventional treatments already available to these families," she said. "We're hopeful that overall family well-being and communication will improve for our military families served through this program."

Recently during a Quarterly Commander's Call, Whittlesey-Jerome spoke to more than 400 airmen at Kirtland Air Force Base about the availability of this program.

"This program has the support of Lt. Col. Bérnabé F. Whitfield, commander of the 58th Aircraft Maintenance Squadron at Kirtland

Air Force Base, who is concerned with the increased numbers of suicides and divorces among his airmen," she said.

Southwest Horsepower in the South Valley and Equine Therapeutic Connections in the North Valley will be conducting the free military family equine groups. Whittlesey-Jerome will provide program evaluation services pro-bono to help the agencies evaluate the effectiveness of the military family equine groups, and she will submit reports to the state on program outcomes.

EAGALA's mission is to become the global standard for equine-assisted psychotherapy and personal development.

"Part of EAGALA's work is to promote the use and scientific measurement of the effectiveness of its EAP model," said Whittlesey-Jerome, who is a member of the association's board.

Prior to being chosen for the board, she served on the organization's research committee. One of her contributions to the organization is creating a graphic model that presents a complete picture containing all of the various components of EAGALA's EAP. This model is currently under review by the leadership of the association.

"An important component of the EAGALA EAP model is that an EAGALA-certified team of professionals—a mental health specialist and an equine specialist—co-facilitate the sessions," she said.

"The sessions consist of solving problems in groups within the context of being 100 percent on the ground with horses. Participants learn to negotiate and develop a mutual relationship with the horses built on trust and respect," she continued. "At the same time, they learn to work together with other participants in new and creative ways that often lead to insight through metaphors that naturally develop in the arena with horses."

In one example, participants are asked to create an obstacle course with props such as traffic cones, plastic pipes, swim noodles, hula hoops and buckets. The task is to get the horses to move through the obstacle without halters or lead ropes. After completion of the task, the group discusses their experience and writes or draws in journals or sketchpads about what they experienced in the session.

"Eventually, I hope to be able to gather additional research data that continues to build an evidence base to further support the use of the EAGALA EAP model," she said.

"EAGALA has 4,500 members word-wide; however, there are many variations of equine therapy currently being used," she said. "If we want to build an evidence base that supports the use of EAGALA's EAP model, practitioners need to be doing the same things in the same ways, and researchers need to measure outcomes using similar tools and procedures. In addition, we need larger studies with more participants. I see this as a possibility as we increase our outreach efforts and develop more university-community partnerships."

Dec. 6, 2015

NMSU Beef Cattle Research Opportunities Have a South African Connection

When New Mexico State University professor Clint Loest and graduate students Eben Oosthuysen and Zeno Bester share information about their beef-cattle research, the New Mexico cattlemen they're speaking with often wonder about their accent.

"People ask me if I'm from Texas," said Loest, a ruminant nutrition expert in the Animal and Range Science Department. "I tell them a little further south—actually, almost to the South Pole."

Loest grew up on a ranch in South Africa and earned his bachelor's and master's degrees at the University of the Free State in Bloemfontein, South Africa. He arrived at NMSU in 2001 after obtaining his doctorate at Kansas State University.

The livestock nutrition research by the College of Agricultural, Consumer and Environmental Sciences team of Loest, Eric Scholljegerdes, Mike Hubbert, Shanna Ivey and Sergio Soto-Navarro has given NMSU something of a rock star status in the beef-cattle industry.

"When you work as a team, it makes things so much better and word gets out about the research," Loest said. "With our facilities on campus, along with the campus ranch and the livestock research centers in Corona, Clayton and Tucumcari, we are able to cover all spectrums of the cattle industry. We are able to study the nutrition of cows and calves on the ranch and follow up with the nutrition of calves in the feedlots."

That attention has brought two more South Africans halfway around the world in pursuit of doctoral degrees.

Oosthuysen was the first to arrive. He has completed his Master of Science degree while at NMSU and is now working on his doctoral degree. Bester joined the doctoral program this year.

"While finishing my Bachelor of Science degree at the University of Pretoria in South Africa, my professor said I should contact Dr. Loest for further study," Oosthuysen said. "When I saw the facility, I knew I needed to be here."

During his research at the Clayton Livestock Research Center, Oosthuysen tested various feedlot receiving protocols on 600 to 700 head of cattle per study.

"Because the cattle-feeding industry in America is so much bigger than at home, I am able to see more cattle on feed in a week than are fed in all of South Africa," he said. "There are very few places in the world that allow the opportunity to do a study on 700 high-stress newly received calves."

Bester arrived in New Mexico after nine years of commercial experience in the feed industry. She, too, attended the University of Pretoria, where she earned her bachelor's and master's degrees in animal nutrition.

"Back home, we all know about Dr. Loest," Bester said. "He is known for the work he is doing in America."

But it was Hubbert, superintendent of the Clayton Livestock Research Center, who brought Bester to NMSU.

"I was looking at either Kansas State or New Mexico State— then I met Dr. Hubbert and was sold on NMSU," Bester said. "I was impressed with his work and his industry connection. He really has his feet on the ground and knows the concerns of the producers."

While the beef-cattle industry differs between the United States and South Africa, both graduate students say the industries taking care of the animals are the same because animals are animals. They are both doing research on animal nutrition and health—specifically in the feedlot.

South Africa's beef industry raises a smaller, leaner animal.

"In South Africa, we raise our cattle differently. We fatten them in a shorter period of time—115 to 120 days. So there is a difference in the way we feed our cattle," Bester said. "Our consumers prefer leaner meat than Americans, who like their meat to be marbled."

Both students see their future in the feedlot aspect of the cattle industry. Oosthuysen said a summer internship with one of the leading feedlot nutritionists in the United States reaffirmed his decision to stay in the Texas/Oklahoma Panhandle region as a feedlot nutritionist.

Bester has seen the global side of the industry and wants to work in that arena.

"We can't produce enough meat just from one country," she said. "So we need to look at the whole food production process from a global perspective. I think with the expertise developed in America, we can benefit different economies across the world. I want to consult in various countries to help them develop their beef-cattle industry."

March 6, 2016

NMSU Extension Specialists Says Chocolate Selection Says a Lot About a Person

You can tell a lot about a person by what they eat, and especially which chocolates they select.

An observant person can learn about someone's background by their food type. Ethnicity, social class, religious practices, fashion and economic status, influence food selection, according to a New Mexico State University Extension specialist

"Since everyone must eat, what we eat becomes a most powerful symbol of who we are," said Sonja Koukel, New Mexico State University Extension Health Specialist.

That same logic can be applied to how a person interacts with chocolate.

"Murray Langham, a psychotherapist in New Zealand, has conducted research that correlates an individual's personality to the chocolates they select," Koukel said.

He published his findings in the book "Chocolate Therapy: Dare to Discover Your Inner Center!"

During therapy sessions, Langham watched his clients select chocolates that he had available. With time, he saw similarities in the people's personalities in association with the shape of the chocolates, type of chocolate, fillings, and even the way they handled the wrapper while eating the candy.

Chocolate therapy can be used as a parlor game or as a therapy to restore, nourish and rebalance the human psyche, Koukel said. She likes to use chocolate therapy as an icebreaker with groups.

"It is fun to have people select chocolates from an assortment and then read what Langham says that selection means about them," she said. "Almost always, like 99.9 percent of the time, you will hear people say, 'That is so me. That's totally who I am.'"

Throughout history, researchers have acknowledged the profound influence of chocolate on a person's physical, mental, emotional and spiritual well-being.

Langham said in his book that his chocolate therapy is concerned with healing the body, mind and spirit through liberation. Once self-realization around chocolate takes place, it allows a person to understand themself better. He said when this happens, many other neuroses and fears just drop away.

During her group presentations, Koukel gives participants a list of personality descriptions associated with the candy's shape and type of chocolate.

"This is the fun part," she said. "There are so many factors associated with the type of filling that I encourage people who want to learn more about themselves to purchase Langham's book."

Here is a brief summary of what the shape means.

- Circle: As a circle person, you love company. In fact, you must be around people or life is not worth living.
- Oval: You move beyond the circle, stretching your limits. You do this by using your feelings for others and, in turn, opening yourself to expressing your thoughts.
- Square: All sides equal, you are balanced and therefore, it's hard for others to push you around. This makes you honest and truthful.
- Rectangle: You are a loyal person who loves sitting or staying in one place. You seem to be a rock for others to lean on.
- Diamond: You make decisions slowly, after internalizing them, and only move on to a new project when you feel from deep within you that it is right.

Here is a brief summary of what the type of chocolate means.

- Milk: As a lover of milk chocolate, you like to live in the past emotionally, to love that sweet, smooth feeling that is the pure essence of childhood.

- Dark: You're a forward-looking person. Your thoughts are always directed towards the future.
- Bitter: A connoisseur of the fine things in life, you know what you're talking about and you are a specialist in your field.
- All chocolate: So you're a person who is flexible and can fit into any situation anytime, anywhere.
- White chocolate: You have an innate sense of fairness. You believe you have the power of the universe at your command.

June 13, 2016

NMSU Extension Turf Specialist Helps New Mexico Golf Courses Save Water

SANTA FE—Drought conditions and water shortages are having an impact on all sectors of society, including recreational landscape areas. In arid and semi-arid environments across the Southwest, the golf industry is trying to find ways to conserve water while maintaining playability and course quality.

For the past five years, The Club at Las Campanas, a luxury golf community in Santa Fe, has been working on implementing water conservation strategies for its two 18-hole courses, designed by golf pro-Jack Nicklaus.

Recently, club management turned to New Mexico State University's Cooperative Extension Service turf specialist Bernd Leinauer in Las Cruces for suggestions on how to resolve a lingering issue.

"In addition to using effluent water, we have reduced the amount of turf on the courses by a third, redesigned and updated the irrigation system and started using wetting agents to help conserve water," said Tom Egelhoff, director of agronomy at Las Campanas. "However, we are still battling wasting water on the tee boxes."

The main problem when irrigating the relatively small area of turf on a tee box with sprinklers is that the water overshoots the area or is blown in the wind, causing it to water the desert around the tee box, which not only wastes water but increases labor costs as plants start to grow in a much larger area.

Leinauer's advice was to use subsurface drip irrigation for the tee box turf.

"Subsurface drip irrigation can save water from 20 to 90 percent of what is used by sprinkler systems," Leinauer said.

"It is not yet economical to use this method for the fairways or greens, but is perfect for tee boxes," he said. "Las Campanas is one of the first golf courses in the nation to install this type of system in tee boxes."

Las Campanas is collaborating with NMSU, the United States Golf Association and irrigation system manufacturers Toro and Rain Bird to install subsurface drip irrigation on six tee boxes. The manufacturers each donated the materials for their systems. USGA awarded a grant to off-set the travel cost to install the system and collect research data.

Leinauer and his colleagues, Elena Sevostianova and Matteo Serena, spent one week at Las Campanas to assist Joel Krause, irrigation superintendent, and his crew with the installation of the subsurface drip systems.

"We installed Toro and Rain Bird systems in three tee boxes each," said Leinauer. "We will collect real-world data on water consumption and quality of turf in these boxes compared to a standard sprinkler system."

Drip lines with emitters 12 inches apart have been installed four inches below the turf at one-foot intervals across the tee box area.

"This system is fairly new for turf areas," Leinauer said. "However, in the irrigation industry, it is not new at all. We've had subsurface drip-irrigated agricultural fields for decades. It's been shown numerous times that this system delivers water efficiently."

While it is not yet practical to have subsurface systems in the fairway and greens, it has been used on bunkers where the slope does not allow water from sprinklers to infiltrate the soil, according to Brian Whitlark, an agronomist with USGA Green Section who assisted with the project.

"Because of the data that will be gathered from this project, USGA awarded NMSU a grant to aid the research," Whitlark said. "USGA supports about a million dollars in research across the country each year."

Both Toro and Rain Bird are working to identify new technologies that allow more effective and efficient irrigation management.

"Collaborative projects with a university like this one are important to us," said Joshua Friell, a principal research scientist at Toro's Center for Advanced Turf Technology. "It allows us to have a third-party verification of the technology and the resulting water savings."

"I hope that we will be able to get meaningful results from this field test and we will be able to document significant water savings, which then can also be implemented on other golf courses across the world," said Samir Shah, Rain Bird marketing and international sales manager.

NMSU Agricultural Outreach Program Receives Regional Honor

A New Mexico State University agricultural program that provides research-based information to the underserved residents of northern New Mexico has received honors from a regional association.

The Rural Agricultural Improvement and Public Affairs Project is the recipient of the Western Extension Director's Association Awards of Excellence. The award was presented during the organization's Western Region Joint Summer Meeting on July 13 in Bozeman, Montana.

"It is certainly an honor for our Rural Agricultural Improvement and Public Affairs Project to be named as a recipient of the Western Extension Directors' Association Awards of Excellence for 2016," said Jon Boren, NMSU associate dean and Cooperative Extension Service director.

"The purpose of this award is to recognize Extension outreach education programming that has achieved outstanding accomplishments, results and impacts in addressing contemporary issues in one or more of the thirteen Western states and territories."

"It is an honor that WEDA has recognized the important work that the RAIPAP has done and is doing for Hispanic and Native American farmers and ranchers in New Mexico," said Jay Lillywhite, NMSU's College of Agricultural, Consumer and Environmental Sciences agricultural economics and business and Extension economics department head, of the program within the Extension Economics department.

"RAIPAP and participating New Mexico Cooperative Extension Service faculty and staff are developing and implementing culturally accepted training programs that are improving farmer and rancher operations and changing in very positive ways the lives of farm and ranch families," said Lillywhite, who accepted the award in Montana for the RAIPAP team.

RAIPAP has worked with Native American and Hispanic farmers and ranchers in northern New Mexico since 1991.

"Northern New Mexico is one of the most economically deprived yet culturally and historically rich regions of the country," said Edmund Gomez, RAIPAP director. "The indigenous farmers and ranchers, who have the oldest history of agricultural production in the continental United States, are threatened due to loss of land, custom, culture, tradition and language."

RAIPAP has assisted 5,000 families with one-on-one, traditional and culturally accepted Extension education programs in areas of sustainable agriculture, value-added agriculture, small business development, and leadership and organizational development.

Initially established with a Kellogg Foundation grant and continually supported by an additional $10 million in U.S. Department of Agriculture outreach grants, RAIPAP has provided programs with assistance from county Extension agent members of the Small Farm and Ranch Task Force and Extension specialists.

"Every three years, we have a strategic planning meeting with our stakeholders and task force members," Gomez said. "This is where we get directions for our programming."

Most recently, the team has worked with the 10 southern pueblos during the three-year Beginning Farmer and Rancher Program, where 58 individuals with less than 10 years of farming or ranching experience participated in workshops on horticulture, animal husbandry and agricultural economics. Participants also received one-on-one assistance to ensure their farm operations would improve.

Through the years, RAIPAP has established the Northern New Mexico Organic Wheat Program in the Taos area; developed the Pueblo Wool Marketing Program; assisted in developing several pueblo and Navajo growers' market programs; and assisted in the development of the Mora specialty livestock program. It also assisted in organizing and expanding the Northern New Mexico

Stockman's Association and the Sangre de Cristo Growers Association.

"Each of these projects helped the producers improve their income," Gomez said. "The wool marketing program doubled the amount of money per pound that the sheep growers received."

The organic wheat program brought an estimated $700,000 into the county through the added-value products by milling the wheat at a mill built in Questa.

"Another area we have strived to improve is the farmers' and ranchers' awareness of USDA programs they can benefit from," Gomez said. "We have held more than 40 USDA and other agency resource fairs in Native American and Hispanic communities. This has bridged a gap in communication between the agencies and the citizens."

RAIPAP developed a minority farmer/rancher directory for northern New Mexico with more than 14,000 Hispanic and Native American producers listed.

Members of the RAIPAP team are Del Jimenez, agriculture specialist; Joseph Garcia, southern pueblo agent; Tory Hoagland, northern pueblo agent; Judy Finley, small business agriculture agent; and Augusta Archuleta, administrative assistant.

During its fifteen years of existence, other team members have included Jaime Castillo, Ted Herrera, Nancy Flores, Ron Walser, Manny Encinias, Sam Fernald, Ursula Rosauer, Pat Melendrez and original project director Andy Nunez

Also helping through position with the Northern New Mexico Outreach Project were Christine Turner, Hayley Melloy Encinias, Tim Tapia, Melissa Long, Jessica Lucero, Lucia Sanchez, Hershal Muniz and Daniel Melendrez.

Sept. 20, 2016

Youth Learn Where Their Food Comes From During NMSU Food Camp For Kids

LOS LUNAS—Three out of four consumers know nothing or very little about farming and ranching, according to a survey by the U.S. Farmers & Ranchers Alliance. That percentage is even higher for youth.

Two New Mexico State University Cooperative Extension Service county agents decided to help youth learn about the agricultural industry in their county by hosting two Food Camp for Kids one-week programs.

"The idea for Food Camp for Kids came about with the understanding that many people are disconnected from where their food comes from, especially youth," said Newt McCarty, NMSU Extension agent in Valencia County. "We wanted to show them where their food comes from with actual experiences of seeing the livestock, honey and berry farms, orchard and dairy that exist in their county."

According to the U.S. Department of Agriculture farm statistics, Valencia County has annual agricultural cash receipts of $76 million for livestock and $10.9 million for crops. It has a wide variety of food production ranging from beef cattle, pigs and lambs to fruit orchards, raspberries and garden vegetables. It also produces products such as packaged meat, milk, honey and flour.

"Food Camp for Kids was a six-day, six-hour-a-day camp for youth ages 9 to 14 that included field trips, hands-on cooking activities and a lot of discussions," said Laura Bittner, NMSU's Valencia County Extension director and family and consumer science agent.

Monday, Wednesday and Friday, the youth visited Hays Apple Orchard and Honey Farm and DeSmet's Raw Milk Dairy in Bosque Farms; 4 Daughters Cattle Feed Lot and Mechenbier Pig Farm in Los Lunas; the organic garden at Green House Bistro and Tome

348

Berry Farm in Tome; Toni Barrow's grass-fed beef farm and Mathews' Custom Meat Processing plant in Belen; and the Valencia Flour Mill in Jarales.

On Tuesday and Thursday, the youth planned a meal, selected recipes, shopped for ingredients and cooked while learning about food safety practices.

"We provided the kids with a hands-on opportunity where they could take the food products they had learned about the day before and actually get into the kitchen and prepare recipes using those particular products," Bittner said.

Volunteers Carolyn Chance and Debby Hasse from the county's Extension Association of New Mexico club taught the youth how to make black pepper biscuits and freezer jam. Hasse, a graduate of NMSU's Master Food Preservation program, taught the youth about canning and freezing fresh produce.

"We set some pretty high expectations of the youth," Bittner said. "They were responsible for capturing the week's activities using iPads from NMSU's Learning Lab."

They used the iPads to take pictures, videos and notes from their interviews with the producers and growers.

"They not only met our expectations, they exceeded our expectations with their technical skills and their presentation to a group of 30-40 adults on Saturday," she said.

What did the youth learn from the week at camp?

"The field trips were really fun and informative," said Shaylee Cordova, 9, of Belen.

"I learned that out of a 1,300-pound cow, only one cup of fluid is not used," said Adrian Rodriguez, 14, of Los Lunas. His brother, Abram Rodriguez, 11, thought it was interesting that the cattle at the feed lot were fed cereal and granola bars that were waste from the cereal factory.

"Pigs sweat through their mouths and hooves," said John Wallace, 12, of Belen. His sister Caelie Wallace, 10, said she learned that baby piglets develop in the womb in three months, three weeks and three days and that a red Angus can be bred by a black Angus cow and a black Angus bull.

"Pigs can weigh as much as 700 pounds," said Aiden Lane, 12, of Los Lunas. "When they are 200 pounds, they send them to the butcher."

"This was the first time I've seen cows being milked," said Dominic Martinez, 9, of Los Lunas.

Rio Romero, 11, of Los Lunas, thought it was cool that the dairy only milked once a day so the mother cow could provide for its babies and the dairymen didn't have to bottle feed the calves.

At the berry farm, the youth thought picking the raspberries and eating them immediately in the field was neat.

Visiting the flour mill, which was built in 1914, was a high point in the field trips for several of the youth. "I liked all of the machines, especially when they were running," said Isaiah Martinez, 9, of Los Lunas.

"I thought it was neat that he had rebuilt everything and that belts from a main shaft in the ceiling turned each machine," said Shauncey Cordova, 10, of Belen.

Oct. 10, 2016

NMSU Researchers Find Natural Immune Stimulator For Chile Plants

Farming is a high-risk business. Crops are planted and a variety of things can impact the harvest, yield and, ultimately, the profit made by the farmer.

Within New Mexico's chile pepper industry, the growers have many potential economic impacting issues to face ranging from adverse weather and labor availability to plant disease pressure.

During the last ten years, these issues have caused the acreage planted and harvested to decrease by 9,000 acres, thus reducing the value of production by as much as $9 million depending on the yield per acre and price per 100 pounds, according to the U.S. Department of Agriculture National Statistics Service.

New Mexico State University's researchers are working with the chile pepper growers to find solutions to controllable issues, such as mechanical harvesting and integrated pest management methods.

"Plant diseases that cause economic impacts to chile production in the Southwest include Phytophthora blight, caused by the plant pathogen Phytophthora capsici; Verticillium wilt, caused by the fungus Verticillium dahlia; and beet curly top, caused by the beet curly top virus that is transmitted by the beet leafhopper," said NMSU College of Agricultural, Consumer and Environmental Sciences graduate student Esteban Molina of Los Lunas.

Growers stay vigilant for these diseases in hopes of preventing total loss. However, in general, plant diseases caused by these pathogens are difficult to control chemically.

In addition, consumer concerns regarding the use of chemicals on edible produce are increasing, causing NMSU researchers to seek alternative ways to combat the diseases.

NMSU's Department of Entomology, Plant Pathology and Weed Science researchers are striving to find integrated pest management methods to help the chile pepper growers in their battle with the diseases.

"We are looking at biocontrol agents for controlling chile diseases," Molina said.

Under the direction of research faculty Jennifer Randall and Rio Stamler, Molina is evaluating the effectiveness of a non-pathogenic Phytophthora species, P. riparia, to prevent diseases.

"Dr. Stamler discovered that P. riparia does not kill chile plants," Molina said. "Since it thrives in riparian environments on decayed biomass, especially cottonwood leaves, we have a readily available source."

P. riparia was tested on chile and other crops planted in the Southwest to be sure that it did not cause disease in these plants.

Molina's assignment as an undergraduate lab assistant was to cultivate the organism found in the Rio Grande watershed.

"I isolated the P. riparia by a technique called leaf baiting," Molina said. "Once lesions form on the leaf they are surface sterilized and plated on a specific media where we cultured the organism to inoculate the chile plants with a liquid culture."

The first stage of the test was to see what effect P. capsici infection would have on the inoculated chile plants.

"We determined that the P. riparia induces resistance to blight," Molina said. "Next, we did a field study comparing treated plants to non-treated ones."

Preliminary results from the field study conducted during the last two years indicate that the P. riparia treated chile exhibited less disease symptoms than non-treated plants.

"Induced resistance using P. riparia increased the fitness of the plants in the field but did not completely alleviate disease pressure," Molina said. "The riparia treated plants produced almost 10 percent more weight and yield."

Molina is conducting further research with P. riparia this year.

"Since it did not completely alleviate the disease pressure, we've decided to combine the treatment with naturally occurring beneficial soil microbes to see if it will increase the fitness of chile plants when exposed to disease pressures in a greenhouse study and in a field trial," he said. "We also need to see if P. riparia can induce resistance to insect-transmitted beet curly top virus in a greenhouse study."

Molina has planted the inoculated plants in a field study at the NMSU research plots in Las Cruces and at NMSU's Agricultural Science Center at Los Lunas this summer.

"There is a lot we don't know about this treatment," Molina said. "During my graduate studies, I will study how the chile plant reacts to the P. riparia so we can understand its mechanisms of protection."

Molina's goal is to help solve problems that impact farmers' profits.

"Hopefully, our research will give the chile pepper growers one more tool in an integrated pest management approach to produce healthier and better-yielding plants to help increase their profits," he said.

Nov. 21, 2016

NMSU Vegetable Researcher Helps Develop More Nutritious Potato

The potato is the number one vegetable consumed by Americans. It is an excellent source of potassium, contains 45 percent of the recommended daily amount of Vitamin C and provides all essential amino acids.

But could the nutritional value of potatoes be improved? That is what U.S. Department of Agriculture research geneticist Kathy Haynes has been asking for nearly 30 years. Her quest for the answer has led her to breed a more nutritious potato, similar to the papa criolla types found in South America.

Haynes' quest has also led to a collaboration with New Mexico State University for field trials to see if the new lines of potatoes can be raised in New Mexico as a specialty crop.

"When Dr. Haynes contacted us, I was very excited," said Stephanie Walker, NMSU Extension vegetable specialist and researcher. "Potatoes are the most widely consumed vegetable, but are low in the antioxidant compounds that are found in the papa criolla types. This research is taking a vegetable that is already loved by people and then making it even more nutritious."

White-fleshed potatoes typically grown in the United States are low in carotenoids that act as antioxidants for healthy eyes. The most well-known carotenoid is beta-carotene, found in carrots.

The carotenoids in the South American papa criolla potatoes, which make the potato yellow-fleshed, are lutein and zeaxanthin, which help prevent age-related macular degeneration. At least one study has suggested that zeaxanthin also improves mental acuity in elderly people.

"Yukon Gold, a yellow-flesh potato that consumers are familiar with, has these carotenoids," Haynes said. "Comparatively, the papa criolla types have 10-20 times more lutein and zeaxanthin than Yukon Gold."

The best food sources of lutein and zeaxanthin currently in U.S. markets are dark leafy greens, collards, kale and spinach.

Haynes has used traditional breeding to develop the papa criollas into a potential commercial potato. Starting with germplasm from Peru, she developed more than 500 breeding lines of the potato during a multiple-year process.

"At first, the plants were only producing pea-size tubers," she said. "But through our breeding process, we now have tubers about the size of a golf ball or larger."

In 2014, after selecting 500 breeding lines with possible commercial traits in her Maine breeding plots, Haynes sought collaboration with NMSU and the University of Florida to conduct field trials in areas with sizable Hispanic populations, hoping to generate interest among people already familiar with papa criolla type potatoes.

Walker planted several hundred breeding lines in Las Cruces and Los Lunas in 2015 and 2016 and helped whittle that number down to 150 in 2016. From the harvest data, about 40 breeding lines were scheduled for continued evaluation in 2017.

"We also plan to plant about 6-10 breeding lines next spring in spacing trials to begin developing production recommendations for growers."

Walker says they have already learned that Las Cruces may be too warm for growing the potatoes.

"The plants were highly stressed from the heat in late spring and the tubers did not develop for many of the lines," Walker said. "However, the lines that did produce a good yield of tubers in Las Cruces may be the basis for breeding lines more tolerant of the conditions in southern New Mexico."

Walker has great interest and passion for pursuing new and unusual vegetables for New Mexico growers and consumers.

"This kind of crop could really be popular with growers' market consumers who are looking for new and exciting vegetables," Walker said.

Haynes said the papa criolla types could be popular with two consumer groups.

"The Hispanic population is increasing in the United States and they are very familiar with this potato from their homeland," Haynes said. "It also will appeal to other consumers who associate color with good nutrition."

Dec. 25, 2016

NMSU's Youth Development Program Provides 4-H Military Partnership Program Statewide.

Paper airplanes and propeller sticks fly around the room as kids chase their flying objects.

This is a special day at the Kirtland Air Force Base youth recreation center. It's National Youth Science Day and the youth are learning about airplane flight and drones.

New Mexico State University's 4-H agents Brittney Sonntag and Nicole Jaynes have brought the national 4-H activity to the youth center. Helping with the activities are volunteers from Sandia Labs. Lockheed Martin, a parent company of Sandia Labs, is a national partner for the science day.

This is just one activity the 4-H agents provide for the children of military personnel through the 4-H Military Partnership program.

Military children face multiple stressors through deployment and other events, which emphasizes the importance of youth development skills that help them process adversity by positively adapting to situations.

"The 4-H club provides youth an opportunity to take on leadership roles, creating the opportunity to communicate and think of other's interests and the needs of other age groups of youth," Sonntag said. "It is critical that military children have the opportunity to develop resiliency skills within their family and community."

Over the last four years, New Mexico 4-H has been working to strengthen its partnership with the military installations in the state. Currently, there are programs at Holloman and Kirtland air force bases, New Mexico Army National Guard in Albuquerque and White Sands Army Base.

"Statewide annually, we have approximately 215 military youth enrolled in 4-H and another 650 military youth reached through 4-H programing at the various installations," Sonntag said.

"There are four main components in the program, health and nutrition; STEM—science, technology, engineering and math; community service; and integration into traditional 4-H programs off-base," Jaynes said.

Fourteen youth participating in a five-day 4-H cooking camp at Holloman AFB learned about nutritional food choices, menu planning, food preparation, food and kitchen safety and etiquette.

At Kirtland AFB, a year-long project combined learning where food comes from with nutritional cooking.

"We decided to reconstruct a garden area on the base and asked Home Depot for help," said Sonntag. "Home Depot donated $500 worth of plants and provided a gardening expert to help design and plan for a successful garden."

With help from military personnel volunteers, the garden was created. An automated drip irrigation system was designed and installed by the youth.

"Throughout the summer, the Kirtland AFB youth center had harvest days," Sonntag said. "The youth harvested the produce then prepared it for consumption and served it with lunch that day."

Twenty-four youths, grades kindergarten through fifth grade, attended a week-long STEM camp at White Sands Army Base, where they experienced science through hands-on activities. They had fun learning about chemical reactions and what happens when different ingredients are mixed together, making Play-Doh, bubbles, Silly Putty and goo.

Eleven youths, ages 9 to 14, participated in a three-day rocketry camp at Kirtland AFB youth center.

"They build three rockets—a construction paper model, a water rocket and a model rocket," Sonntag said. "At the conclusion, the model rockets were launched."

Community service projects at the various installations included participating in the Read Across America Celebration and making no-sew blankets for Animal Humane of New Mexico.

"An important aspect of the 4-H Military Partnership is to have the military youth participate in traditional 4-H programs so they become involved in the community where their installation is located," said Sonntag. "One way to do this is to have the military youth enter their projects in their respective county fairs. The New Mexico military youth entered over 400 projects."

Future plans are being made for a leadership-building activity of rafting on the Rio Grande south of Taos. The activity is being offered to all military pre-teens and teens. They will be joining the Bernalillo County 4-H Council members in this activity.

"This will be a big event, getting everybody together for a leadership day," Sonntag said. "It will be interesting seeing what other activities evolve from this gathering of the youth."

The 4-H Military Partnership between Bernalillo County Urban 4-H and Kirtland AFB has already established a working relationship that the youth enjoy.

"The kids really look forward to 4-H Day," said Lucy Burbach, recreational specialist at Kirtland AFB youth recreation center. "I really appreciate Brittany and Nicole. They have vast knowledge of various activities such as cooking, jewelry making and sewing. They have helped me a lot with our photography club."

March 13, 2017

Register Now: New Mexico Youth Ranch Camp Headed Back to CS Ranch in June

CIMARRON—Cimarron is known for the Philmont Scout Ranch, where Boy Scouts from across the nation come each summer for an experience of a lifetime camping in the Northern New Mexico wilderness.

This year a different group of youth will be heading to Cimarron for an experience of a lifetime that could help them make career decisions.

New Mexico State University's College of Agricultural, Consumer and Environmental Sciences will hold its annual New

Mexico Youth Ranch Camp at the CS Cattle Company's 130,000-acre ranch at the foot of the Sangre de Cristo mountain range near Cimarron.

"Last year, this location allowed our campers to see a real-life working ranch," said camp director Jack Blandford, NMSU Cooperative Extension Service program director in Luna County. "The CS is a working cattle and hunting operation and has been family owned and operated since 1873. We all are excited to be returning to the ranch this year."

The CS Cattle Company was founded by Frank Springer and his brother Charles, whose initials are used for the ranch name and historic brand. Les Davis, the grandson of Frank Springer, took over management of the CS in 1947 and today, his children continue managing the operations.

The youth ranch camp is administered each summer by NMSU's Extension Service. It began in 2011 at the Valles Caldera National Preserve. Since then more than 150 youth have participated in this unique opportunity to gain a greater appreciation of the science and opportunities in agriculture.

"We are proud to offer this one-of-a-kind program for the future cattle producers of our state," said Jon Boren, NMSU College of ACES associate dean and director of the Extension Service. "The collaboration between our Extension specialists, county Extension agents and members of the ranching industry has provided an opportunity for the youth to learn about the many aspects of managing a ranch and natural resources."

NMYRC is a week-long, hands-on, college-caliber educational experience for youth ages 15-19. Each day is filled with information necessary to manage a ranch, including all things beef, marketing and economics, natural resources, and range land management. At the end of each day, one camper receives the Top Hand award for their outstanding participation in that day's activities.

Throughout the week, the youth are compiling information to design their team's own ranch management plan, which they present to a panel of judges from the beef industry and NMSU on Friday in competition for the coveted team jacket.

"You don't have to just be in ranching to attend this camp. It offers a wide variety of career avenues," Blandford said. "I encourage any youth within the age group to apply."

July 23, 2017

"Bee" Healthy: NMSU Researchers Study Medicinal Benefits of Oregano for Bees

ALCALDE—An oregano farmer, a beekeeper and a researcher with New Mexico State University are investigating the medicinal benefits of oregano for bees and whether these benefits are transferred to humans through honey.

"Our goal is to examine and promote Monarda fistulosa as a new crop or accessory planting to affect bee health and also produce a hive product and field crop that can be processed in a number of ways," said Rob Heyduck, senior research specialist at NMSU's College of Agricultural, Consumer and Environmental Sciences' Sustainable Agriculture Center at Alcalde.

Monarda fistulosa, a member of the mint plant family commonly called wild bergamot or bee balm, is known as Oregano de las Sierra for its oregano flavor.

"There are 60 plants that produce the flavor of oregano," said Embudo farmer Todd Bates, who is cultivating the plant normally found wild in the mountains. "The flavor comes from the chemical compounds that also give the plant its medicinal qualities."

It is those medicinal qualities that Zia Queen Bees owner Melanie Kirby is interested in.

"Bee health is of critical importance in pollinator productivity," Kirby said. "As a beekeeper, pollinator productivity is becoming more and more challenging due to weather fluctuation, increase in pest and disease issue, compromising habitats and management practices."

After placing beehives in Bates' field for a couple of years, Kirby thinks there are possible health benefits from the bees feeding on the Monarda flowers.

Bates and Kirby approached NMSU researcher Heyduck to conduct a study. NMSU's College of ACES received a U.S.

Department of Agriculture specialty crop block grant to finance the study.

"To analyze Oregano de la Sierra and its effects on bee health and potential human health benefits through value-added products, we are coordinating with several additional institutions and laboratories both in-state and through the USDA Agricultural Research Service," Heyduck said.

The study is located on a site in the northern Rio Grande Valley and Sangre de Cristo mountain range. Nucleus honeybee colonies established by Zia Queen Bee are located at the three sites.

"We are collecting nectar directly from the flowers and bee-gathered nectar, as well as honey from the hives," Kirby said. "We are also gathering pollen from the hives."

The collections are scheduled for pre-flowering, middle of flowering and after flowering.

Don Hyder and Eric Miller, professors of biology and chemistry, respectively, at San Juan College in Farmington, are using gas chromatography to analyze the nectar and honey samples to determine chemical compounds.

"These compounds, including carvacrol, thymol, p-cymene, have shown bactericidal, viricidal and miticidal activity in previous research," said Heyduck. "We are hoping the analysis will show that these medicinal compounds are in the honey."

"Among herbalists, oregano has provided relief from respiratory and digestive symptoms," Bates said. "It would be wonderful if these properties were also gained from the honey."

Kirby and Heyduck are also collecting bees for analysis of their health.

"By feeding bees in isolation and free-choice, we are seeking to determine a potential bee preference and evaluate the parasite loads of bees fed different diets," Heyduck said. "We are sending the live bees to Jay Evans at the USDA-ARS Bee Research Laboratory in Beltsville, Maryland, to have the bees analyzed for specific viruses and diseases."

Bees preserved in saline solution are being sent to the Bee Information Partnership, a nation-wide beehive health database.

"We are adding our findings to that database to have records of these exact hives as they progress," Heyduck said. "Population samples of Varroa mite, a parasite threatening honeybees worldwide, will be taken at multiple times from the project hives and will serve as an indicator of oregano's effect on bee health."

Regarding the outcome of the research, Heyduck said, "Todd works with oregano as a herb you can add to food. We hope that this research will bring about natural value-added products. Also, using the Oregano de la Sierra plant in revegetation mixes, habitat enhancement, and pollinator gardens could add something medicinal for the pollinators in the area."

August 14, 2017

NMSU Extension Service Helps Santa Cruz Farmer Improve Forage Quality, Yield

SANTA CRUZ - When Mario Madrid decided it was time to renovate his pasture and make beneficial use of the land's water rights, he turned to New Mexico State University's College of Agricultural, Consumer and Environmental Sciences for help.

"My family's land was covered by bi-annual grass and full of weeds. It was barely edible for my horses and it was not adding any protein to their diet," Madrid said of the six acres of land that his father had farmed. "Yields continued to decline."

His father had farmed the land as long as Madrid could remember. In the past, there had been great stands of forage, but in recent years things had run down as his father grew older.

After many trips to Isleta and Tome to purchase quality hay, the team roper reached a turning point.

"I knew I wasn't making hay anywhere close to that quality, so it was a motivation to do something better," he said. "I thought, 'I've got pastureland and water rights, I can learn to raise better quality hay.'"

The NMSU graduate in civil and structural engineering knew the university's Cooperative Extension Service could help him.

Tom Dominguez, NMSU Santa Fe County Extension agricultural agent, began consulting Madrid.

"That's what the Extension Service does, we provide research-based information free of charge," Dominguez said. "People don't know that we are here to help them one-on-one."

Several Extension specialists also provided specific information about forage crop varieties, weed control and pest management.

Forage specialist Leonard Lauriault, from the NMSU Agricultural Science Center in Tucumcari, helped Madrid select a forage type.

"We had orchard grass in the pastures when I was a kid," Madrid said. "I discovered cool-season grasses have a longer growing season than the warm-season grasses in north-central New Mexico. I selected orchard grass because of its yield potential and protein content. I also added alfalfa, so I now have a 70-30 mix of the two plants."

Extension weed specialist Leslie Beck showed him how to identify the weeds, and forage specialist Mark Marsalis, from the NMSU Agricultural Science Center in Los Lunas, taught him which herbicides he needed to use to manage the forage pasture.

"Their help really has paid off, this year, the fields are 95 percent weed free because I applied the herbicide they recommended in the spring," he said.

He also attended the field day at the NMSU Sustainable Agriculture Science Center in Alcalde and a forage grower workshop in Los Lunas to gain more information.

"I really learned a lot," Madrid said. "One thing I realized was that I had to bring myself up to speed to be able to ask the right questions and to be able to understand what their feedback meant."

Irrigation water management was another area Madrid wanted to improve.

"Mario wants to show his irrigation district that he is putting his water to good use," Dominguez said. "It is a big push among acequia associations and irrigation districts for individuals to put their water to good use, so rights are not bought, reallocated or adjudicated away from the land."

Madrid called on his engineering knowledge in grading and water flow as he leveled the land for better irrigation water flow.

"Even though I'm spending the same amount of time irrigating, I'm not opening the gate as far, so I'm using less water," Madrid said. "There is more water in the ditch flowing downstream to my neighbors while I'm irrigating."

The result of Madrid's investment of money and time is paying off with beautiful green fields. The first cutting of the 2.8 acres this year generated 106 bales of hay to feed his horses.

"They were really baled tight, so it came out to 1.4 tons per acre," he said. "My second cutting yielded 239 bales and an average of 3.0 tons per acre. I'm hoping to go over six tons per acre by the end of the season."

With planting an additional 1.5-acre field later this summer, Madrid expects to provide enough hay for his use and have hay for sale next year.

Through determination and the help of NMSU Cooperative Extension Service, Madrid has reached his goal of producing quality hay for his performance horses, as well as earning money to recover the costs he initially invested. Just as important is his stewardship of the land and beneficial use of his allocated water from his irrigation district.

NMSU Graduate, Social Entrepreneur Helping to Feed the Hungry

As a student at New Mexico State University, Jose Rodriguez discovered a passion for helping people and an entrepreneurial way to do it.

During annual food-drive service projects, Rodriguez saw the impact of helping others.

"While the food drive was fun, there were some impactful moments when we would actually go into people's homes and see that they did not have food in their cupboards," Rodriguez said. "We discovered that here in our community, people are living almost in third-world conditions. One home we visited didn't even have electric power. When you hear their stories, you just can't help but get teared up on something like that."

Those moments planted a seed in Rodriguez that sparked his ideas about how to help alleviate poverty. The way to finance that ambition was discovered during an independent-study class focused on social entrepreneurship.

A social entrepreneur recognizes immediate social problems but also seeks to understand the broader context of an issue that crosses disciplines, fields and theories.

During his studies, the finance and economic major in the College of Business learned that a little effort can go a long way from established social entrepreneurs such as Muhammad Yunas, founder of the microfinance movement through the Grameen Bank in Bangladesh.

He learned that a social entrepreneur competes in the marketplace with all other competitors but is inspired by a set of social objectives. This is the primary reason for being in the business.

After graduation, Rodriguez and fellow College of Business student Aron Jones wondered how they could raise money to help alleviate poverty. ROJO Ink was born as a business where the profit would be used to help people.

"We decided we could make custom T-shirts and then, working with organizations that send food aid, we could finance sending food to the hungry," he said. "Every order helps us pay to host meal-packing events."

During its eight years of existence, ROJO has provided over 500,000 meals by financing meal-packing events organized by their customers.

The first was in Las Cruces in 2010, where NMSU students and community members helped pack 100,000 meals for Haiti earthquake victims.

"We now finance one or two smaller events annually with our customers around the nation," Rodriguez said. "These are fun events where people contribute a couple of hours to combining the meal ingredients in sealed bags."

Rodriguez has his vision set on other ways to help people. One is right in his community of Las Cruces—Camp Hope.

"I've seen and studied a lot of programs helping homeless people. Camp Hope is a fairly good model," he said of the tent-to-rent program. "They want to take the tent community to the next level by building 40 permanent three-sided structures that will protect the people from the elements, wind and sun."

Rodriguez wants to help "knock this project out." While this project is not in ROJO Ink's marketing promise of sending meals, he says it makes sense to do it.

"We have a standing offer to finance some of these structures as soon as they get the project organized," he said. "We also want to get other people involved in financing the project."

The young social entrepreneur doesn't see himself as a hero nor wants to be put on a pedestal. He just wants to help his fellow human beings.

Sept. 29, 2017

PNM Grant Helps NMSU Expand Public School Agri-Science Program in Las Vegas

LAS VEGAS, N.M.—Most students learn how plants grow by reading textbooks. Next spring, students in the Las Vegas City School District from kindergarten through high school will see the process with their own eyes.

For 11 years, middle school students, grades 6-8, have had the opportunity to learn by doing in a self-sustaining greenhouse and garden at the New Mexico State University Extension and Research Youth Agricultural Science Center on the middle school campus.

With the reorganization and consolidation of schools within the district, Peter Skelton, NMSU College of Agricultural, Consumer and Environmental Sciences associate professor and director of the science center, is expanding the program district-wide.

Through the "A New Century of Service" grant program celebrating Public Service Company of New Mexico's 100 years of doing business in New Mexico, PNM Resources Foundation has awarded a $10,000 grant to support the Seed-to-Plate program expansion.

"The PNM Centennial Seed-to-Plate project is creating a holistic K-12 farming program across the district," Skelton said. "The partnership with PNM, the Las Vegas City Schools, the San Miguel Economic Development Corporation and NMSU will enhance education and economic development opportunities and create a collaborative community space."

In preparation for the spring, raised-garden boxes are being built at the K-3 Los Ninos Elementary School; next door, at the 4-6 grade Sierra Vista Elementary School, a greenhouse is being built; and at the junior high-high school complex, a multi-functional high tunnel greenhouse is being built by the FFA and vocational education students.

"We want to expand on the success we have had with our middle school program," Skelton said. "When we look at data from our research, we can tell that the kids were not getting much science before they got to sixth grade."

The integrated learning experience in sixth grade changed the students' motivation and attitude toward learning as they enjoyed being in the greenhouse. Having the multi-functional high tunnel at the secondary level schools will allow that enthusiasm to continue.

"During our hands-on projects, we gave context to the content teachers are teaching in the classroom," Skelton said. "Kids see how their food grows and enjoy the fruit of their labor."

The K-3 teachers will begin introducing basic agricultural concepts to the students as each classroom will have its own raised garden.

"I'm really interested in the integration of literacy, numeracy, agriscience, and outdoor classrooms and learning through Center programs," Skelton said. "A K-12 model allows us to intervene educationally at a younger age, enhance current programs, and provide the connection between the science and real-world growing opportunities in secondary education."

Ultimately, the students will be raising vegetables that will be served in the school cafeteria and donated to community hunger relief.

"We did this on a small scale at Memorial Middle School. Now we have the opportunity to do this at a larger scale and impact the education of more students," Skelton said. "We want the kids to learn about growing fresh and nutritious food and the science of it. I'm really hoping that we will get some interest from teachers in supporting production in the high tunnel during the summer for sales at local farmers' markets."

Ultimately, Skelton hopes the program allows the students to develop the skills necessary for them to sustain themselves by growing their own food, or develop a business, or to develop entrepreneurial skills that all add to the local economy.

"We are a growing enterprise," he said.

New Mexico Educators Gain Business Perspective as Woodrow Wilson MBA Fellows

A group of educators is seeing their profession through a different lens.

The Woodrow Wilson Fellows are developing new tools to improve their leadership skills through the New Mexico State University College of Business online Masters of Business Administration program.

"When I began the program, I had the educational tools that I would use all the time," said Colette Martinez, an instructional specialist with Southwest Region Education Cooperative. "Now I have another set of tools that are my business tools. I've learned that there are strengths in both sets of tools and how they can work together to really produce great results for students."

The Woodrow Wilson MBA Fellows in Education Leadership was launched in 2015 in partnership with the New Mexico Public Education Department, NMSU and the University of New Mexico to develop a new model in education leader preparation, equipping graduates to lead schools across the state. Only two states are involved in the program, New Mexico and Indiana.

"The Woodrow Wilson National Fellowship Foundation began the program because they think there are some leadership skills that are in an MBA program that can be useful to any organization, especially school leaders," said Andrea Fletcher, assistant dean and director of the Woodrow Wilson Fellowship program.

The first cohort of nine students completed the two-and-a-half-year program this summer. An additional 40 education professionals are currently in the program.

"They gave us a different perspective, a different insight to being a leader and managing schools a little more effectively," said Estrella Becerra, coordinator for Pre-K programs at Gadsden Independent School District.

"It's not about fixing kids. It's about fixing the structures in order to support our teachers and, therefore, our students," said Lydia Polanco, principal of Mesilla Elementary School, Las Cruces Public Schools. "It's allowed me to look at the systems within the school to see what's working, to see what's not working."

The educators participated in the online MBA program alongside business professionals, which is unique to the other Woodrow Wilson Fellows programs.

"We actually felt both groups learned significantly from each other and really helped to broaden their way of thinking," Fletcher said.

The course work included negotiations, finance, litigation, data analysis, marketing, and other business-related topics designed to provide the students with a solid background in business practices and the problem-solving and people skills needed to be successful leaders.

Once a month, the educators meet face-to-face with professors for sessions related specifically to education.

"Through this format, the Fellows are making connections from the course work to what it looks like as school or district leaders," Fletcher said.

"Typically, you would see us utilizing finances more as a reaction rather than being proactive," said Vangie Barela, principal at Jornada Elementary School, LCPS. "Our courses have taught us how to strategically plan and align all of our finances to our goals and vision."

She added that all school administrators should be expected to take the negotiation class "because you're constantly negotiating whether it be with the community, political members of education, as well as your parents and even your students. I've learned there isn't always a winner or a loser."

The program culminated with a capstone project that was a problem presented by school and district leaders.

"We saw them being very purposeful and thinking about using data, all sources of data, to analyze the problem," Fletcher said. "They were thinking very strategically about the change process and the implementation process."

"The final project allowed us to apply our learning to an issue we work with every day," said Wendi Miller-Tomlinson, assistant superintendent for teaching and learning LCPS. "I think our project is viable and attainable. We could actually implement a couple of the projects."

One project was the creation of a dual-language medical pathway at one of the high schools.

"A Las Cruces high school had zero proficient with their English language learners," Fletcher said. "They also knew that they were constrained by resources. They didn't have enough teachers to really do a good job with the program. Our fellows went in and did a lot of research about what is working well across the country and they developed the concept of the dual-language medical pathway."

Another project was a way to make LCPS's Challenger Space Center able to serve the students and be financially sustainable.

"They created a plan that changed the center's mission not just to be an educational experience for middle school students but also to be a community resource," Fletcher said. "The plan recommended moving the center to a 501(c)(3) organization with a community board of directors."

"As principals, we really want our community to be developed more in the area of science education," said Toni Hull, principal of Mesilla Valley Leadership Academy, LCPS. "We looked at the Challenger Center and said, 'How can we really, truly, make it something that we can leverage in our community to help our kids, and also the adults and businesses in the community?' We think our plan could do that."

Dec. 16, 2017

NMSU Extension Program Encourages Navajo Families to Raise Backyard Gardens

GALLUP—When driving north from Gallup on U.S. 491 to Shiprock, passing through the barren, arid terrain, it is hard to imagine fields of corn, squash and beans, and fruit trees thriving in this corridor of northwestern New Mexico and the Navajo Nation's eastern region.

For decades, Native Americans living in this area grew the traditional Three Sisters—corn, squash and beans.

As the climate has changed in recent years and access to water has decreased, many families have ceased to raise gardens. Health issues, such as obesity and diabetes, have increased as the access to fresh fruit and vegetables has decreased in the Navajo Nation.

New Mexico State University's College of Agricultural, Consumer and Environmental Sciences is working with community leaders and families in the small rural communities along the corridor to bring back the tradition of family gardens.

NMSU's Cooperative Extension Service has obtained funding for a program to revive the tradition from the U.S. Department of Agriculture's Rural Development's Rural Business Development Grant program and the Northwest New Mexico Council of Governments located in Gallup.

"Market Connect is a program to help families, communities and schools develop new gardens," said Michael Patrick, NMSU Extension specialist and economic development coordinator. "The program will also provide families information on the nutritional value and health benefits of fresh fruit and vegetable consumption."

The northwest region of New Mexico is a food desert, with the majority of families having little or no access to fresh produce and other affordable healthy foods due to low income and geographical isolation.

"What really opened my eyes was seeing the convenience stores along Highway 491 not having fresh fruits and vegetables on their counters or stands," said Sharon Sandman of Sheep Springs. "They have replaced nutritious food with junk food that contains sugar, salt and fats."

The average drive time to the nearest full-service grocery store providing access to fresh fruit, vegetables and other healthy foods is forty-five minutes.

Sandman began promoting backyard gardens seven years ago to her neighbors, family and friends. She met Patrick through the U.S. Department of Agriculture's Stronger Economies Together program he coordinates in New Mexico.

"Sharon manages the Market Connect program," Patrick said. "Her efforts have begun to spark the interest and willingness of families, grandparents, parents and children to work together in the Navajo tradition of producing and consuming healthy food."

During the 2017 growing season, 19 families were raising backyard gardens. Four schools and three chapter houses also had some form of gardens. The program assists the gardeners with fencing, soil supplements, tools, water hoses and drip irrigation lines. An additional grant has provided a hoop house at the Sheep Springs Chapter House garden.

Sandman is working with Jesse Jim, NMSU Tribal Extension agent; Carole Palmer, horticulturalists and food systems specialist with Community Outreach and Patient Empowerment; Sadie Lister, field coordinator for the Native American Producers Success; Wayne Franklin, Navajo Department of Agriculture; and Flix Nez, Dine College in Tsaile, Arizona.

The group conducts horticulture and food preparation and preservation workshops at various locations along the corridor.

Market Connect has launched dedicated farmers' markets at local chapter houses to provide access to fresh produce.

"Two of these farmers' markets were created in Sheep Springs and Naschitti," Patrick said. "Six producers provided produce to Sheep Springs and four to Naschitti. The produce was sold out at both markets. Proceeds for the gardening families, though modest, made a big difference to them."

An additional economic development incentive the program provides is giving families a chance to learn business skills and marketing of the products they grow themselves and gain education to continue farming after the project ends.

"In addition, the gardening families all reported that they themselves were eating more fresh produce," said Sandman. "The program is helping to reestablish an important tradition of our culture."

Three NMSU Seniors Have Adventure of a Lifetime in Red Bull 'Can You Make It?'

Three New Mexico State University seniors participated in an adventure of a lifetime during the Red Bull "Can You Make It?" competition in April.

Team Naray, consisting of Emilio Baca of Belen, Torbyn Nare of Albuquerque and Jonah Kennon of Roswell, traveled from Budapest, Hungary, to Amsterdam, Netherlands, in one week.

The adventure came when they had no money or credit cards. They had to receive help from people and pay with cans of Red Bull energy drink.

As 200 teams of three college students fanned across Europe from five starting points, the kindness of people was demonstrated time and time again.

"This was a life-changing experience for all of us," said Baca, a College of Business marketing and small business management major.

"It was a mini-version of life," said Kennon, a College of Business music business and marketing major. "Some days, we wondered what we had gotten ourselves into. There were ups and downs and struggles, but other times things were great."

"So many things happened during the week," said Nare, a College of Arts and Science computer science major. "We met some incredible people."

As Team Naray traveled through Hungary, Croatia, Slovenia, Austria, Germany and the Netherlands, the Sigma Chi fraternity brothers discovered people under the age of thirty were more willing to help them accomplish their goal of reaching Amsterdam in seven days.

"In Croatia, the people were incredible," Kennon said. "We got a good jump on the race's point competition and got some good advice about our journey's route."

While Baca plans to return to Croatia this summer for an internship, he said the country that stands out in his mind is the Netherlands.

"The hospitality there was amazing," Baca said. "People were outwardly trying to help us. People who didn't know about the race would stop and ask what we were up to. Everyone we met tried to help us out."

While the goal was to arrive in Amsterdam in seven days, the champion was determined by who earned the most combined points from three areas—checkpoint challenges, adventure challenges and social media support.

"We had to go to checkpoint cities in each country," Baca said. "After checking in, we had to do a challenge that represented one of Red Bull's extreme sports to earn additional cans of Red Bull energy drink."

Team Naray rode bicycles up a hill to a castle in Ljubljana, Slovenia; made hockey goals at the Olympic Park in Munich, Germany; yodeled at the Olympic ski jump arena in Innsbruck, Austria; performed magic tricks in Nuremberg, Germany; and played a video soccer game against the number 5 FIFA player in the world in Cologne, Germany.

"The adventure challenges were like a scavenger hunt," Baca said. "We had a list of things we needed to do to earn points."

The highlight of the adventure challenges for the owners of Naray & Co, a music and media production company, was meeting a music producer and using his sound studio to create a rap song in one hour. They were among seventeen teams that accomplished this challenge.

Other activities ranged from hugging someone for sixty seconds, jumping rope with a professional boxer and playing Elvis' "Blue Suede Shoes" on the air guitar with a street musician to teaching twenty people a dance, creating a special effects video and staying in a five-star hotel.

"It was late when we were looking for the five-star hotel in Munich," Nare said. "We went to several but were turned down.

They said if the marketing person was there, they probably could. Finally, we found one—the Lovelace—that was amazing."

Social media participation included what they posted along the trip and how many viewers kept up with their adventure.

"My fifth-grade teacher, Carla Dale, showed our posts to her class every day and gave a lesson on where we were," Baca said. "We really appreciate everybody who followed us on social media."

With thirty minutes left to check in at the finish line, Team Naray ended their adventure in Amsterdam.

"I was excited to be back in the Netherlands," said Kennon, who studied abroad there last year. "It's my second home. Ending the race here was the reason I wanted to come on this trip."

They had traveled 1,171 miles and used 140 cans of Red Bull energy drink to accumulate enough points to finished 28th overall. Of the 18 teams from the United States, only one other finished higher, University of Louisiana at Lafayette's The Cajuns, who were 15th.

"This experience showed us that we're more capable than we initially thought," Nare said. "We will use this experience as we head to Los Angles in pursuit of our dream of being in the music industry."

May 13 2018

NMSU Collaborates in New WIC Point of Sale System at Lowe's Markets in Las Cruces

A collaboration of federal and state agencies, a grocery store chain and New Mexico State University researchers has produced a way to help participants in the Supplemental Nutrition Program for Women, Infants and Children program maximize the use of available supplemental benefits, including their cash-value benefits for authorized fruits and vegetables.

With the assistance of NMSU's College of Business Consumer Behavior Lab, collaborators Lowe's Market, New Mexico's WIC agency and the U.S. Department of Agriculture have developed a new point-of-sale system that was launched on April 11 at Lowe's two Las Cruces stores.

Mihai Niculescu, co-director of the Consumer Behavior Lab, and Stephanie Rogus, assistant professor in the College of Agricultural, Consumer and Environmental Sciences' Family and Consumer Sciences Department, spent several years working with the grocery chain in developing the new system. The study was funded by a USDA Economic Research Service grant.

"This collaboration is exciting," said Rob Ybarra, Lowe's director of marketing. "We have developed a win-win solution that is helping not only the WIC participants but our other customers as well to make healthy food choices at check out. Since starting this new system, sales of healthy items at our check stands have quadrupled."

WIC provides federal grants to states for supplemental foods, health care referrals and nutrition education for low-income pregnant, breastfeeding and non-breastfeeding postpartum women and to infants and children up to age five who are found to be at nutritional risk.

In New Mexico, participants access their WIC supplemental food package benefits using an electronic benefit transfer card. In addition to their supplemental food packages, women and children participants receive cash-value benefits in WIC to obtain authorized fruits and vegetables.

"WIC participants are given cards that are funded each month for the purchase of healthy food, especially fresh fruit and vegetables," Niculescu said. "If they don't use all of the funds by the end of the month, the remaining funds are removed from the card when the next month's credit is applied."

The NMSU study found that WIC participants feel bad about starting a purchase transaction and then discovering they could buy more fruits and vegetables when they get the receipt that shows the balance on their card.

"They have a choice to go back to the produce department for additional healthy food and then return to the checkout line," Niculescu said. "But most of the time, they just leave the store and forfeit the money."

Working with New Mexico's WIC agency, Lowe's Market redesigned its computerized system to allow cashiers to tell the WIC participant how much remains on their WIC card before the sales transaction is completed.

"This is a great example of using technology to try to enhance the effectiveness of USDA nutrition assistance programs—by making it easier for WIC shoppers to use all of their fruit and vegetable vouchers," said Lisa Mancino, an economist with USDA's Economic Research Service and USDA's co-investigator on the research project.

In addition, the store has located fresh fruit and vegetables at checkouts to allow the customer to easily use the remainder of their credit.

"This subtle change can make a big difference for WIC participants," said Sarah Flores-Sievers, New Mexico WIC director. "Having healthy food within arm's reach at the checkout counter makes it much easier for participants to use any amount of remaining funds on their benefit card no matter how small, without increasing wait times for everyone in line."

"We had one common purpose—to give all customers the opportunity to make healthier choices," Ybarra said. "Besides having the usual snack items available at the checkout line, now they have healthy choices for those quick purchase decisions. The increase in our sales demonstrates that when you give customers alternatives to eat healthier, oftentimes they make healthier selections."

May 16, 2018

NMSU Launches Website Featuring Newly Trademarked Jujube Cultivars

ALCALDE—AmeriZao is the new trademarked name for jujube fruit trees tested by New Mexico State University's College of Agricultural, Consumer and Environmental Sciences.

"Since these cultivars are originally from China, where Zao is the word for this fruit, I wanted to keep the traditional name in the trademark," said Shengrui Yao, NMSU Extension fruit specialist. "AmeriZao cultivars are American jujubes since they have been propagated and tested in New Mexico."

The 34 varieties receiving the new trademark are those propagated from cultivars Yao received from China in 2011. She has studied each cultivar for traits that will thrive in New Mexico's various climate zones. Gradually, she will publish the top performers in each region and for different purposes.

"Jujube fruit trees are an excellent alternative fruit for growers in northern New Mexico," Yao said. "The trees bloom from late May to early June, so late frosts will not prevent fruit from setting. They also do well in semi-arid conditions."

Yao has discovered that jujube trees, also known as Chinese dates, already exist around the state, but owners are often not aware of what type of tree it is or how to use the fruit. She has collected fruit from various locations, plus those raised in her study, for annual fruit-tasting events.

"People really like the different flavors that each cultivar offers," she said. "They are excited about having the fruit in their diet."

To help people learn more about each cultivar, Yao and NMSU's media production department have developed a website that features photos of each cultivar and information about the plant and its fruit.

"When you search the Internet for information about the jujube fruit, there are not many high-quality photos," Yao said. "Our website has photos I have taken of each cultivar during my research."

Yao hopes the NMSU website at aces.nmsu.edu/jujube will help people identify the cultivar of jujube they may currently own or help growers select cultivars in the future.

"Occasionally, plants bought from retailers are mislabeled, or a person discovers a jujube tree on their property from previous owners. This website allows them to compare their tree's fruit with the photo to see what cultivar they have," she said.

The photographs are grouped according to the best use of the varieties—drying, fresh eating, multipurpose or ornamental.

"People have different desires for using the fruit," Yao said. "They can look for the variety that matches their intended use of the fruit."

Yao has continued to propagate the cultivars but does not have the facility or staff to produce the plants for retail sale.

"The next step for providing these trees for commercial fruit growers is to partner with nurseries to produce the quantity necessary for that size of the market," she said.

Sept. 17, 2018

Meadow Lake Youth Earn Bicycles Through NMSU Extension Program

MEADOW LAKE—This summer, 11 Meadow Lake youth enjoyed riding a new bicycle after the surprise Meadow Lake Kids Club end-of-school party in May.

Receiving the bike wasn't a free ride. They had to earn it.

Meadow Lake Kids Club is an after-school program hosted by New Mexico State University's Cooperative Extension Service in Valencia County. For the past five years, the youth and their parents or guardians have met at the Meadow Lakes Community Center every other week for a variety of fun and educational activities, including snacks provided by a local church.

"We've had a great partnership with the First United Methodist Church in Belen," said Laura Bittner, NMSU's Valencia County program director. "Besides making healthy snacks once a month for club meetings, the community outreach committee has provided a meal during the winter holidays for all of the youth participants and their families."

The church members also give the youth an end-of-school-year tote bag filled with books, games and art supplies to enjoy during the summer months.

"Each year, we seem to take it up a notch," said Elaine Wilson, mission committee chairperson for the First United Methodist Church in Belen. "This year, we decided to give a bicycle to each of the club participants."

Committee members got the idea from a Methodist Church in Texas where bicycles for youth was a Sunday school class project.

"We started talking about what a great thing it would be for these kids," Wilson said. "One of the problems in impoverished areas is the lack of good nutrition and good exercise. So we felt the bicycles would be a good exercise for these children."

When Bittner was told about the church members' idea, she decided it was important that the children were not just given a bicycle but that they would have an opportunity to earn a bicycle.

"So, I had a conversation with the youth telling them they had an opportunity to earn a prize of significant value," Bittner said. "After explaining what prize, significant and value means to the youth, they helped establish criteria that they felt could be accomplished in a five-month period of time in order to earn the prize."

The youth had very grand ideas about the types of things they could do, but with Bittner's guidance, they narrowed the criteria to a very doable but still challenging list of activities.

The expectations included having a 95 percent attendance record at school, reading five age-appropriate books, obtaining a letter of recommendation and support from a teacher or school administrator, attending six of seven kids club meetings, walking or running two laps around the waking path at the community center at each club meeting, participating in a cleanup activity at the community center, contributing two non-expired canned food items to a local food pantry, participating in a community service project for four people living in Meadow Lake and performing ten acts of service for their family without being asked.

"The benefits of this program extend so much further than just kids earning a bicycle and a congregation gathering funds together to be able to purchase bicycles," Bittner said. "While we were putting together food baskets to be delivered, one of our youth kept questioning why we were giving away food to people we didn't know and why we needed to do this particular project. After delivering the food to the last home, she came to me and said, 'I feel so good in my heart.' That project could be a life-changing moment for her."

Meanwhile, the Methodist Church was raising funds to purchase the bicycles.

"Our congregation is small but very giving," Wilson said. "We did better than what we ever dreamed. With the help of a grant from the United Methodist New Mexico Conference, we raised over $4,000. We thought we'd probably make just enough to purchase bicycles. We not only bought the bicycles, but we bought each child a bike helmet and each bike a utility basket, bike lock and a bright light."

On May 14, the big surprise was revealed to the youth. After a supper provided by the church members, the youth watched as a pickup truck pulled a trailer from in front of the bicycles and revealed what a prize of significant value looked like—eleven shiny new bicycles.

The Meadow Lake Kids Club is one example of how NMSU Extension programs successfully engage with, rely on, and benefit from community involvement.

"I can't say enough about the partnership. I can't say enough about the congregation and the way they support the projects. And I can't say enough about partnering with Laura Bittner and the Extension office," Wilson said. "We are a small congregation, so when it comes to projects that we have a lot of heart and passion for, we may not have the ability to make the full-time commitment. Laura and her group make that commitment and we're just a good support system for that. It's a win-win situation for both of us and we plan on a long future with the Extension office."

"Not only do we have youth learning valuable skills, but we also have a wealth of adult volunteers supporting, encouraging and caring about our youth," Bittner said. "Our volunteers contributed so much more than a monetary gift, they assisted our youth in developing personal characteristics, such as goal setting, accountability, social responsibility and commitment. There is something so powerful that occurs when adults invest time in youth and when youth realize people care about them who absolutely do not have to."

Nov. 11, 2018

NMSU Farmington Research Center Participating in Potatoes USA Variety Study

FARMINGTON—Approximately 5,000 semi-truck loads of potatoes leave the Four Corners region every year. The spuds are headed to dinner tables via retail stores and snack processors.

The dinner potatoes are grown by Navajo Agriculture Products Industry, while those headed to potato chip processing are grown by Navajo Mesa Farms, an independent contractor renting NAPI farmland.

Located in the middle of the potato fields is New Mexico State University's Agricultural Science Center at Farmington, which is conducting variety trials to help the two producers improve their crop quality and yield.

Potatoes produce more revenue per acre than any other crop that can be produced in the Four Corners region.

NMSU is one of 12 land-grant university research farms in the United States conducting potato variety trials in cooperation with Potatoes USA, a grower's group.

Potatoes USA is an industry-funded marketing organization that promotes five main potato products: fresh table-stock potatoes, fresh chipping potatoes, seed potatoes, frozen potato products and dehydrated potato products.

"Producers pay 3 cents a hundred-weight to Potatoes USA to provide services that help customers around the world increase demand for potatoes," said Charles Higgins, president of Higgins Farms Inc. and consultant through Potatoes USA. "The organization invests in marketing and product management research to help grow the potato business."

NMSU has benefited from the organization's investment in research through grant funds for equipment specific to potato research.

"This year, variety trials of 33 table cultivars and 22 chip cultivars were conducted at the Farmington research center fields," Higgins said. "We are looking for chip varieties that have better chemical stability from storage for potato chips and varieties that have a better appearance for supermarkets."

Since NMSU established the research farm fifty years ago on the mesa south of Farmington, variety trials of an array of crops have been done to help NAPI and Four Corners region agricultural producers be more profitable.

"We are combining research and practical experience to obtain the best results," said Aaron Benally, NAPI organic/conventional crop director. "The variety trials at NMSU help us to not waste time and money on crops that will not produce well in our environment and climate."

As consumer trends shift toward organic produce, NAPI has expanded its farming practice to include organic potatoes.

"Because of regulations regarding what chemicals can be used on organic fields, we are transitioning a portion of our farm in order to help NAPI determine which organic crops they might want to grow by looking at pest control methods that are best for their operation," said Kevin Lombard, superintendent of NMSU's Farmington facility.

NMSU has conducted extensive research on evapotranspiration at the Farmington facility. Water research has determined consumptive use indexes and efficient water application strategies on crops grown in the area. This information has helped NAPI and other agriculture producers to be better stewards of water in the semi-arid region.

Water application research includes determining the water-use production function of the crop. This project includes developing and evaluating formulae to predict water application and consumptive use of the crop.

NMSU assistant professor Koffi Djaman, whose professional field of expertise includes soil and water resources, irrigation engineering and crop response to irrigation, has extended the water research into the potato fields where he is measuring soil moisture with soil probes that transmit data to office computers and cell phones.

Sensors in the probe at four-inch intervals measure the soil moisture content at different depths.

"With this system, we can tell when we need to water and how much irrigation water is needed," Djaman said. "After a rain, we can determine how deep that moisture has gone and add the amount needed to meet crop evapotranspiration efficiently."

The partnership between NMSU, NAPI and Potatoes USA is helping the region contribute one percent of all potatoes produced in the United States.

Feb. 2, 2019

4-H Program in Albuquerque Elementary School Turning School's Grade Around

ALBUQUERQUE—Albuquerque Public Schools principals are turning to the 4-H Youth Development program to spark students' success. Eight schools are implementing programs to help students.

Collet Park Elementary School principal Stephani Treadwell was looking for a way to provide experiential learning opportunities for her school's students when she contacted New Mexico State University's College of Agricultural, Consumer and Environmental Sciences' 4-H Youth Development program in Bernalillo County.

The first-in-the-nation "4-H in the School" program is helping to improve the school's performance.

The result has been a decrease in behavioral issues, an increase in school attendance, an improvement in student subject proficiency and an increase in school-wide scores.

"Our students were not retaining the information they had been proficient in the prior week," Treadwell said. "We realized that new information is retained when it is connected to the knowledge that is already gained through an experience. The majority of our students live in poverty and have not had a wide variety of experiences to link classroom learning to."

When Treadwell did an Internet search on experience and learning, the first item listed was 4-H and experimental learning.

The educational administrator contacted NMSU's Cooperative Extension Service office in Albuquerque and a successful collaboration began.

4-H agents Brittany Sonntag and Nicole Jacobs helped Treadwell develop a plan to integrate the 4-H curriculum into her school.

"We believe Collet Park Elementary is the first school in the nation to implement the 4-H club model and curriculum during the school day," Sonntag said. "The results are amazing."

"We dove into the 4-H curriculum and we love it," Treadwell said. "We implemented school-wide 4-H clubs in 2016, with the addition of teachers using subject kits in their class curriculum the following year.

Each Friday afternoon, during the last hour of the school week, the students attend 4-H clubs that they chose featuring a variety of projects ranging from art, woodworking, and crafts to weaving, knitting, cooking and gardening.

"The classroom teachers are the project leader. They have picked a subject they enjoy and want to share with the students," Treadwell said. "Each club has officers and they begin each Friday with the 4-H Pledge and business meeting, then work on the project activity."

Besides doing hands-on projects, the students are learning to be responsible for their homework assignments.

"The students have to complete all of their homework for the week before they can participate in the 4-H Club activities," Treadwell said. "So sometimes you will see a student in the back of the classroom working diligently to get their assignments done."

The teachers are seeing the benefit of the program during their regular class activities.

"The kids are experiencing things, then thinking about what it is that they have experienced and how they have grown through the process by going back and analyzing the activity," said Nancy Zulic, fourth-grade teacher. "They are also becoming more verbal. They are able to talk about what they are learning. I think it has improved their overall performance as students and problem solvers."

The success of "4-H in the School" is evident in the student's performance on the Partnership for Assessment of Readiness for College and Careers testing during the 2017-18 school year.

"The second year, we began seeing a huge growth on our monitored month-by-month testing," Treadwell said. "The kids had a 16 percent proficient in language arts at the end of the year and the next year, they were 47 percent proficient."

Collet Park Elementary chronic absenteeism has also decreased, from 23 percent to 7 percent. "We have seen students tell their parents they don't want to miss school, especially leaving early on Friday afternoon, because they want to participate in the 4-H club activities," Treadwell said.

Before starting the program, Treadwell averaged a couple of suspensions a month, this year, she has had no suspensions.

The school's school-wide score has increased by 6.33 points and is .75 points away from increasing to a "B" school.

Three years after Treadwell contacted the Bernalillo County 4-H agents, there are now eight schools in Albuquerque developing ways to use 4-H to spark their students' success.

"We have also been working with school districts from surrounding counties in New Mexico to implement this program," Sonntag said. "We are actually working with some other states as well so they can find a way to integrate 4-H into the school day."

Looking to the future, Sonntag and Jaynes are taking the current national 4-H curriculum and aligning it with the common core.

"That way, teachers will be able to teach directly from the kits without concern that it does not align with the required common core," Sonntag said.

February. 17, 2019

NMSU, Santa Ana Pueblo Gathering Water Data for Wine Grapes Grown in the Southwest

SANTA ANA PUEBLO—What is the optimal amount of water to raise quality wine grapes?

That is the question New Mexico State University's viticulture specialist Gill Giese and Pueblo of Santa Ana's Tamaya Vineyard manager Jim Peterson will investigate this summer when the pueblo's 30-acre vineyard north of Albuquerque enters its third production year.

"Compared to other crops, such as corn and alfalfa, wine grapes can use less water. In many years they don't use much more water per acre than cotton, and wine grapes have a greater potential economic return," Giese said.

With water becoming a valuable commodity, Santa Ana Agricultural Enterprise is gathering data for the U.S. Department of Agriculture Natural Resource Conservation Service regarding the amount of water used for growing grapes, alfalfa and corn.

"We received a grant from NRCS to gather data regarding the amount of water we use as well as how much fertilizer and compost is applied," Peterson said. "We want to learn the optimal amount of times to water with our drip irrigation system."

Giese is joining the study to gather additional data.

"We want to define the crop quality and quantity and then match the amount of water we need to get to that target," Giese said.

Giese installed three one-meter-long frequency domain reflectometry probes to track the water as it moves through the soil profile. Data will be gathered weekly. Climate and grape development data will also be recorded.

"In addition, we will do some pressure chamber readings to gauge and correlate vine water status to soil moisture levels to see how irrigation scheduling impacts vine performance and water use,"

Giese said. "We plan to gather this data at different periods of growth—bud burst, flowering, veraison and at harvest. We want to know how much water the plant is actually using versus how much it really needs at each of the stages." Although this has been done in other wine regions, it has not been done under New Mexico conditions.

When growing wine grapes, vineyard managers often withhold water while the grapes are developing to control the berry size.

"When growing wine grapes, your goal is the quality of the skin and its integrity. Because that's where most of the flavor, aroma, color, and the impact of the phenolics are located that define a quality wine," Giese said. "The seeds are also important, but the fleshy pulp is sugar water."

But a grower doesn't want to restrict water too much because they will reduce the yield by physically restricting the berry and vine growth.

"Timing matters," Giese said. "There is an optimal amount of water needed at specific times to produce the targeted quality and quantity."

Currently, there are 516 vineyards growing grapes on 1,153 acres. Annually the 45 wineries in New Mexico produce approximately 350,000 gallons of wine.

As the wine industry in New Mexico continues to grow, water management will become an important factor in our sun-rich and semi-arid environment.

"Working with Jim Peterson at the Santa Ana vineyard will give us real-life data," Giese said. "This information will help current producers fine-tune their irrigation and, in the future, when someone is planning to put in grapes and they need to know the amount of water that it will take to grow quality wine grapes."

NMSU Extension, Community Collaborate to Address Food Insecurity

LOS LUNAS—New Mexico is ranked 50th in the nation regarding food insecurity, with the highest percentage of its residents not having consistent access to enough food for an active, healthy life.

In rural Valencia County, food insecurity is a pervasive issue, particularly for the 32 percent of youth under age eighteen who live below the poverty level, according to a U.S. Department of Agriculture Economic Research Service 2017 report.

Food insecurity is strongly associated with learning disabilities, decreased productivity, physical and mental health issues, chronic disease and poor family life.

When Laura Bittner, New Mexico State University's Cooperative Extension Service family and consumer sciences agent in Valencia County, learned that some of the students at Los Lunas Schools' Century High School experience food insecurity, she knew something had to be done.

"There are many national 'backpack' programs for students who do not have food at home, but there are very few national programs addressing this need for high school-age students," Bittner said. "Most of the programs available to high school students are managed on a local or community level. Through 'backpack' programs, food is presented to children at the end of the school week, providing something for them to eat during the weekend."

Bittner, with the support of her county advisory board members, decided it was time to help the 176 students at Century High School, a school designed to give students an opportunity to regain class credits, getting them back on track toward graduation.

Since the first week of the 2018-2019 school year, all Century High students have been offered a "snack pack" containing non-perishable food requiring no refrigeration or electricity to prepare.

Snack packs are distributed on Thursday afternoons because not all students at Century are required to attend school on Fridays.

The Nutrition on Weekends program has taken on a life of its own. The community has risen to the challenge of donating funds and food and packing and transporting the snack packs to the school for distribution.

"Since August, over 3,000 snack packs have been distributed," Bittner said. "We started with $5,000 seed money and as of March 1, we have received $20,000, including $13,933 donated by 91 individuals or organizations from 17 states through the NMSU Foundation 'Make A Statement' crowdfunding campaign."

In addition to the "Make A Statement" campaign, local organizations, Los Lunas Rotary Club, four churches and individual community members have donated food and money.

Church members donate different types of canned food each week, such as peanut butter, peaches or vegetables. They are also packing 500 snack packs each month.

"People really do care. They want to volunteer. They want to help. They want to be part of a solution addressing different issues," Bittner said. "But people don't always know how to direct their desire to help. A big part of this program's success has been educating the community about food insecurity in the state and in their community. I can't begin to express the incredible, ongoing community support for this outreach effort."

The impact of the NOW Snack Pack program goes beyond providing food. Students realize people they don't even know care about their success.

"We have conducted surveys with the students and their parents or guardians to learn how they feel about the program," Bittner said. "When asked in an open-ended question how or if the snack packs have helped them as students, one-fifth of the students wrote the snack packs helped them with their focus, productivity and motivation at school."

Bittner added that 68 percent of students reported sharing the content of their snack packs with someone at home—a sibling, a grandmother, or a niece, nephew or cousin.

"I recently ran into a student shopping with his father," Bittner said. "They shared with me that the father has diabetes. The son shares his snacks with his father, leaving them in their vehicle, ensuring his father has something to eat when his sugar level drops."

In another survey, the students were asked how the snack packs made them feel.

"We had a number of students that wrote that it made them happy and they added that they were really grateful that so many people cared about them," Bittner said.

"This community collaboration is ideally how we want our Extension programs, or our outreach efforts, to work," Bittner said. "Especially when you look at how great the needs are in some of our communities. The ability to address those needs isn't accomplished by one person. It requires the community as a whole stepping up to solve or address the issue."

March 13, 2020

NMSU Extension Beef Heifer Replacement Project Introduces Youth to Cattle Industry

LOS LUNAS—Six youths from Bernalillo, Torrance and Valencia counties are on a 12-month journey learning about the cattle industry by participating in the New Mexico Beef Select Heifer Replacement Project.

The youth are the second cohort to participate in the program offered by New Mexico State University's Cooperative Extension Service in Valencia County.

Participating in the year-long program are Chelby Kenney, Erica Garcia, Kara Batie, Marisol Olivas, Myra Olivas and Taylor Rolan.

"While raising and developing a replacement beef heifer, the youth gain knowledge about the beef industry through Zoom workshops and seminars," said Newt McCarty, NMSU Extension agricultural agent in Valencia.

Through college-level instruction, participants learn about the science behind raising cattle, from genetics and fertility to nutrition and immunology.

While creating a business plan, the youth learn about industry and consumer trends—everything from grass-fed beef to feedlot production.

As they raise a heifer, they maintain records of the animal's weight, average daily gain, and the cost involved in raising the animal.

"The seminars open with Beef Quality Assurance training, where each participant earns their certification," McCarty said.

Learning about feed and nutrition includes a field trip to Onate Feed Mill in Albuquerque, where participants see how commercial feed is made.

"The first big decision the youth have to make is in regard to how they will breed their heifer," McCarty said.

Before those decisions are made, the youth attend seminars in reproduction anatomy and endocrinology, along with expected progeny difference, sire selection and reproduction technologies.

"This year, we have opened the seminars to the cattle producers," McCarty said. "If producers are interested, they can contact me for the date, time and place."

When it is time to breed their heifer, veterinarian Sarah Loya gives the hands-on youth experience while they learn about synchronization and artificial insemination.

In addition, the youth learn about animal health and welfare, how to handle their heifer, the importance of range management, and complete the Masters of Beef Advocacy training through National Cattleman's Beef Association.

As the youth care for the pregnant heifer, they turn to the business side of a cattle operation as they develop a marketing plan and present their business plan to industry professionals.

"Not all youth raising a heifer are interested in a project this comprehensive and intense, but those who do are stand to reap big rewards," McCarty said. "Just completing the project is a huge accomplishment. Therefore, each participant will receive their choice of a buckle or jacket. The two participants who excel the most have a chance of earning a total of $3,000 in scholarships."

Awarding of scholarships is determined by a points system based on pre and post-exams, written and oral presentations, record keeping, monthly activity and financial reports, participation in seminars and activities, and completion of the Masters of Beef Advocacy course.

Two college scholarships will be awarded, with the high point receiving $2,000 and the reserve high point receiving $1,000.

Oct. 25, 2019

NMSU Research Proving 'Tough Love' Helps Tree Seedlings to Survive in Harsh Environment

Giving forest tree seedlings a fighting chance to survive when planted on wildfire-scared mountains in New Mexico and the Southwest is the goal of New Mexico State University researchers.

Researchers and land managers have had poor success in getting planted seedlings to survive, with an average survival rate of 25 percent.

Many things play into the survival rate of the seedlings, including growing and planting techniques, climate and precipitation, temperature and animal activity in the area.

Research in nursery protocols at NMSU's John T. Harrington Forest Research Center at Mora is proving that "tough love" impacts the seedling's survival rate.

"It comes down to producing seedlings that are going to be successful on a given specific site," said Owen Burney, NMSU associate professor and superintendent of the facility. "In forest restoration, the goal is long-term. In thirty-forty years, you want the area to be a forest again. But there are critical front-end concerns, details that go into improving seedling survivability."

The research team hypothesized that drought-conditioned seedlings would develop structures and processes that make the plant hydraulics and water use more efficient within the seedling.

"In short, can we train plants to function with less water so they are better adapted to the harsh planting site?" Burney said the research that is the first of its kind in the United States.

Ponderosa pine and aspen seedlings are the tree species being used in the study.

"Normally, nurseries water at a rate that does not happen in nature," Burney said. "We wanted to see how plants adapt to reductions in the amount of watering. We developed a scientific procedure that stresses plants to just above wilting point."

Burney and his research team discovered a physiological change in the plant's tissue that transport water and nutrients from the roots to the stem and leaves.

"Through microscopic analysis of the xylem elements, we discovered that there was a greater abundance of the xylem in plants that were stressed," Burney said. "This translates to building a buffer against drought environments."

He explained the results as if there were ten drinking straws in the control plants and 100 in the drought-tolerant plants. When the harsh conditions took away four of the straws from both groups, the ones with more straws were more likely to survive.

The true test came when 800 ponderosa pines were planted north of Flagstaff. Of the plants, 400 were normal nursery protocol and 400 were drought-conditioned.

"The field test was on a really harsh, dry site," Burney said. "This study was designed for all the plants to die, but they didn't. Out of the original 800 seedlings, 109 survived. Of the survivors, 92 were the drought-conditioned trees."

Along the Way

During the research, Burney and his team discovered they needed to develop a better way of watering the seedlings in the greenhouse.

"Using the overhead sprinkler system worked fine as the seeds germinate, but once there is foliage on the plants, the water does not reach the root systems evenly," Burney said. "We needed a more consistent irrigation system."

The team developed a system that watered the plants from the roots up.

"We created a sub-irrigation system where the seedling racks are placed in a water-tight platform that we fill with water," he said. "This allows the potting medium to absorb the water evenly."

Measuring the amount of water in the soil and plants was part of the scientific procedures to determine when to water the drought-conditioned seedlings.

"We accomplished creating a scientific sub-irrigation system for our entire greenhouse, which is actually the largest such system in use," he said.

Oct. 13, 2020

NMSU Developing Perfect Green Chile Pepper for Mechanical Harvest

There are many variables in producing the perfect New Mexico green chile pepper.

Consumers select the flavor profile and pepper pod size, shape, thickness and color. Agricultural producers want a high-yielding plant with picture-perfect pods that are easy to harvest. Food producers want chile peppers with no stem and no damage to the pod.

New Mexico State University researchers have developed what is on its way to being the perfect chile pepper for mechanical harvest.

"After many years of traditional selective breeding, we have a new advanced green chile line with the proposed name NuMex Odyssey," said Stephanie Walker, NMSU chile researcher and Cooperative Extension Service vegetable specialist.

The new green chile line, Odyssey, is the result of the NMSU College of Agricultural, Consumer and Environmental Sciences' ongoing efforts to resolve issues associated with harvesting green chile.

"Because of difficulty in obtaining people to hand-harvest the green chile, we have been working on a mechanized harvest system," Walker said. "We began by identifying a harvester manufactured in Israel that gives us the most efficient pick of the chile compared to other machines tested."

While testing various harvesters, the research team realized they needed some changes in the plant and chile pod.

"We worked on plant architecture and fruit attributes that would mechanically harvest better," Walker said. "We needed the plant to have a strong, single stem with fewer basal branches. The low-lying lateral branches interfered with the machine, causing it to uproot the plant. We also found that fruit setting slightly higher on the plant and also detaching from the plant with less force contributed to a cleaner mechanical pick."

Fixing these traits in Odyssey resulted in higher mechanically harvested yield, with significantly less fruit loss in the field, compared to standard commercial green chile varieties.

While this plant architecture helps the harvest efficiency of the plant, Walker said another really exciting thing about the Odyssey variety is the destemming—pedicel removal—efficiency of the fruit.

"For green chile processing, we needed the pedicel—stem and calyx—to come off the fruit easier and cleaner," she said. "Often when you pull the pedicel off of other varieties, you might either break it and partially leave it on the fruit, or you break the chile fruit."

Pedicels perfectly detached from Odyssey fruit 68 percent of the time as opposed to 34 percent for AZ 1904 and 24 percent for NuMex Joe E. Parker.

"With Odyssey, we get very good, clean breaks," she said. "This will also help hand-harvesting."

Pedicel removal is very important for the quality of commercially processed green chile.

"In a processing plant where you are getting thousands of pounds of chile through the system, you have to remove the stem, or otherwise it creates woody material in the processed food," said Walker, who began her work with chile as a quality control supervisor in a processing plant.

"Currently, with the 100 percent hand-harvest system, the people actually remove the pedicel out in the field," she said. "When it doesn't come off easily, they sometimes break the fruit, which causes yield and quality loss."

Ultimately, how does Odyssey taste? After taking a bite from the green chile pod, Walker declared, "Delicious New Mexico chile flavor, although very mild." The new variety's heat factor averages between 300 and 400 Scoville units.

Watch Walker talk about the new variety on YouTube, youtube.com/watch?v=Eoevm6aXHZI.

Dec. 15, 2020

NMSU Studying Ponderosa Pine Trees Seed Sources for Future Forest Management

A warmer, drier climate is predicted to be the norm for the already historically arid forests of the Southwest.

Climate change is a natural occurrence. Plant life has been able to adapt to that pace of change genetically and with a natural migration of plants to environments where they can survive. Seed dispersal and the rate of climate change were in sync.

However, the influence of humans through the burning of fossil fuels, releasing of methane gases, and other activities has accelerated the changing climate. Most plants and trees are unable to keep up with this rate of change via seed dispersal.

New Mexico State University's College of Agricultural, Consumer and Environmental Sciences is researching many areas to help agriculture and forestry professionals adapt to the changing climate.

A seven-year study at NMSU's John T. Harrington Forestry Research Center at Mora is providing land managers and researchers with data regarding seed source selection as they restore forests after severe wildfires.

Ponderosa pines from 75 source locations ranging from southern New Mexico and Arizona to British Columbia in the north have been growing in the northern New Mexico environment. A total of 3,000 seedlings were planted at the research center.

"The idea of the project is to build an understanding of how the movement of seed sources will work in a changing climate based on this northern New Mexico location," said Owen Burney, NMSU associate professor and superintendent of the facility.

"This study will go far into the future and will additionally aid forest land managers in assisted migrations projects. These projects examine the movement of seed, via tree planting, from southern locations to northern ones in order to put seed dispersal and the rate of climate change back in sync."

The study was originally developed by the late John Harrington, who, during his twenty years of research, helped develop forest regeneration and restoration in New Mexico.

Preliminary results show that the southern sources are doing better than the northern seeds.

"Trees from the southern sources are, on average, significantly larger than both the local and northern sources," Burney said of the trees planted at the agricultural experiment station and in natural environments in the region.

"Trees from the northern sources have begun to show a decline in growth with some mortality," he said. "As we look at a future climate in the north that is warmer and drier, which will maybe match northern New Mexico's present climate, we now know that Colorado to British Columbia sources are not going to do very well."

The study is being used by federal and state agencies across the southwestern United States to develop seed transfer guidelines regarding the range of environments that various source seeds can tolerate.

"This information will be used by land managers to assist in the restoration of burned landscapes," Burney said. "As they take into consideration the present climate and changes in the near future, they need to figure out where they are going to get their seed."

Seed collection and the production of these seedlings in nurseries are critical to the restoration needs around the world, including the Southwest.

"A lack of seed and nurseries around the world, as well as the Southwest, limit any assisted migration and restoration effort," Burney said. "As we continue the research on where to plant trees, we still need to build up the seed collection and nursery systems to support these efforts that will only continue to grow into the future."

About the Author

As one of the first women sports writers in Texas in the 1980s, Jane Moorman discovered she was the only soprano in the press box. She was an award-winning journalist during her thirty-one-year career at two community newspapers in Texas and New Mexico. Besides writing about sports and general news, she contributed columns about life as she saw it. She currently lives in Albuquerque, New Mexico.